BETTING ON THE FARM

BETTING ON THE FARM

Institutional Change
in Japanese Agriculture

**Patricia L. Maclachlan
and Kay Shimizu**

CORNELL UNIVERSITY PRESS ITHACA AND LONDON

Publication of this book was made possible, in part, by a generous grant from the Office of the Vice President for Research at the University of Texas at Austin.

First published 2022 by Cornell University Press

Library of Congress Cataloging-in-Publication Data

Names: Maclachlan, Patricia L., author. | Shimizu, Kay (Kaoru), author.
Title: Betting on the farm : institutional change in Japanese agriculture /
    Patricia L. Maclachlan and Kay Shimizu.
Description: Ithaca [New York] : Cornell University Press, 2022. |
    Includes bibliographical references and index.
Identifiers: LCCN 2021041484 (print) | LCCN 2021041485 (ebook) |
    ISBN 9781501762123 (hardcover) | ISBN 9781501762147 (pdf) |
    ISBN 9781501762130 (epub)
Subjects: LCSH: Agriculture, Cooperative—Japan. | Agriculture and
    state—Japan.
Classification: LCC HD1491.J3 M333 2022 (print) | LCC HD1491.J3 (ebook) |
    DDC 338.10952—dc23
LC record available at https://lccn.loc.gov/2021041484
LC ebook record available at https://lccn.loc.gov/2021041485

For Catherine, Jonah, and Hana

Contents

Tables

Figures

Preface

We like telling stories. But one of the drawbacks of social science scholarship is that storytelling must adhere to strict standards of objectivity and relevance. This is a shame, since so many of our memorable experiences in rural Japan these past several years must be left untold.

Take, for instance, the day in June 2017 when we risked our lives in the Mount Aso region of Kumamoto Prefecture—a day we touch on in more "objective" terms in our epilogue. The culprit: Hironaga-san, a gregarious, seventy-five-year-old retired math teacher and amateur photographer. We had hired Hironaga-san through a local friend to drive us around for a day of interviews in the mountains, along with Kay's five-month-old daughter, Hana, and a kind, middle-aged nursery-school teacher who was Hana's nanny for the day.

Hironaga-san drew up outside our Kumamoto City hotel at the appointed hour in an ancient, duct-taped Mitsubishi minivan that drew snickers—and, later, tears—from at least one member of our little entourage. How that van managed to accommodate us and our baby gear was a mystery, for every inch of it seemed to be taken up by something: Hironaga-san's camera equipment, cooking utensils and a sleeping bag (Hironaga-san liked to sleep outdoors), books about birds and plants and bugs, and even some dead bugs. More worrisome was the fact that only one of the five seats had a functioning seatbelt. (We assigned that seat to Hana.)

As we pulled out of the hotel parking lot, we realized that the minivan also wanted for air conditioning and shock absorbers. But no matter. It was a lovely, sunny day, and we were headed into one of the most beautiful regions of Kyushu.

The real trouble started about forty-five minutes in, when we pulled off the highway and began to ascend the narrow, winding roads into Mount Aso. Hironaga-san cheerfully navigated the treacherous terrain with pedal to floor and just one hand on the steering wheel, regaling us with tales of past adventures over the din of the engine and the wind whistling through the open windows. Clutching our handrails and lurching in unison from side to side, we watched in fright as descending trucks barreled past. Unperturbed, Hironaga-san grabbed a harmonica with his free hand and started to play. "Any requests?" he yelled into the back seat.

After nearly an hour of this, we pulled into a rest stop. The last straw for the nanny came when Hironaga-san retrieved a lug wrench from the back of the van and proceeded to tighten the bolts on his wheels. She would have left us for good at that point had she found an exit ramp.

Obviously, we made it through that day. And what a day it was. Hironaga-san thoroughly endeared himself to us by supplying us with snacks, entertaining Hana, and even asking some sharp questions of our interviewees. Together, we surveyed what remained of the damage wrought by the massive Kumamoto earthquake of April 2016—gashes rippling through farmland, entire hillsides missing. And we met with farmers, local government officials, and a town mayor. Most significantly, we bore witness to the enormous economic and demographic challenges currently facing rural Japan.

How farmers and particularly agricultural cooperatives are responding to those economic and demographic challenges is the central story of this book. To tell that story, we have become indebted to a long list of individuals and institutions. Heartfelt thanks to Sera Kikuko, of Kumamoto City, who introduced us not only to Hironaga-san but also to several of the individuals whose experiences are chronicled in this book. Sera's warm hospitality and generosity opened doors to a side of Kumamoto Prefecture that we never would have discovered on our own. We are also very grateful to Governor Kabashima Ikuo of Kumamoto Prefecture, Mayor Umeda Yutaka of Yamato, and Hamada Yoshiyuki of the Kumamoto prefectural government for their time and generous assistance.

In Nagano Prefecture, Miyamura Chiaki, head of the Karuizawa Lion's Club, introduced us to a number of our interviewees, among them Yanagisawa Toshihiko of Sunfarm Karuizawa, who generously granted us several interviews and offered helpful introductions and advice. We also thank Koizumi Minoru, an organic farmer in Karuizawa, and Inayoshi Masahiro of Sunfarmers in Shizuoka Prefecture for their time and insights. And in Tokyo, the following individuals patiently answered our incessant questions and opened doors to further interviews: Kamei Zentarō, formerly of the Tokyo Foundation; Kōno Tarō, LDP Diet member from Kanagawa Prefecture; Matsukata Shichirō and his colleagues at the Ginza Rotary Foundation; Noda Takeshi, LDP Diet member from Kumamoto Prefecture; Hayashi Yoshimasa, LDP Diet member from Yamaguchi Prefecture and former minister of agriculture; and Takagi Yūki, formerly of the Ministry of Agriculture, Forestry, and Fisheries (MAFF) and frequent commentator on agricultural issues. Our thanks to you all.

We owe a debt of gratitude to Yamashita Kazuhito of the Canon Institute for Global Studies—a former MAFF official and one of Japan's foremost agricultural economists. Yamashita met with us countless times over the years, arranged for and accompanied us on two fun-filled fieldtrips, introduced us to some of our interviewees, and made helpful book recommendations. We thank him for everything he has taught us—and for his friendship.

We presented portions of our research at the following institutions: the Weatherhead East Asian Institute at Columbia University, the Asian Studies Program at Georgetown University, the Graduate Institute for Policy Studies (GRIPS) in Tokyo, Harvard University's Program on US-Japan Relations, the International Studies Association, the Japan Studies Association of Canada, the Center for Japanese Studies at the University of Michigan, the Midwest Political Science Association, the Asian Studies Center at the University of Pittsburgh, the Walter H. Shorenstein Asia-Pacific Research Center at Stanford University, the Center for East Asian Studies at the University of Texas at Austin, and the Department of Political Science at the University of Toronto. We thank these institutions for hosting us and their members for their insightful comments and suggestions.

Special thanks to Ilia Murtazashvili and Jennifer Brick Murtazashvili of the University of Pittsburgh, who offered us excellent logistical and theoretical advice when this project was still in its infancy. And to the two anonymous colleagues who reviewed earlier versions of this manuscript for Cornell University Press, your constructive criticisms and encouragement are deeply appreciated.

Patti thanks the Mitsubishi Heavy Industries Professorship of Japanese Studies and the Subvention Grants Program at the University of Texas at Austin, and Kay, the Weatherhead East Asian Institute at Columbia University, the Abe Fellows Program of the Center for Global Partnership, and the University of Pittsburgh's Central Research Development Fund, Japan Council, and the Japan Iron and Steel Foundation and Mitsubishi endowments. Kay also thanks Takenaka Harukata, her host at GRIPS for several semesters, and Kohno Masaru, her host at Waseda University during her tenure as an Abe Fellow. And we are both grateful to Ikeda Yuka, Yano Tomoko, and Yoshida Marin for their skillful research assistance, and to Gill Steel, of Doshisha University, who helped us nail the title of our book.

Roger Haydon, our initial editor at Cornell University Press, gave generously of his time and expertise, making the writing and publication processes far less stressful than they could have been. We thank you, Roger, and wish you a long, happy, and travel-filled retirement! And our sincere thanks to Sarah Elizabeth Mary Grossman, our editor who deftly ushered this project to completion.

We are also immeasurably grateful to the many representatives from Japan Agricultural Cooperatives (JA), government officials, and especially farmers whom we interviewed for this project—some several times—but who chose to remain anonymous. Thanks to you, we were granted a glimpse into Japanese farming and rural society that was simply extraordinary.

And a shoutout to Hironaga-san, whom we happily hired again on return trips to Kumamoto Prefecture. In 2018, he picked us up in a new minivan—same model and color scheme as before but a bit newer, with functioning seatbelts and a somewhat smoother ride. Hironaga-san had suffered a heart attack after our 2017 visit, but he had recovered well and was in fine spirits. Perhaps, someday, we will have an opportunity to recount more stories about our time with Hironaga-san and many others like him who helped make our fieldwork so fun and interesting.

For readers who wish to access the data set we assembled in support of our analysis in chapter 4, we invite you to contact us directly. We would also like to note that while this book has undoubtedly benefited from the generous support of individuals and programs mentioned above, we alone are responsible for any potential shortcomings.

Finally, we thank our families for their encouragement and patience since 2014, when we launched our collaboration and started disappearing for stretches of time into the Japanese countryside. Hana and her older brother, Jonah, who were both born after we started our research, accompanied Kay on many a fieldtrip; they are now devoted connoisseurs of the tasty fruits of Japanese farming. It has been eighteen years since Catherine visited Japan, and COVID-19 is making it hard for Patti to fulfill her promise to take her back any time soon, but she knows that her mother will one day make good on that promise. These three kids made us less productive, but they put our work in proper perspective. It is to them that we lovingly dedicate this book.

Abbreviations

ABL	Agricultural Basic Law
ALA	Agricultural Land Act
APC	agricultural production corporation (*nōgyō seisan hōjin*)
Chūōkai	central union of agricultural cooperatives (prefectural)
CRR	Council on Regulatory Reform (Kisei kaikaku iinkai)
DPJ	Democratic Party of Japan
FLCB	farmland consolidation bank (*nōchi chūkan kanri kikō*)
Gentan	rice acreage reduction program
HBFA	Hamlet-based farm association (*shūraku einō soshiki*)
ICC	Industrial Competitiveness Council (Sangyō kyōsōryoku kaigi)
IOF	investor-owned firm
JA	Japan Agricultural Cooperatives
JA Zenchū	Zenkoku nōgyō kyōdō kumiai chūōkai (National Central Union of Agricultural Cooperatives)
JA Zenkyōren	Zenkoku kyōsai nōgyō kyōdō kumiai rengōkai (National Mutual Insurance Federation of Agricultural Cooperatives)
JA Zennō	Zenkoku nōgyō kyōdō kumiai rengōkai (National Federation of Agricultural Cooperative Associations)
Keidanren	Japan Business Association
Keizairen	prefectural economic federation (of agricultural cooperatives)
LDP	Liberal Democratic Party
MAFF	Ministry of Agriculture, Forestry and Fisheries
METI	Ministry of Economy, Trade and Industry
MOF	Ministry of Finance
NGC	new-generation (agricultural) cooperative
Nōrinchūkin	Nōrin chūō kinko (Central Cooperative Bank for Agriculture and Forestry, or JA Bank)
PARC	Policy Affairs Research Council (LDP)
SCAP	Supreme Commander for Allied Powers
Shinren	prefectural credit federation of agricultural cooperatives
SMD	single-member district
SNTV/MMD	single nontransferable vote / multimember district system
TPP	Trans-Pacific Partnership

Note on Transliteration

In this book, we note Japanese names in the Japanese order (family, given). In cases when scholars publish in English, we write their names in the Western order. We use the modified Hepburn system to transliterate Japanese-language words into English, except for widely recognized placenames like Tokyo, Osaka, and Kyushu.

BETTING ON THE FARM

ADAPTING TO THE MARKET

Institutional Change in Japan Agricultural
Cooperatives (JA)

Japan Agricultural Cooperatives (JA),[1] a massive network of agricultural enterprises ostensibly owned and operated by and for their farmer-members, has long been a powerful fixture in the Japanese farm sector. For generations, leaders in the JA system pressured local co-ops to operate as passive cogs in a large agricultural machine that channeled minimally processed rice and other raw products into the system's distribution networks and JA's farm-input and other services to local farmers. For as long as this arrangement ensured producers a position in the middle class, few resisted JA's one-size-fits-all services and high commissions. But as rural populations shrink and age, as agricultural markets liberalize and the demand for rice decreases, as domestic food supply chains grow more diversified and competitive, and as farm incomes decline, JA's traditional approach to agricultural production is losing credibility.

In response, a small but increasing number of Japan's 652 local cooperatives are breaking out of the traditional JA mold and embracing more profit-oriented business models designed to put more money in the pockets of farmers.[2] JA Echizen Takefu is at the cutting edge of this trend. Under the able leadership of Tomita Takashi, a former stockbroker, the Fukui Prefecture co-op has professionalized its management team and expanded its organization by establishing subsidiaries, one of which manufactures low-priced fertilizers for the co-op.[3] It was one of the first co-ops in the country to sell rice grown with low levels of agricultural chemicals and to differentiate rice prices according to finely graded product "taste scores" (*shokumichi*). It defies JA's middlemen and distribution channels by negotiating face-to-face with independent farm suppliers and selling its products directly to consumers.⁴ And Takefu is venturing into risky niche consumer markets; its high-priced, brand-name Princess Shikibu rice, for example, has gained a foothold in Japan's already saturated rice market. To an economist, Takefu's efforts to run itself like a business are a rational response to changes in consumer demand and other market forces. But when compared to JA tradition, they are nothing short of radical.

While Takefu and other local co-ops strive to adapt to changing market forces and in ways that serve the financial interests of their farmer-members, far more co-ops seem stuck in the JA traditions—even at the expense of shrinking farmer incomes. For many years, this is what JA's national leaders have seemed to prefer, as evidenced by their willingness to retaliate against "upstart" co-ops by withholding essential services. Indeed, fear of censure from JA's prefectural and national leaders is so pervasive that many co-op officials who flock to Takefu's facilities for inspection tours refuse to reveal their identities.⁵ Put simply, as some co-ops attempt to chart a new, more market-conforming approach to agricultural cooperation, many more are entrenched in a status quo that JA leaders seem determined to defend.

What explains these divergent behaviors within JA? Why have JA organizations been changing more at the local level than at the national level? Why do some local co-ops behave like for-profit corporations, while others do not? How, finally, does reform unfold at the local level?

In addressing these and related questions, this book pushes institutional analysis in new directions. For in addition to exploring why and how institutional change occurs, ours may very well be the first major study to systematically explain *variations* of change among otherwise similar units of analysis. In so doing, we make careful conceptual distinctions among institutions as *rules of the game*, both formal and informal, *organizations*, and *strategies*. While our primary objective is to explain variations in strategies across different co-ops, we also emphasize the dynamic interaction among all four types of institutions during the reform process. To do this, we bring a mix of qualitative and quantitative methodologies to our analysis, including scores of interviews with a variety of stakeholders and policy makers and the statistical analysis of an original data set of 105 local agricultural cooperatives in six prefectures—an unusually large sample of isomorphic units of analysis for the purposes of analyzing institutional transformation.

As we answer our questions, we take a fresh look at the conditions for change among co-ops and in the Japanese agricultural sector more broadly. First, we explore the effects on formal and informal rules, organizations, and strategies of two sets of slow-moving structural changes that challenge many countries today: market liberalization and demographic decline and aging. There is no shortage of academic analyses of the impact of market transformations or demographic change on the modern Japanese political economy,[6] but we still know very little about the interactive effects of these two processes and their impact on institutional change. With its gradually liberalizing markets and oldest population in the world, Japan is an optimal laboratory for examining these interactions. And the Japanese farm sector, where the population is shrinking and aging at rates much faster than the national average, offers us a unique setting for exploring these processes up close.

Second, we reassess the impact of Japanese government policies on the propensity for change among co-ops and their farmer-members. While scholars are often correct to criticize policy makers for not doing enough to resolve the many challenges confronting the Japanese farm sector,[7] we emphasize how even small-scale government adjustments to the formal rules that buttress farming and agricultural cooperation can generate incentives for cultivators and co-ops to reform their organizational structures and business strategies in ways that conform to changing market signals.[8] There may be no deregulatory "big bangs" in Japanese agriculture comparable to Prime Minister Hashimoto Ryūtarō's (1996–1998) dramatic deregulation of the financial sector during the 1990s, but the cumulative effects of the government's piecemeal reforms over time can be quite transformative. Indeed, we make the case that years of small-scale policy reforms have unleashed grassroots support for further change in the farm sector that will likely gain momentum regardless of future levels of government engagement.

Third, while other analyses of co-op reform tend to focus on important incentives generated by legal and policy developments at the national level,[9] our exploration of cross–co-op variations in strategic change also includes close attention to *local* variables.[10] From area-specific natural resource endowments to the presence of local agents of change and the ways in which farmers organize themselves (or not) behind new strategies, these local variables generate many of the opportunities for and *limits* to—and there are many of them—co-op reform. Microlevel analysis also enables us to understand exactly how the slow-moving demographic and economic changes noted above combine with local opportunities and constraints to produce the distinctive outcomes of a co-op's reform process.

Our focus on the local conditions of co-op change also positions us to demonstrate how the achievements of reformist farmers and co-ops are helping to push JA's notoriously stubborn national organizations to provide a more conducive environment for reform throughout the co-op network. That one of the wellsprings of reform within the broader JA system is local has important implications for the future of change not only for JA itself but also for the farm sector more generally.[11]

Although *Betting on the Farm* is primarily a book about institutional reform in Japan, it should also be of interest to development scholars. But while most development studies tend to explore change in developing economies,[12] the story of Japanese co-op reform can be read as a case study of the limited opportunities and many challenges confronting institutional transformation in mature economic systems, where institutions are relatively stable and the stakeholders numerous. It is our hope, moreover, that our emphasis on agricultural cooperatives will be relevant to scholars of change in well-established labor unions, professional organizations, and other "self-organized enterprises" and their associated federations.[13]

Our study should also interest readers concerned with business and agricultural economics, not least by poking holes in the conventional wisdom that Japanese agriculture is nothing but a declining industry. To be sure, agricultural, forestry, and fisheries products contributed just 1.2 percent to Japanese GDP in 2017, which is less than the Organisation for Economic Co-operation and Development (OECD) average of 1.5 percent.[14] And it cannot be denied that the farm sector faces a precarious future as it grapples with deepening economic and demographic challenges. But in our fixation on what ails Japanese agriculture, we overlook the scope and significance of the changes that have already occurred, as well as the potential for more change in the future. Some farmers and co-ops are venturing down rapidly diversifying food supply chains, creating value-added opportunities both for themselves and for domestic food processors and retailers, and in so doing, transforming the way food travels from farm to table. Cashing in on Japan's reputation for producing high-quality food, some are even participating in *global* food supply chains by learning how to export—a dramatic change from a generation ago when "adapting to globalization" meant little more than blocking food imports.[15] Again, we demonstrate how these bold new farmer and co-op strategies reflect broad economic and demographic pressures, new legal and regulatory incentives, and a variety of local variables. When all is said and done, some farmers and co-ops are becoming more competitive not only because they must but also because they can.

In exploring these issues, we also touch on the fate of the family farm. Until recently, farming in most countries was controlled by family farms and supported, in many cases, by agricultural cooperatives. But this model has come under threat—especially in developed countries—as markets liberalize and farm populations shrink. How can traditional family farms and co-ops ensure stable agricultural output and producer incomes when the number of farmers is declining and agricultural prices are more volatile? Some countries, including the United States, have met these challenges by corporatizing and expanding farm enterprises, including cooperatives. In Japan, however, a combination of precedent, politics, and geographic constraints has restrained the incorporation and expansion of many types of farm enterprises, thereby contributing to the continued predominance of small-scale family farms and traditional cooperatives. But Japanese co-ops are under no less pressure to change the way they do business than agricultural enterprises elsewhere. As we explore how Japanese farms and especially co-ops have made these adjustments, we illustrate the ways in which old economic institutions can adapt to new market incentives.

This is not to suggest that farmers' and co-ops' gradual embrace of freer markets symbolizes the beginnings of an inexorable march toward a neoliberal future and concomitant rejection of the sorts of institutional complementarities and communitarian values that have come to define Japan's "coordinated market economy."[16] To be sure, some Japanese economists and even government officials would like to see exactly that. But while we emphasize the need for some degree of competitive market reforms for co-ops—and Japanese agriculture more generally—to survive into the future, we also recognize that the universal principles of agricultural cooperation and Japanese historical precedent have generated enduring expectations for co-ops to contribute to the well-being of struggling rural communities. Co-ops are not "corporations" in the narrow sense of the term. They are economic membership organizations that strive not only to advance the material well-being of their members but also to exercise stewardship over farmland and irrigation systems and contribute a range of collective goods to rural communities. How individual co-ops juggle the trade-offs between their economic and social missions as "rural revitalization" ascends to the top of the Japanese national agenda is an important underlying theme of this study.

Concepts and Theories

In our analysis of variations of reform within JA, we employ some of the concepts and insights of institutionalism theories.

At their most fundamental level, institutions are the enforceable "rules of the game in a society."[17] By defining and limiting "the set of choices of individuals,"[18] institutions operate as abstract arenas of human interaction that incentivize cooperation and agency and constrain certain types of behavior.[19] As such, institutions can both reflect and help entrench the distribution of power among actors in a corresponding environment.[20] Institutions are also "relatively enduring" and hence sources of stability and predictability in social life.[21]

There has long been a tendency in the social sciences to indiscriminately apply the term *institution* to a broad range of phenomena. This usage runs the risk of muddying the meaning of institutions and of the processes that contribute to their transformation. To minimize these pitfalls, we distinguish among four types of institutions in the political-economic context: formal and informal rules, organizations, and strategies.

Formal rules usually take the form of laws, regulations, and other types of codified constraints, while informal rules consist of norms, conventions and codes of conduct, mindsets or worldviews, and the like.[22] Both types of rules function as constraints on human behavior but are enforced in different ways; while formal rules are subject to official enforcement by the state or other established authorities, informal rules are usually enforced by peer pressure or other manifestations of social expectation.[23] Formal and informal rules are interconnected in that norms and conventions can come to reflect the constraints and opportunities of formal rules over time. As Gretchen Helmke and Steven Levitsky argue, some informal institutions complement or reinforce formal rules, while others compete with or challenge them.[24] The interconnections between formal and informal rules can range from the relatively simple, as in the case of the regulations and codes of conduct that bind individuals to their workplace, to the complex, as in modern markets, which are vast constellations of formal and informal rules that help shape the interrelated choice sets of a broad range of economic actors.[25] It is important to note, finally, that while our analytical objectives warrant careful distinctions between formal and informal rules, in reality, the two can combine to produce something much more than the sum of their parts. Hugh Heclo was evidently mindful of this when he defined institutions as "inheritances of valued purpose with attendant rules and moral obligations."[26]

As Douglass North observed, organizations are "groups of individuals bound by some common purpose to achieve objectives." If rules open and circumscribe opportunities for action in a society, "organizations are the players" that are "created to take advantage of those opportunities."[27] Rooted in time and space, organizations are the operational expressions of formal and informal rules. As with formal versus informal rules, the distinction between rules and organizations should not be overstated; in many cases, rules without organizations to represent or implement them amount to little more than empty platitudes, while it is impossible to conceive of organizations devoid of supporting rules. We remain mindful of these conceptual complementarities in our analysis. And to further clarify how rules help shape organizations, we take our cue from Elinor Ostrom by distinguishing among two broad types of formal rules: those that are exogenously imposed on organizations by government authorities or organizations at a higher level of an organizational hierarchy and those that are endogenously generated.[28] As we shall see, the origins of rules can have a major impact on the scope for change. For now, suffice it to say that organizations serve as concrete arenas for agency—for actors, in other words, to translate opportunities and choices into action. And by "action" in economic settings, we mean strategies: an organization's goal-oriented, enforceable action plans or repeated behaviors for maximizing the potential returns on available resources within existing market settings.[29]

While North's explanations of "institutional"—that is, "rule"—change in market settings emphasize the interactive effects between formal and informal rules, on the one hand, and organizations, on the other hand,[30] we add strategies to the equation in the expectation that tracing the dynamic interrelationships among these four types of institutions offers greater insights into the conditions for and sequencing of events within the reform process. These processes can unfold in a variety of ways. Changes to the formal rules that define organizations, for instance, can increase or decrease profit-making opportunities, thus leading to strategic reforms and/or changes to an organization's governance and management systems. Alternatively, changes in norms, conventions, or mindsets may trigger strategic and/or organizational changes by challenging the legitimacy of existing organizational structures and/or strategic choice sets.

It is also possible that strategic changes can lead to reforms of universal formal rules. In one scenario, strategic shifts among a few maverick economic organizations can trigger a sea change within the underlying normative context that in turn encourages the diffusion of those strategies among a broader population of organizations. In time, governments may be incentivized to introduce regulatory and legal reforms to accelerate that diffusion. Of course, real life is never so simple; poor information, weak leadership, the demands of vested interests, and a host of other social, economic, and political impediments can slow these dynamic processes or derail them altogether. Nevertheless, we see evidence of such interactive processes at work in the case of agricultural cooperative reform, a subject to which we now turn.

JA in Theoretical and Historical Perspective

The JA Group—a large nested hierarchy of cooperative organizations that parallels the national, prefectural, and municipal levels of the Japanese government[31]—embodies many of the formal and informal rules of postwar Japanese agricultural cooperation. Four large federations warrant our attention at the national level: JA Zenkyōren, which oversees the network's extensive life and non–life insurance services; Nōrinchūkin (Commonly known as JA Bank), the group's banking arm and one of Japan's largest financial institutions; Zennō, which provides agricultural inputs and product processing and marketing services to farmer-members; and finally, Zenchū, the powerful "control tower" (*shireitō*) of the JA Group and primary JA spokesperson within the government policy making process.[32] (For the purposes of this study, we focus primarily on Zennō and Zenchū.) At the next level are several dozen prefectural federations (*rengōkai*) that are organized by function and linked to corresponding national federations. And at the grassroots level, JA is anchored by two types of cooperatives: as of November 2017, 629 commodity-specific, special-purpose co-ops (*senmon nōgyō kumiai*) and, more importantly for our purposes, 652 multipurpose agricultural cooperatives (*sōgō nōgyō kumiai*),[33] the primary interface between farmer-members and the broader JA system.

Japan's multipurpose co-ops approximate what many Western agricultural economists term the "traditionally organized agricultural cooperative," which is a "user-owned and controlled business from which benefits are derived and distributed on the basis of use."[34] On paper, Japanese co-ops resemble their foreign counterparts in that they seek to reduce farmer risks and maximize—or at least stabilize—farmer incomes by all but guaranteeing farmer-member access to farm inputs and agricultural markets and by collectively representing farmers in negotiations with more powerful wholesalers, processors, and retailers. The co-ops also help safeguard farmer property rights—most notably the rights of farm households (*nōka*) to own and receive an income stream from farmland; in return for a minimal investment, farmers gain membership in an organization that empowers them to focus their resources on improving the productivity of their individual farm enterprises.[35] But as its name suggests, Japan's "multipurpose" co-op is internationally distinctive in that it offers not just one or two essential agricultural services but also a panoply of banking, insurance, and even social welfare and recreational services. Even more distinctive is JA's historical role as an influential electoral intermediary between farmers and Japanese political parties.[36] As we shall see, these distinctive features have weakened the capacity of some JA organizations to adapt to changes within the Japanese food supply chain.

For decades after World War II, the food supply chain was shielded from international competition and propped up by generous subsidies that catapulted some agricultural prices well beyond international levels. Within that supply chain, JA dominated food—and particularly rice—production while food processors and retailers operated within their own more-or-less discrete spheres of economic influence further downstream. Hence, when it came to product collection and distribution, the typical co-op was strategically incentivized to do little more than gather and lightly process the raw product of its farmer-members and channel that product up JA's hierarchical distribution system, or *keitō* (i.e., prefectural economic federations and then Zennō),[37] which then forwarded it to wholesalers or other buyers; since farmers already stood to reap returns far beyond competitive market prices, there was no compelling need for the co-op to add value to its products by engaging in sophisticated branding or marketing strategies. For rice, Zennō divided raw product into broad grades and paid farmers uniform prices within each grade with only minimal attention to variations in product quality; end-use consumers, for their own part, had no choice but to purchase their rice at licensed vendors and at highly inflated prices. As such, the food supply chain was remarkably immune to the vicissitudes of market signals like price and consumer demand.

Although local co-ops could have done more to keep farm production costs down and increase the prices paid to farmers for their raw product, the government's agricultural policies nevertheless positioned them to do well by their farmer-members, the vast majority of whom grew—and continue to grow—rice. By 1970, total farmer incomes from agricultural and off-farm pursuits were on par with those of urban worker households. Against this backdrop, a set of norms and conventions took root that roundly contradicts the notion of the rational farmer—of the individual cultivator who responds to economic incentives to advance his or her material self-interest.[38] In what amounted to an agricultural *mindset*,[39] the typical (i.e., small-scale, part-time) farmer viewed himself as a passive participant who produced commodities for distribution into the broader food supply chain and who looked with some disdain on risk-taking and the naked pursuit of profit. Scholars have shown that norms function as informal institutions when they are entrenched in concrete organizations and subject to enforcement;[40] this was certainly the case with what we call the passive-producer mindset, which was grounded in the organizational fabric of the traditional farm village and local co-ops and enforced by peer pressure. This complementarity between informal rules and local organizations helped traditionally organized agricultural co-ops—and the JA system more generally—survive well beyond their "best by" date.[41]

By the mid-1980s, agricultural stakeholders and pundits alike were well aware that JA's strategies were unsustainable as pressures for agricultural market liberalization mounted and the already shrinking farm population showed ominous signs of aging.[42] Following the 1990 collapse of the economic bubble, a confluence of economic and political developments magnified these structural fault lines in the agricultural sector and plunged JA into crisis mode. As the decade unfolded, Zennō's dominance in the rice market and in the provision of fertilizers, machinery, and other farm inputs began to decrease as waves of unprecedented domestic deregulation expanded competition within the food supply chain and supporting markets. The prices co-ops could offer farmers began to plummet as international pressures during the Uruguay Round of General Agreement on Tariffs and Trade (GATT) trade negotiations forced the government to reduce rice and other food-related subsidies. JA's influence in bureaucratic and political corridors declined as electoral reform rendered the political parties less dependent on votes mobilized by interest groups. And JA braced for a steadily declining membership as the rates of farm population shrinkage and aging accelerated; at an average age of nearly sixty-eight years,[43] Japanese farmers are, as of 2020, among the oldest in the world. Finally, and perhaps most problematically for the future of agriculture, the diminishing economic fortunes of farming spawned a severe shortage of farm successors (kōkeisha). In response to these and related economic and demographic challenges, both JA and the government found themselves under mounting pressure to reform the formal rules and the organizational and strategic foundations of agricultural cooperation.

As farmer incomes derived from agricultural pursuits declined, cultivators reassessed their relationship to JA. Some seemed incapable of—or unwilling to—change. A few all but abandoned JA and navigated markets on their own. Many others kept one foot in their local co-op, picking and choosing from among its offerings much like a diner at a cafeteria.[44] Meanwhile, as they learned to adapt to changing market conditions, small but growing numbers of farmers increasingly perceived themselves not only as producers but also as competitive, risk-taking, profit-seeking farm managers (keieisha) and entrepreneurs.[45] Although Japan has yet to spawn a coherent, market-conforming mindset that serves as a clear, unifying alternative to the passive-producer mindset of old, for the sake of simplicity, we refer to this admittedly amorphous constellation of norms and conventions as Japanese agriculture's emerging *entrepreneurial* mindset. Yet another challenge to the legitimacy of the old JA system, these new values and expectations sparked a backlash from more conservative farmers and no small number of personnel up and down the JA hierarchy.

It was in this context of a deepening agricultural crisis and conflicting approaches to farming that the pace of strategic change among local co-ops picked up speed. From the rogue behavior of Takefu, which remains part of JA in name only, to the more modest efforts of other local co-ops to adapt to changing economic and demographic conditions, some co-ops are now implementing more market-oriented strategies, by which we mean production, branding, marketing, and distribution strategies that respond more directly to consumer demand and that stand to increase co-op and farmer profits. Other co-ops, however, have failed to take these steps.

Explaining Institutional Change in JA

These dramatic variations in co-op change highlight JA's advantages as a case study of institutional reform. JA presents a rare opportunity to specify clear units of analysis, which is essential to understanding the causes and processes of institutional change. Institutions scholars often focus on multicentered institutions at very high levels of aggregation,[46] such as political regimes,[47] social welfare and other policy clusters,[48] or even entire economies.[49] This complicates efforts to untangle the interplay among formal and informal rules, organizations, and strategies within the reform process. Like regimes or policy clusters, JA is a nested hierarchy of rules of agricultural cooperation and their representative organizations,[50] but with one key advantage: the organizational structure of that hierarchy is crystal clear and generally unsullied by overlaps with other organizational arenas. More importantly, JA offers us highly discrete units of analysis in the form of local multipurpose cooperatives. The fact that there are so many of these units in Japan, moreover, allows us to hold constant certain macropolitical and economic variables like regime and market type as we identify the mix of factors that drive change at the local level.

Nevertheless, explaining institutional change is no easy task, not least because scholars have yet to agree on what exactly it means and how it unfolds. For years, theorists assumed that change was the exception to the norm of institutional stasis. Mature institutions, they argued, were like "dried cement"—nearly impossible to uproot.[51] Changes that did occur were classified as one of two types: radical or incremental. Radical change was usually depicted as the product of "critical junctures": relatively rare, short-term windows of opportunity triggered by exogenous shocks during which existing formal and informal rules are wholly or partially suspended, thus expanding the range of choices available to—and the relative power of—agents of change.[52] Incremental path-dependent change, by contrast, was deemed far more common,[53] particularly for economic organizations.[54] Path dependence refers to the endogenously produced, self-reinforcing legacy of past actions that constrain choices in the present and future, thus buttressing the power of key institutional stakeholders.[55] Under conditions of path dependence, scholars assumed, change tends to be minimal, piecemeal—at the margins.

Interestingly, the history of JA's national organizations duplicates this older, starkly dichotomous interpretation of institutional change. During the postwar occupation of Japan (1945–1952), the cooperative system inherited from the prewar period was thrust into a critical juncture during which the formal rules of the cooperative game were rewritten to entrench new kinds of agricultural property rights and other legal reforms. In short order, JA's market-distorting practices took firm root, subject to strict top-down controls within the JA hierarchy and supported by government policy. Since then, JA organizations at the national level proved remarkably sticky, succumbing to reform only when not doing so posed an existential threat to the survival of the JA network; even then, the changes that were introduced did little to significantly alter the fundamental distribution of organizational power within the JA pyramid. In short, change at this level has been narrowly path dependent and incremental.

A major reason for the institutional rigidity of JA's national organizations is rooted in their relationship to market forces. In theory, economic organizations operating in competitive markets should respond quickly and flexibly to price fluctuations and other market changes.[56] But JA's national organizations are not purely "economic"; nor have postwar Japanese agricultural markets been particularly "competitive." Zenchū, JA's control tower, is a deeply politicized, *administrative* organ that has a long history of aggressively lobbying government and political parties for policy favors, such as inflated rice prices, generous farmer subsidies and tax breaks, and curbs on rice imports. It was able to secure these favors from the government by operating as a semiofficial branch of the state in the implementation of postwar agricultural policies and by delivering the farm vote behind sympathetic conservative politicians in rural districts. Zenchū then used its political heft to ensure that competition within the agricultural sector was kept to a minimum.

Meanwhile, the near absence of meaningful market competition for JA's main commodity, rice, ensured that Zennō was spared exposure to what Paul Pierson calls "the measuring rod of price"—the fundamental mechanism through which information about the rapidly changing market is conveyed to market participants,[57] thus signaling to them the conditions under which strategic reform may be necessary. Indeed, the upper organizational echelons of JA were so market insensitive that when rice prices began to decline from the mid-1990s in response to the partial liberalization of the rice market and the long-term decline in consumer demand, this tier did relatively little to promote the kinds of reforms that would have enhanced the competitiveness and profitability of its core agricultural services. Instead, JA at the national level initially compensated for its mounting losses by imposing higher input prices, fees, and service commissions on co-ops and hence their farmer-members and by expanding its lucrative credit and insurance services to nonfarmers—especially in rural areas that were underserved by private-sector firms. In short, JA stayed afloat through rent seeking and the diversification and expansion of its services away from farming. Barring the imposition of curbs on its noncore functions and/or the elimination of rent-seeking opportunities, JA's national organizations continued their support of the institutional status quo. They remained, in other words, in a situation of path-dependent, self-reinforcing "lock in."[58]

If institutional change at the national level of JA has, for the most part, been defensive, it can be transformative at the local level—and in ways that resonate with more recent theorizing about the potentially innovative effects of path-dependent institutional change over time.[59] To be sure, some kinds of institutional reforms at the individual co-op level are, at best, narrowly path dependent and incremental, or simply impossible. One (institutional) reason for this is that many of the formal rules of agricultural cooperation are imposed on individual co-ops by either national or prefectural governments or higher-level organizations in the JA hierarchy—rules that regulate a broad gamut of co-op features and responsibilities, from the co-op's role in the provision of certain financial services to the professional qualifications of members of the co-op's all-important board of directors (*rijikai*). These exogenous formal rules narrow the co-op's room to maneuver. But at the grassroots level, where co-op employees interact closely with individual farmers in the processes of agricultural production and co-op service provision, co-ops have a significant degree of freedom to devise and adjust locality-specific rules for the management of local agricultural resources—what Ostrom calls "operational rules."[60] These are the rules that set product-specific production standards, that enable co-op monitoring of farmers as they comply with those standards, that establish and administer organizational linkages between co-op branches and their members, that define how farmland is to be mobilized in support of co-op goals, and so on. And to a significant degree, they are the product not of directives issued from higher-level JA authorities but of spontaneous, face-to-face interactions between co-ops and their farmer-members over time. Together, they give shape to the broad—and often interrelated—production, processing, branding, marketing, and other strategies that distinguish otherwise isomorphic co-op organizations from one another. Over time, changes to these small-scale, endogenously generated operational rules that help define co-op strategies and organizations can add up to major shifts in the way individual co-ops do business. In some instances, moreover, they can stimulate bottom-up pressures for change within the broader JA hierarchy and even within the formal-legal foundations of agricultural cooperation.

The local co-op is incentivized to engage in market-sensitive strategic reform not only by the relative flexibility of local operational rules but also by the immediate impact of prices and other market signals on its membership base. Consider some of the services that the co-op is expected to provide its farmer-members: administering member orders for seeds, farm machinery, and other inputs; collecting raw product for distribution to market and paying farmers for that raw product; advising individual cultivators on how to cut production costs and, to that end, coordinating the sharing of expensive farm implements; and so on. It is in part through participation in these and other co-op services—and through comparisons of the economic returns of co-op services to those of alternative providers in today's increasingly competitive market—that the entrepreneurial farmer learns about what her or his options are. In cases where the co-op is insensitive to price and simply rides the coattails of nationally orchestrated service diversification or rent seeking, it is that farmer—that *entrepreneurial* farmer—who balks at the neglect and the weak returns on her output and who is most likely to defect from co-op services. ("Defection" from JA rarely entails a wholesale repudiation of JA membership. Today, as before, nearly 100 percent of Japanese farmers remain members of JA co-ops.) But the more farmers distance themselves from co-op services, the more co-op coffers are depleted and the co-op falls short of its mission as an agricultural enterprise. Ceteris paribus, co-ops that wish to curb farmer defections have no choice but to adapt their agricultural strategies and supportive operational rules and organizations to shifting price and other market signals, in ways that put more money in the pockets of their farmer-members.[61]

But, as we know, *ceteris* is not always *paribus* in the world of Japan's multipurpose co-ops; some co-ops take the plunge into institutional reform, while others do not. How, then, can we explain these variations in local co-op change?

One possible explanation is that variations in strategic reform are driven by local demographic conditions. It almost goes without saying that co-ops in farmer populations that are shrinking and aging will have good reason to introduce strategic changes that make local farming more financially rewarding to future generations. But this point should not be overstated. Demographic decline poses an existential threat to virtually all co-ops and to Japanese agriculture in general. Like climate change, however, it is one of those slow-moving structural threats that everyone knows about but few act on, since its worst effects will be felt in the future rather than today. To be sure, the future has arrived for many Japanese farm communities in the form of severe successor shortages and a concomitant rise in abandoned farmland and shuttered homes and small businesses. And yet some co-ops facing severe demographic stress will conclude that reform is futile. Simply stated, demographic decline, on its own, is a poor predictor of institutional change at the local co-op level.

Our data analysis explores other potential predictors of why some co-ops change while others do not, the most robust of which is the ratio of regular co-op members (*sei kumiaiin*), or active farmers with co-op voting rights, to associate co-op members (*jun kumiaiin*), nonfarmer (or retired-farmer) residents of a co-op's jurisdiction who lack voting rights but are entitled to the co-op's financial and other nonagricultural services. Nationally, the number of associate members now significantly exceeds that of regular members,[62] which is symptomatic of the growing importance since 1990 of the JA system's lucrative credit and insurance services relative to its farm-oriented services. It is our position that the higher the ratio of regular members to associate members, the more likely a co-op will engage in strategic adaptation to market signals; when the reverse is the case, co-ops tend to remain price-insensitive proponents of the status quo. This insight should be interpreted as no more than a general rule of thumb, since some co-ops with more associate than regular members have been known to introduce significant strategic changes on behalf of their farmers.

A more compelling set of reasons for variations in co-op reform has to do with local conditions that can vary dramatically across—and even within—individual co-ops. Of particular note is the mix of local resource endowments and product-specific market conditions. Some co-ops are simply better endowed than others in terms of climate and soil conditions to produce the kinds of crops that can do well in today's variegated agricultural markets. For example, co-ops in areas that are naturally positioned to grow high-end vegetables can be incentivized to engage in strategic change by expanding consumer demand and high prices for these products. By contrast, change will be much harder in co-ops that can produce little more than rice, since the demand for and price of rice has been dropping over the past generation. For reasons that have to do with the idiosyncrasies of today's rice market, however, co-ops in regions that produce Japan's highest-quality rice face stronger economic incentives to change.

While resources and corresponding prices and other market conditions can be important motivators of enduring, market-conforming strategic reforms that benefit farmers, they are by no means sufficient. Two additional conditions must be met, one of which is the presence of local agency. Leaders are essential to defining and articulating the goals of institutional change, identifying measures of success, and devising road maps for transforming ideas about change into reality. These insights are not new; theorists have long observed that institutional reform cannot occur in the absence of proactive agents of change.[63] But while many studies of institutional change tend to be either implicitly or explicitly focused on the actions of leaders occupying prominent positions in organizations, a degree of agency can emulate from the *members themselves* in membership organizations like cooperatives, as Ostrom's landmark work underscores.[64] To be sure, in instances like these it will also be necessary for co-op personnel to exercise a significant degree of agency, especially in the co-op–wide implementation of complex, value-added strategies requiring specialized skills. A focus on leadership is also important for what it reveals about how slow-moving demographic and economic changes shape the co-op reform process, for it is co-op leaders and other agents of change who interpret the demographic challenges for a co-op, who actively learn about changing market opportunities, and who oversee the necessary steps for adapting co-op strategies to those opportunities.

The second, non-resource-related prerequisite for enduring, market-conforming reform is farmer organization behind new strategic goals. And the reason for this is simple: no strategy in economic membership organizations can effectively take root unless the members themselves support it and are appropriately organized to participate in its implementation. As a result, organizing farmer-members behind co-op strategies is one of the change agent's most important tasks, although this task is harder in some co-ops than in others. Complementary farmer organizations can take a number of forms, from product-specific production committees at the grassroots level to arrangements at the hamlet level and beyond for pooling farm inputs and labor and/or coordinating production. What matters is that these arrangements open opportunities for *communication* and *deliberation* between farmers and the local multipurpose cooperative and in ways that simplify the introduction of and farmer conformity with the many operational rules that compose specific co-op strategies.[65] Effective farmer organization and co-op strategies are flip sides of the same coin, for in the words of one of our key interviewees, co-ops as membership organizations "are only as strong as the farmers they serve."[66]

While the variables noted above play out in most—if not all—cases of co-op change and nonchange, the manner in which they interact with one another in the reform process can vary dramatically and unpredictably from co-op to co-op, and even within co-ops. We must also be mindful of the possibility that natural disasters, economic downturns, agricultural policy changes, and a raft of other unforeseen developments can derail or slow the reform process, even in co-ops that appear primed for effective change. And the reverse is also possible. Price increases and the opening up of new sources of demand, for instance, can make all the difference to a co-op that has been struggling to change. The point here is that while there may be certain prerequisites for strategic reform, they are no guarantee of successful reform outcomes; those outcomes are also shaped by the timing and sequencing of institutional change, historical contingency, and other contextual factors, many of which, like resource endowments, are beyond a co-op's control.

The processes of strategic reform are also influenced by farmer mindsets, which tend to vary in response to a co-op's distinctive history and/or mix of resources and product-specific market signals. Cultivators in those vegetable-producing co-ops, for instance, tend to be quite market savvy and entrepreneurial, largely because they have decades of experience working in relatively open and competitive markets. Again, these are the types of farmers who are most likely to hold their co-ops to high standards and exercise a degree of agency—and to defect from co-op services if they can get a better deal elsewhere. In co-ops like these, leadership among co-op personnel is important, but farmers themselves may generate reformist initiatives, (re)organize themselves, and, in a bottom-up flow of influence, galvanize more proactive leadership among co-op personnel than what otherwise might occur. What is more, reform in these contexts can be quite sweeping. By contrast, farmers—usually part-time farmers—in co-ops with rice monocultures have had far less experience with competitive markets and are thus more likely to harbor passive-producer mindsets and to rely unquestioningly on their co-ops. In these cases, strategic reform depends almost entirely on the presence of proactive leadership among co-op personnel, and the reform process is a far more time-consuming and top-down affair. And since passive producers are usually less willing to abandon their old strategic habits and put their trust in co-op leaders, co-op reform tends to be more path dependent and less sweeping. Finally, the risk of failure in these cases is quite high, for if farmer mindsets do not change in ways that reinforce the strategic reforms motivated from above, the reforms and their underlying organizations might very well unravel once reformist co-op leaders leave the scene. In sum, farmer mindsets on their own are very weak predictors of whether a co-op will or will not change. But they can have a significant impact on the patterns of the reform process as well as on the scope and long-term effectiveness of reform.

In the past, reformist farmers and co-op leaders were in a distinct minority. Most farmers—particularly Japan's legions of part-time rice cultivators—were enmeshed in passive-producer mindsets. Co-op leaders, for their own part, were constrained by the top-heavy distribution of power within JA's hierarchical organizational structure and the capacity of Zenchū and Zennō to veto local co-op actions. The shortage of innovative co-op leadership was further reinforced by the selection process of the co-op's all-important board of directors; directors were drawn from and elected by the co-op's rank-and-file (read conservative) membership. Generally speaking, those change-oriented leaders who did step forward did not conduct themselves as assertive purveyors of market-oriented mindsets—profit-seeking co-op managers who could build enduring farmer organizations behind significant strategic reforms and who were willing to risk censure as they bypassed JA networks, like Takefu's Tomita Takashi. Instead, most limited themselves to changes that conformed closely with JA's normative and strategic precedents.

But the reformist impulse is now on the rise. Market developments that have enabled more ambitious farmers to break out of the traditional mold of passive production are strengthening farmer-member expectations for co-op change in some parts of Japan. And stronger market signals and changes to the legal context of agricultural cooperation—those exogenously imposed rules that help demarcate broad opportunities for co-op change—are encouraging more co-op personnel to step forward as change-oriented leaders. In the late 1990s, for example, the government amended the 1947 Agricultural Cooperative Law (Nōgyō kyōdō kumiai hō, "Co-op Law") to encourage co-ops to select certified full-time farmers and nonfarmer business managers and other "professionals" to their boards of directors, the assumption being that these individuals would bring new strategic ideas into the co-op.[67] Following the Abe government's 2015 amendments to the Co-op Law, the inclusion of such individuals on co-op boards is now mandatory. These changes increase the likelihood that more market-oriented norms will take root within a co-op and that farmer-members will mobilize (or be mobilized) behind corresponding co-op strategies.

The market-oriented strategies and organized relationships with farmer-members adopted by some reformist co-ops are inspiring other co-ops to embrace change. One telling indicator of this is the busloads of co-op personnel who routinely flock to Takefu for inspection tours.[68] Meanwhile, a confluence of trends appears to be challenging institutional inertia elsewhere in the JA hierarchy. As more and more entrepreneurial farmer-members loosen their dependence on JA services by buying some of their inputs and marketing all or portions of their raw product outside of the keitō, JA's national organizations can no longer compensate for lost income by coercing co-ops back into the fold, charging high input prices and service commissions, or increasing co-op reliance on credit and insurance services—services that are now well past their peak. This is due in no small part to government interventions that have weakened JA's rent-seeking opportunities. The government's liberalization of rice markets during the 1990s and post-2013 partial dismantlement of the nearly fifty-year-old rice price acreage reduction program known as *gentan* have reduced JA's access to the inflated commodity prices and administrative controls needed to impose rents on farmers. In its determination to accelerate the momentum of co-op reform, the Abe government also amended the co-op law to weaken the veto powers of JA's national organizations over local co-ops by stripping Zenchū of its right to require and carry out mandatory audits of local co-ops, once a mainstay of Zenchū's capacity to "advise" (read pressure) the co-ops, and by barring national and regional service providers from retaliating against local co-ops that refuse to sign up for a full roster of services. Once complicit in the installation and perpetuation of JA's market-distorting practices, the government has, to a modest but significant degree, increased JA's exposure to that all-important "measuring rod of price." In response to these interactive changes in the legal and regulatory context of agricultural cooperation and to the growing momentum toward market adaptations among local co-ops, JA's national tier is taking its first tentative—but meaningful—steps toward encouraging market-oriented strategic reform at *all* points in the JA hierarchy.

The Book in Brief

The following chapters develop the themes and arguments presented above in theoretical, historical, and comparative perspective.

In chapter 2, we set the stage for our subsequent analysis of JA reform by identifying what JA is changing from. Specifically, we explore Japan's postwar (1945–1990) interpretation of agricultural cooperation; examine the legal/regulatory, normative, organizational, and strategic foundations of the JA system that emerged out of the critical juncture of the early postwar period; analyze the synergies between the Liberal Democratic Party (LDP) government's redistributive policy stance toward the farm sector and JA's economic dominance; and explain the divergent predispositions toward institutional change at the national and local levels of the JA system.

Chapter 3 explores how farmers—the bedrock of co-ops—have changed since the early 1990s. We demonstrate that while family farms continue to dominate the Japanese agricultural landscape, they have grown more diverse in their preferences, mindsets, and production and management strategies. These changes are products of two sets of developments: deepening demographic and economic challenges and changing market opportunities generated by the government's gradual shift away from redistributive policy supports toward structural reforms designed to encourage more productivity and profit in the farm sector. These changes, we argue, are generating new reformist impulses within the co-ops, in part by raising the specter of farmer defections from the JA system.

In chapters 4–6, we analyze how and under what conditions JA organizations have responded to the developments chronicled in chapter 3. Chapter 4 demonstrates how JA's national organizations initially introduced path-dependent reforms to the JA organizational hierarchy and expanded their lucrative nonagricultural services. We then draw from our data set of 105 co-ops and other statistical sources to illuminate variations of strategic change among local co-ops by testing a series of hypotheses about the relationship between local economic, demographic, and other conditions, on the one hand, and indicators of strategic changes for increasing farmer incomes, on the other hand.[69]

Since quantitative methods can be inadequate when it comes to explaining both why and how the strategic reform process unfolds as it does in specific contexts, chapters 5 and 6 engage in qualitative case-study analysis. Chapter 5 explores the interactions among resource endowments and their corresponding market opportunities, agency, farmer organizations, and broader institutional factors in the reform processes of two co-ops with diverse product lines. The first case, in Kumamoto Prefecture, is one of top-down reform in a co-op with relatively passive farmer-members, while the second, in Nagano Prefecture, shows how strategic reforms can be carried out through partnerships among more entrepreneurial farmers, a proactive co-op, and, surprisingly, Zennō. In chapter 6, we explore strategic reform in rice-centric co-ops—those that produce and market more rice than any other product. Here, we illustrate how the measuring rod of price wields its influence over the reform process differently than in co-ops with more diverse product lines, and for one simple reason: rice prices have been declining over the last generation. In our analysis of two co-ops in Niigata Prefecture, we argue that, to do well, reformist rice-centric co-ops with a competitive product and strong farmer organizations must not only satisfy certain resource and market, organizational, and agency conditions but also place a premium on the timing of their reforms and on the co-op's acquisition of sophisticated marketing skills. Along the way, we explain why even hardworking, reform-oriented co-ops in today's challenging rice market may fail to stabilize farmer incomes, let alone increase them.

In chapter 7, we do two things. First, we explore JA's contemporary self-reform (*jiko kaikaku*) agenda and accelerated efforts during the second Abe Shinzō government (2012–2020) to transform the formal-legal foundations of Japanese farming and agricultural cooperation. In contrast to those who argue that self-reform is mere lip service or, at best, a half-hearted effort to comply with government reform objectives, we make the case that the JA Group now faces strong incentives—some of them endogenous—to promote reform at all levels of the JA pyramid. These include the growing capacity of entrepreneurial farmers to defect from JA services, limits to the expansion of JA's nonagricultural services, the gradual erosion of rent-seeking opportunities, and precedents set by reformist local co-ops. Second, we draw from the experiences of a reformist Niigata Prefecture cooperative to underscore the formidable challenges confronting contemporary farm communities and to make the case that the future of both Japanese agricultural communities and local multipurpose cooperatives depends on the further empowerment of local stakeholders.

By way of conclusion, we shift gears with a brief epilogue that takes a deeper dive into those slow-moving demographic and economic transformations that have catapulted Japanese farming and rural villages into a crisis of existential proportions. In our narrative of the struggles of a remote, mountainous community of Kumamoto Prefecture, we remind the reader of how farming is woven into the economic and social fabric of rural communities, how the painful economic and social trade-offs inherent in agricultural and co-op reform can reverberate far beyond the farm, and how JA remains an integral component of rural Japan's uncertain future—for better or for worse.

THE POSTWAR JA MODEL
1945–1990

Farming is risky business in free market settings. Farmers face uncertain incomes caused by commodity prices that fluctuate in response to everything from weather changes to shifts in the political winds. Their voices are overpowered in the marketplace by large wholesalers, food processors, and retailers. And their efforts to secure their futures by expanding their farms or diversifying their products are often thwarted by the reluctance of for-profit financial institutions to extend them credit.[1]

For more than two centuries, farmers in many countries have formed horizontal associations called cooperatives as an antidote to the many risks and challenges that inevitably arise when markets fail them. In their traditional form, co-ops put farmers first by serving their material and social-welfare interests through the provision of low-cost services and by giving them sovereign oversight of co-op management. Some co-ops fall short of these ideals, however, and JA more than most. By the early 1980s, JA's powerful national associations resembled large, self-interested corporations that trampled the freedoms of local cooperatives and raised costs for farmers. Put simply, JA had lost sight of the very farmers it professed to serve.

How and why did JA get this way?

The answers to this question are rooted in the institutional choices that shaped the early postwar formation of JA organizations and their subsequent path-dependent evolution, and in a conducive political environment fueled by an electoral exchange relationship between JA and the ruling LDP. Following a brief comparative and theoretical overview of JA, this chapter explores these points in turn. We then identify the basic organizational and strategic features of JA's national and local organizations, analyze the farmer mindsets that reflected and reinforced those features, and explain why change has always been more likely at the local level than at the national level. To conclude, we show how JA's extraordinary features and departure from basic co-op principles have intensified the need for organizational and strategic reform among member organizations while simultaneously limiting the scope for such change.

For several reasons, we date the end of JA's long postwar era at 1990. First, it was during the mid-1980s that postwar agricultural production peaked and the JA system reached organizational and strategic maturity.[2] Second, the abrupt collapse of the economic bubble in 1990 marked a turning point in JA history by deepening an economic and demographic crisis in the farm sector and triggering a gradual transformation of the legal, economic, and political contexts of agricultural cooperation. This confluence of trends in turn generated momentum among policy makers and stakeholders behind agricultural and JA reform. But before we can explain why and how JA organizations and strategies have been changing (or not) since the early 1990s, we must first understand what JA is changing *from* and how its institutional past constrains future reform. To that end, we begin our analysis by exploring how postwar JA measured up to the principles and practices of agricultural cooperation.

JA in Theoretical and Comparative Perspective

The Traditionally Organized Agricultural Cooperative in Theory and Practice

The "traditionally organized agricultural cooperative" is a form of "self-organized enterprise."[3] It is typically defined in the agricultural economics literature as a "user-owned and controlled business from which benefits are derived and distributed on the basis of their use." Those who own and control the co-op, in other words, are those who use it, and the co-op's ultimate purpose is to maximize user—that is, farmer-member—benefits.[4] As such, a co-op differs from the investor-owned firm (IOF), in which the degree of ownership and control is proportionate to the amount of equity capital invested and in which the owners of the firm are not necessarily its patrons.[5] The co-op also differs from the IOF in its generally nonprofit orientation and firm commitment to the *social* mission of enhancing individual farmer lifestyles and the integrity of rural communities.[6]

Traditionally organized agricultural co-ops have a long and storied history. In the early nineteenth-century rural United States, they first developed in reaction to the rise of commercial markets and concomitant decline in the number of small-scale firms that could provide farmers with competitively priced supplies.[7] By century's end, they were spreading throughout struggling British colonies with the support of imperial authorities.[8] Co-ops, in other words, were antidotes to imperfect markets.[9] In marked contrast to Anglo-American, free-market economic values, however, the traditional agricultural cooperative embraces principles and practices that border on the socialistic. Membership is open and voluntary. Co-op ownership rights are restricted to farmer-members,[10] and voting rights are usually distributed according to the "one farmer, one vote" equality rule.[11] Farmers invest modest funds in the co-op, the returns on which vary in relation to their patronage of co-op services.[12] And co-op members are usually entitled to sell all their raw product to the co-op, although they are under no obligation to do so.[13] Co-ops also practice democratic, "bottom-up" governance.[14] In smaller co-ops, the farmer-members can govern themselves directly. In larger co-ops, local farmer-members normally elect candidates from among their own ranks to serve on the co-op's board of directors, which oversees hired management,[15] and they expect those directors to remain accountable to them.

Traditionally organized farm co-ops can vary in several ways. In terms of function, four types of co-ops predominate. *Purchasing*—or farm-supply—co-ops take orders from their farmer-members for farm inputs (like fertilizers, seeds, and machinery), purchase those inputs from manufacturers, and then sell the inputs to their members at or near cost. Some purchasing co-ops also serve nonfarmer members by offering household appliances, lawn and garden supplies, and even grocery and restaurant services. Second, *marketing* co-ops, the most common type of co-op, collect the raw product of their farmer-members and then sell it to wholesalers or consumers, ideally at prices that advantage producers. Third, *service* co-ops specialize in addressing one or a few specific farmer needs, such as the artificial insemination and transport of livestock, product testing, crop drying and grain storage, farm credit and insurance, and, in rural communities lacking alternative providers, housing, utilities, health care, funeral services, and the like. All three types of co-ops levy commissions on their members for services rendered. Finally, *agricultural production* co-ops comprise entire communities that collectively own farmland and farm implements and that make all production decisions jointly. Production co-ops are common in Russia, central and south Asia, and Israel (kibbutzim) but are rare in the United States and Europe.[16] As we explain in later chapters, however, variations of these co-ops are now taking root in Japan.

While purchasing co-ops can service many different types of farmers, marketing co-ops are usually limited to a specific product line (e.g., dairy, wheat, citrus). It is therefore not uncommon for farmers to belong to more than one co-op at a time. Some larger co-ops in the United States, Canada, and Europe supply a mix of purchasing, marketing, and/or other services to their members; the (pre-reform) Saskatchewan Wheat Pool and its counterparts in other Canadian prairie provinces, for instance, operated at once as purchasing and grain-marketing co-ops.[17] Farm credit functions, however, are normally confined to special-purpose co-ops; with a few exceptions, including some German co-ops, these co-ops do not also offer input and/or marketing services.

The traditionally organized agricultural co-op also varies in terms of its organizational reach. Most co-ops are local in scope, but some participate in federations that span entire regions and beyond. Finally, and as chapter 4 further explains, co-ops have grown larger in recent decades through mergers and acquisitions, and new types of co-op organizations—and federations of co-ops— have appeared at the local, national, and even international levels.

No matter what their service profile, organizational structure, or geographic reach, the ultimate objective of the traditionally organized agricultural cooperative remains the same: to empower farmers by reducing their risks and increasing their incomes. By routinizing farmer access to farm inputs, distribution channels, and credit and other services, co-ops reduce farmers' transaction costs and lower their exposure to price volatility.[18] By collectively representing farmers in negotiations with wholesalers, processors, and retailers, they strengthen farmers' bargaining power in the food supply chain. These services in turn help farmers reap the benefits of their property rights, most notably access to a long-term, stable income stream—ideally the maximum possible income stream—from farmland.

Farmers and their communities are not the only ones who stand to benefit from traditional agricultural cooperation. According to the "competitive yardstick hypothesis" proposed by the American agricultural economist Edwin G. Nourse during the 1920s, well-functioning, not-for-profit cooperatives with sufficient—but not overwhelming—market share can incentivize market competitors to behave more efficiently and fairly.[19] And when that happens, advantages accrue to actors throughout the food supply chain, from the farm household, which earns a higher income from farming, to the urban consumer, who gains access to high-quality, fairly priced foodstuffs.

The traditionally organized cooperative originated at a time when small family farms were the predominant type of farm enterprise and global competition in food production was insignificant. Commodities—dairy, rice, wheat, corn—were relatively undifferentiated; value-added processing was minimal to nonexistent; consumer food preferences were simple, and knowledge about branding and other sophisticated marketing strategies was, at best, rudimentary. For as long as these conditions persisted, farm co-ops had no need for highly skilled managers, complex organizational networks, or sophisticated business strategies.[20] The business of the co-op was simple: to provide inputs or other services to members and/or to collect raw product for minimal processing and then sale and shipment to wholesalers and retailers. Recently, however, the diversification, industrialization, and globalization of agriculture has obliged agricultural co-ops around the world—including in Japan—to rethink their organizational structures and strategies, a topic we explore in later chapters. For the remainder of this chapter, our aim is to understand and explain postwar Japan's distinctive take on *traditional* agricultural cooperation.

JA

In some ways, postwar Japan's version of the traditionally organized agricultural cooperative has conformed with the principles and practices outlined above. Japanese farmer-members "own" and invest minimal sums in their co-op,[21] and on paper, at least, they receive returns on their investments in proportion to their patronage of co-op services. Voting rights are distributed to farmer-members only, and each farmer receives only one vote regardless of farm size or patronage of co-op services. Finally, the co-ops have come to practice a form of representative democracy in which farmer-members elect boards of directors from among their own ranks; the board is in turn responsible for overseeing hired management and other employees.

In other ways, Japanese co-ops have departed from international cooperative principles and practices, most notably in terms of the sheer scope of the functions they perform. Whereas most co-ops in Europe and North America specialize in a discrete set of services and, in the case of marketing co-ops, offer them to only certain types of farmers,[22] Japan's multipurpose agricultural cooperatives (sōgō nōgyō kumiai) offer purchasing, marketing, credit, and other services to *all* farmers. But that is not all. Until very recently, multipurpose co-ops were also *legally required* to serve as agents of government farm policy and to contribute collective goods to their farm communities, from the reclamation, improvement, and irrigation of farmland to the dissemination of information and the provision of agricultural education programs. They also offer an inordinately wide range of financial, social-welfare, retail, and recreational services to their communities, including home and personal loans, insurance policies, pensions, medical and hospital services, elder-care and funeral services, grocery stores (A-Co-op), gasoline, wedding planning, movie theaters and beauty parlors, libraries, cooking instruction, travel and real estate services, and even, in some cases, car and tombstone sales. There is virtually nothing that the co-op cannot do or provide. It is a general store (*nandemoya*)[23]—a one-stop shop for public and private services that is open to farmers and nonfarmers alike. It is the countryside's largest employer. And in many rural communities that have been poorly served by private-sector providers, its status as "more than co-op" has rendered it all but indispensable.

A second distinguishing feature of Japan's multipurpose co-ops is that for decades, membership and participation in co-op services was voluntary in principle, but not in practice. Farmers were *required* to open co-op bank accounts and to conduct their transactions with the co-op through those accounts—a practice that enabled the co-op to monitor individual members. The co-ops also curbed farmer defections by threatening to cut off their access to co-op-managed irrigation systems and other essential services.[24] They even made it difficult for farmers to give up their membership; farmers had to be approved by the co-op before taking such a step, and the waits could be interminable. Not surprisingly, the rate of farmer membership in the co-ops consistently neared 100 percent, far surpassing European or North American rates.[25] And it remains at that level today. This extraordinary rate reflects JA's historically dominant position as an agricultural service provider; its role as a semiofficial, administrative arm of the state; and, as we shall see, the norms and practices of the JA network.

Third, JA has stretched the customary boundaries of agricultural cooperative membership to include not only active farmers—or regular co-op members (sei kumiaiin)—but also vast numbers of associate co-op members (jun kumiaiin): retired farmers and nonvoting, nonfarmer residents of the co-op jurisdiction who are entitled to the co-ops' financial and other nonagricultural services. Since 2009, JA's associate members have outnumbered its regular members by significant margins.

Fourth, local co-op leaders have historically been far more accountable to prefectural and national authorities in the JA hierarchy than to the farmer-members who elected them. JA Bank (Nōrinchūkin) and Zenkyōren, the national associations for JA banking and insurance, respectively, have set the terms for farmer credit and insurance sales at the co-op level. Zennō and its corresponding prefectural economic federations (keizairen) have orchestrated the co-ops' purchasing and marketing services. Until recently, Zenchū—the "control tower" (shireitō) of the JA Group—and its prefectural equivalents (chūōkai, unions of agricultural cooperatives) monitored the co-ops' financial affairs and management practices while serving as the main conduit for co-op contact with Japanese politicians and officialdom. Even ordinary co-op employees have been subject to top-down manipulation, as evidenced by their obligation to fulfill onerous quotas (noruma) for the sale of JA products to the co-op's farmer-members.

Finally, and perhaps most significantly for our purposes, JA organizations have done a poor job of maximizing financial returns to farmers. They have overcharged for farm inputs and extracted generous commissions on services rendered. And in their fixation on profits, they have often neglected to give farmers their financial due. In many respects, JA organizations have prioritized their own financial well-being and longevity over the interests of their farmer-members.

To the extent that agricultural co-ops should function as organizations of, for, and by farmers, JA is an anomaly. Power is concentrated at the national—rather than local—level of the JA system. And JA benefits accrue as much, if not more than, to nonfarmers and JA organizations as to farmer-members. Meanwhile, JA has grown so large over the decades that it has weakened rather than strengthened competition in agricultural markets. So much for Nourse's "competitive yardstick" theory.

As chapter 4 explains, traditionally organized agricultural cooperatives around the world have been pressured to change as farmers adapt to the diversification, industrialization, and liberalization and globalization of agriculture. Adding to these pressures in JA's case are controversies surrounding its extraordinary multifunctionality, its associate membership, and its top-down flow of authority. But how did JA come by these distinctive features in the first place?

The Historical and Institutional Foundations of the JA System

JA's Postwar Critical Juncture: The Occupation

Critical junctures can function as cradles for significant institutional change. Rare and relatively short periods in history that are often precipitated by disruptive events like wars and economic crashes, critical junctures empower agents to make bold institutional choices by loosening the normal rules of the game. Some of the reforms that can emanate from these periods are exogenously imposed, while others are endogenously generated; as we note in chapter 1, specifying these institutional origins is essential to understanding subsequent "self-reinforcing path-dependent processes,"[26] including the capacity of organizations for future change.

The US occupation of Japan (1945–1952) and its immediate aftermath marked a critical juncture in the history of Japanese agricultural cooperatives and the farm sector more generally. Triggered by defeat in war, imposed primarily by the Supreme Commander for Allied Powers (SCAP), and enabled by the suspension of many long-standing rules of Japanese political engagement, the institutional reforms introduced during this period helped put the agricultural cooperative system on its distinctive postwar path. Some of those reforms were transformative. Others warrant our attention because of their unintended consequences. Also noteworthy were the paths not taken. The cumulative result of these myriad changes and nonchanges was a postwar co-op system that ran afoul of many of the principles and practices of traditional agricultural cooperation.

The 1947 Agricultural Cooperative Law can be read in part as an example of missed opportunities. If SCAP had had its way, Japanese co-ops would have emerged from the legislative process looking very much like the traditionally organized co-ops we examined above.[27] Convinced that autonomous, democratically constituted local co-ops were key to improving the "economic and cultural well-being" of Japanese farmers,[28] SCAP upheld the principles of US and European agricultural cooperation as models for Japan to emulate.[29] SCAP's vision was not without historical precedent in Japan. By the Tokugawa (1603–1867) period, for example, a type of co-op with distinctly democratic features had become a fixture of local Japan. Known as kō, these voluntary associations included arrangements for pooling credit and other resources that members could draw on to weather short-term crises; farm-labor (yui) kō helped cultivators reduce production costs.[30] As Tetsuo Najita observes, although some types of kō were subject to varying degrees of government regulation, many had emerged spontaneously as self-help organizations that operated outside of the "formal . . . political order" and that reflected a "shared organizational consciousness" based on mutual trust.[31] This spirit of autonomous, grassroots cooperation for the purposes of mutual aid imbued a range of spontaneous local experiments with agricultural and other cooperative organizations until well into the twentieth century.[32] Spontaneity also marked the establishment of purchasing co-ops (kōbai kumiai) and marketing co-ops (hanbai kumiai) in the Meiji-era sericulture and tea sectors as they grappled with the unforeseen opportunities and challenges of expanding foreign trade.[33]

The postwar Japanese government, for its own part, championed an alternative, state-led approach to agricultural cooperation that was rooted in a more recent history—the early twentieth century.[34] Two types of cooperative organizations dominated the agricultural landscape at that time: farm associations (nōkai) and the more ubiquitous, but misleadingly named, industrial cooperatives (sangyō kumiai). Authorized by legislation passed in 1899 and controlled by rural landlords, farm associations promoted the diffusion of new technologies and other agricultural improvements, largely at the government's behest.[35] The industrial cooperatives, by contrast, were rooted in the 1900 Industrial Cooperatives Law (Sangyō kumiai hō), which authorized the government to guide the formation and subsequent development of co-ops in a range of sectors that were struggling with the negative externalities of capitalism.[36] In response to expanding commercial markets that challenged vulnerable family farms and regional distribution systems, the Industrial Cooperatives Law drew from German models to provide for discrete purchasing, marketing, credit, and other service co-ops in the agricultural sector. Within a few short years, the law was amended to authorize the co-ops to form prefectural federations and to cross functional lines,[37] thus laying the groundwork for the postwar JA system's three-tiered organizational structure and its hallmark multifunctionality. The co-ops' role as semiofficial administrative organizations (*gyōsei soshiki*)[38] also intensified during this time as the state gradually tightened its controls over the co-ops, appointed mayors and other village officials to lead them, subjected them and the farm associations to waves of organizational reform, and prodded farmers to join.[39] These efforts culminated in the passage of the 1943 Agricultural Associations Law (Nōgyō dantai hō), which forced the industrial cooperatives and the farm associations to merge into agricultural associations (*nōgyōkai*), a type of wartime control association (*tōseikai*), and made farmer membership compulsory. The law also tasked the reconstituted co-ops with implementing the food rationing system established by the 1942 Staple Food Control Act.[40] Unlike the voluntarist, democratic organizations envisioned by Western theories of cooperation or even the premodern kō, the wartime farm co-ops were first and foremost instruments of the authoritarian state. But this was of little concern to early postwar Japanese authorities, who viewed them as optimally positioned to alleviate a deepening food crisis caused by failed rice harvests, the suspension of food imports from Japan's now former colonies, a war-torn distribution network, a rationing system that was trying the patience of a restive public, and a burgeoning black market for foodstuffs.[41]

Between March 1946 and July 1947, SCAP and the then Ministry of Agriculture and Fisheries battled long and hard over their conflicting visions of agricultural cooperation, producing multiple drafts of what was to eventually become the 1947 Co-op Law.[42] In accordance with SCAP's preferences, the Co-op Law identified the core mission of agricultural cooperation as the economic and social elevation of farm households and adopted the principle of one vote per farm household regardless of farm size.[43] But in most other respects, the law reflected the farm ministry's vision. Contrary to SCAP's—and the Ministry of Finance's (MOF)—preference that credit functions be separated from the local co-ops, as per US custom, the law endorsed the now well-established practice of co-op multifunctionality. The farm ministry's justification for this was that combining credit and other co-op functions under one roof would facilitate rice deliveries; less well publicized was the ministry's fear that a separation of functions would put farm credit under the control of its rival—the MOF.[44] The provision strengthened the monopoly potential of the co-ops by permitting them to extend credit to their members that could then be used to purchase other co-op services.[45] The legislation further defied SCAP's wishes by exempting the multipurpose co-ops from the 1947 Anti-Monopoly Law and prohibiting the establishment of more than one co-op per village. Grounded in the logic that stepped-up competition would harm the co-ops' already precarious financial health, these provisions strengthened JA's first-mover advantage in the agricultural sector.

Other Co-op Law provisions worked at cross-purposes to the co-ops' core mission of serving farmers. The introduction of the nonvoting associate cooperative membership, for example, was intended to grant former landlords and other nonfarm enterprises access to certain co-op services without empowering them vis-à-vis the co-op's regular farmer-members. This step toward member inclusiveness may have boosted the co-op's social and economic legitimacy at the local level by strengthening its role as a village solidarity group (*sonraku kyōdōtai*).[46] The problem was that the law's architects could not have foreseen that the number of associate members would one day exceed that of regular members or that co-op revenues would grow far too dependent on nonagricultural services.[47] The provision, in short, had the unintended consequence of deflecting the attention of JA leaders from the (less profitable) agricultural interests of their farmer-members, thus indirectly violating the early postwar goal of releasing farmers from the control of nonfarmer actors.[48]

While the Co-op Law distanced the co-op system from some of the internationally recognized principles and practices of agricultural cooperation, the consequences—both intended and unintended—of postwar land reform combined with JA policies and other incentives to help keep family farms small, increasingly part-time, and heavily dependent on co-op services.

By transferring the bulk of Japanese farmland from the politically powerful landlord class to their former tenants, land reform created a vast population of farm households (nōka) that owned, on average, just one hectare of farmland. Land reform also prevented those farms from growing substantially larger by imposing draconian restrictions on farmland ownership and transfer rights. Enshrined in the 1952 Agricultural Land Act (Nōchi hō, ALA) against the wishes of farm-ministry officials who championed structural reform,[49] the restrictions included a ban on absentee ownership, the imposition of strict upper limits on the amount of land a farm household could own, controls on farmland leasing, and the stipulation that only farm households (and schools and villages)—and not nonfarm corporations—could own and cultivate farmland. Finally, the reforms empowered village agricultural committees (nōgyō iinkai)—themselves composed of local farmers—to approve the sale, leasing, and conversion of farmland in their jurisdictions.[50]

To be sure, these stipulations placed welcome curbs on excessive tenancy and the return of the reviled landlord class. But they also generated all manner of agricultural inefficiencies. As Mary G. McDonald explains, by ensuring that farmland could only be acquired through birth or adoption or marriage into a farm household, they excluded many potential players from the primary sector.[51]

And they helped keep farms inordinately small by enmeshing farmland leasing in a thicket of red tape, thereby forcing ambitious farmers who sought to expand their holdings to borrow land informally from family and friends.[52]

Most significantly for our purposes, land reform and a spate of complementary changes combined to produce a large population of part-time, small-scale farm households, virtually all of whom focused on rice cultivation. There are two main types of part-time farm households: those that earned more than 50 percent of their total household income from farming pursuits and those that earned less than 50 percent from farming. For much of the postwar era, the latter group outnumbered the former by a wide margin. Part-time farming was in one sense a natural corollary of land reform; many farmers needed nonfarm employment because their holdings were simply too small to support their families. But it was also a product of the deliberate industrialization of the countryside, which provided cultivators with plenty of opportunities for off-farm employment, and of generous property and other tax breaks that incentivized part-time cultivators to remain on the land. Finally, advances in agricultural technology dramatically simplified rice cultivation, thereby enabling farmers to till their paddies after hours or to delegate the job to the "three *chans*": *ojīchan* (grandpa), *obāchan* (grandma), and *okāchan* (mom). Outnumbering their full-time counterparts by a ratio of more than five to one by 1990, these part-time households formed—and continue to form—the heart of JA's regular membership base.

JA organizations saw to it that most farm households remained small—too small to turn their backs on the convenient services of the ubiquitous, multipurpose co-ops. It exercised its formal authority to recommend candidates for local agricultural committees, which had authority over farmland consolidation. It ignored or rejected calls for structural reforms that would have decreased the size of its membership base. Many local co-ops, meanwhile, took advantage of their freedom to devise many of their own "operational rules" to set the terms of regular membership as liberally as possible, thereby admitting even the smallest and most inefficient of noncommercial cultivators.[53] All the while, JA organizations zealously upheld the one-farmer, one-vote rule, never mind that this rule weakened the voices of less numerous—but more efficient—full-time farmers, many of whom, not coincidentally, grew less dependent on co-op services as the years unfolded. To this most fundamental of co-op principles, JA remained firmly committed.

The Organizational Centralization of JA

JA also parted company from international co-op norms in its top-heavy, pyramid-shaped system of organizations. Two developments shaped this distinctive

structure. First, the co-ops' official designation as state agents ostensibly war-
ranted the presence of network organizations that could coordinate not only the
collection and distribution of rice and other agricultural products but also the
dissemination of official directives and subsidies to local farmers.[54] Second, questions about co-op competence in the wake of lower rice prices triggered by US-led
austerity measures (the 1949 Dodge Line) and increasing co-op debt were fueling
calls by the early 1950s for the empowerment of supralocal organizations over the
managerial and fiscal affairs of the co-ops.[55]

As long as SCAP was around to voice its misgivings about government med-
dling in co-op affairs, the organizational centralization of the co-op system proceeded in fits and starts. The history of Zennō (Zenkoku nōgyō kyōdō kumiai
rengōkai, or the National Federation of Agricultural Cooperative Associations) is
a case in point. In keeping with SCAP's opposition to multipurpose prefectural
and national associations,[56] two separate national associations were established
in 1948, one to oversee purchasing functions (Zenkoku kōbai nōgyō kyōdō
kumiai rengōkai, National Federation of Purchasing Agricultural Cooperative
Associations) and the other to orchestrate the network's marketing services
(Zenkoku hanbai nōgyō kyōdō kumiai rengōkai, National Federation of Marketing Agricultural Cooperative Associations). In 1972, well after the watchful eye of
SCAP had disappeared, these two federations merged to form the powerful, multifunctional entity we know today as Zennō. Zennō and its predecessors proved a
mixed blessing for local co-ops and farmers. On the one hand, they alleviated
farmers' exposure to economic risks by guaranteeing their access to essential
farm supplies and agricultural markets. On the other hand, they compromised
local co-op independence and proved costly to local farmers, for in the absence of
meaningful competition in the primary sector, the organizations were free to
charge inflated prices and commissions for their services.[57]

The centralization of other functions and organizations in the JA system accelerated after national sovereignty was restored to Japan in 1952. In 1954, as
part of a broad effort to stabilize the management and financial affairs of struggling local co-ops,[58] the government established Zenchū (Zenkoku nōgyō kyōdō
kumiai chūōkai, or the National Central Union of Agricultural Cooperatives)
and corresponding chūōkai at the prefectural level. Building on prewar proto-
types and authorized through an amendment to the Co-op Law, the prefectural
unions oversaw agricultural extension and educational services for farmers, carried out essential research and surveys, settled disputes within the co-op system, issued proposals to government policy makers, and even helped mobilize
the vote during elections.[59] Zenchū and the prefectural-level central unions were
also empowered to provide auditing (kansa) and management (shidō) services
that for many local co-ops were mandatory; while they undoubtedly saved many

a co-op from financial ruin, these services widened opportunities for Zenchū and their prefectural counterparts to influence local co-op affairs.[60]

Finally, the government streamlined the provision of financial services to farmers. The centralization of agricultural credit had been completed well before the war with the 1923 establishment of JA Bank.[61] Thanks largely to regulations that required farmers to receive government subsidies and payments for their products via their JA bank accounts, JA Bank and its prefectural affiliates (shinren) became the only available source of savings and credit for postwar Japanese farmers. In 1951, the government authorized the establishment of Zenkyōren (National Mutual Insurance Federation of Agricultural Cooperatives) to coordinate the provision of life and nonlife insurance products to cultivators; in 1958, Zenkyōren was permitted to establish prefectural organizations.

The centralization of power within the upper echelons of the JA system was buffeted by several practices, one of which was the imposition of sales quotas on co-ops and their employees. No matter the task—bank loans, insurance policies, the sale of farm inputs, the marketing of crops—virtually every full-time employee had a quota to fulfill, and those who met or exceeded it were openly rewarded. Top-performing co-ops were also rewarded by higher-level JA leaders with well-publicized cash prizes during widely attended ceremonies; in time, nothing worried the co-ops more than *not* receiving these distinctions. Indeed, the quotas grew so important that a failure to comply with them was enough to disqualify candidates for co-op leadership positions. From Zennō's perspective, the quota system helped ensure co-op dependence on its input and marketing services. For the Japan Fair Trade Commission, however, it was a misuse of JA power. From the early 1980s, the commission stepped up its official investigations into the practice.

The centralization of JA power was also fueled by mergers of local co-ops. During the early 1950s, some local co-ops voluntarily merged to keep up with merging villages, whose boundaries the co-ops increasingly duplicated for administrative purposes;[62] other co-ops lacked the financial strength or leadership to survive on their own.[63] Many had to be cajoled into merging. In the name of administrative efficiency, the government introduced a string of measures between 1956 and 1988 to speed things along, including the authorization of prefectural governors to encourage co-op mergers in their jurisdictions. Zenchū, for its own part, did all it could to promote ever greater economies of scale at the local co-op level, especially in the wake of agricultural price decreases following the 1973 oil shock and efforts during the 1980s to expand JA's financial offerings in anticipation of financial deregulation.[64] Critics viewed this outside interference in the administrative decisions of local co-ops as a gross violation of the spirit of co-op autonomy.[65]

Between 1960 and 1990, mergers reduced the number of multipurpose co-ops from 12,050 to 3,574 and increased the average number of regular members per co-op from 480 to 1,551. (By late 2018, there were just 649 co-ops with an average of 6,545 regular members.)[66] This expansion in the co-ops' economy of scale may have enhanced the profitability of JA's financial services over time, but it diminished the quality of many co-op services geared toward farmers. As expanding co-ops grew more geographically diverse and the average number of regular members per co-op increased, it became harder for co-op leaders to address the specific needs of each farm region in its jurisdiction and to offer individualized advice to farmers. Finally, and as a subsequent section elaborates, a concomitant decline in rural community cohesiveness diminished the capacity of farmer-members to systematically communicate with top co-op officials and to hold them accountable.

Farmers—in theory the ultimate beneficiaries of agricultural cooperation—were becoming mere consumers of co-op services and spectators of co-op governance.[67]

The Political Foundations of JA Dominance

By the time Japan's famous 1956 Economic White Paper had proclaimed the end of postwar economic recovery, most of the rules, norms, and organizations of the postwar co-op system were in place. But it was by no means inevitable that JA would become the agricultural powerhouse that it did by the early 1980s. In fact, from the vantage point of 1961, JA's future looked much different.

That year, the LDP government spearheaded the enactment of the landmark Agricultural Basic Law (ABL) in response to the white paper's observation that a productivity gap was developing between the farm sector and Japan's burgeoning manufacturing sector, and with it an income gap between rural and urban households. This was a pressing political issue, not least because, with 13.27 million Japanese—or 30 percent of the total workforce—working on the land in 1960, agriculture was still the country's largest "industry."[68] Any government that ignored the emerging productivity and income gaps did so at its peril.

To close those gaps, the ABL called for structural reforms to boost farm productivity. The recommended reforms included the deregulation of farmland to enable farm consolidation and a reduction in the number of inefficient farms,[69] the diversification of production away from rice,[70] and the introduction of incentives for greater producer responsiveness to consumer demand.[71]

But, with a few noteworthy exceptions that we explore in chapter 4, LDP-led governments did not fully embrace the spirit and objectives of the law. This was because structural reform stood to trigger a major political backlash by creating winners and losers in the farm sector. Had the government moved to expand farm size and diversify production, some farmers would have prospered while many more smaller, part-time farmers would have been pushed off the land. This would have been political suicide for the LDP, which had just committed itself to doubling the incomes of ordinary Japanese over the next decade and was facing electoral challenges from the Japan Socialist Party. And it would have been bad for JA, since fewer farmers would mean declining co-op membership. Product diversification, meanwhile, would have decreased farmer dependence on the co-op system, for while it was one thing to rely on JA's relatively uniform distribution channels for rice, a product that is easily pooled and transported and that can be stored for lengthy periods, it was quite another for fruits, vegetables, and other perishables that were distinguished by multiple gradations in strain and quality and that required speedy delivery to market.[72]

To close those rural-urban gaps, then, successive LDP governments implemented *redistributive* policies that did little to improve agricultural productivity but much to line the pockets of farmers—especially part-time farmers—and solidify JA dominance. Those governments weakened—or outright vetoed—legislative efforts to promote farm consolidation. They gave farmers generous tax breaks and funded rural factory construction and public works projects that provided part-time producers with off-farm employment. They blocked foreign rice imports. And they kept domestic rice prices extraordinarily high. Rooted in the 1942 Staple Food Control Act and originally intended to stabilize the food supply during and immediately after the war, rice price supports dragged on until the early 1990s.[73] Under the scheme, government rice (*seifumai*) followed a set route as it moved from farm to table: the co-ops would purchase the bulk of rice from their members at high, government-subsidized prices; that rice would then wind its way through first a prefectural economic federation and then Zennō (or its pre-1972 marketing predecessor), ending up in either official storehouses or at local wholesalers or vendors licensed by the Food Agency, a bureau of the Ministry of Agriculture, Forestry and Fisheries (MAFF).[74] Since consumer rice prices, while high by international standards, were deliberately set lower than producer prices, the scheme strained government coffers; by 1965, Japan was paying more in agricultural subsidies than any other country.[75]

The LDP's commitment to redistribution was reinforced by its electoral ties to JA. There had long been a natural political affinity between most farmers and conservative politicians after land reform transformed tenants into landowners, thus weakening radical tendencies in the countryside.[76] The national co-op network proved an effective vehicle for mobilizing those conservative sympathies. JA's electoral wing, known today as the farmers' political leagues (nōseiren), mobilized farmer-members behind individual LDP politicians in lower house elections under single nontransferable vote, multimember district (SNTV) rules. It also gathered the farm vote behind sponsored candidates (rieki daihyō giin, lit., interest representative Diet members) in the upper house's national proportional representation district; most of these candidates were former farm bureaucrats who could represent JA's interests in the political and bureaucratic worlds. And JA provided the LDP with invaluable electoral endorsements and campaign volunteers. In these ways, JA helped compensate for the LDP's small membership base and weak organizational presence at the local level.[77]

JA and the LDP benefited from the exchange relationship. Zenchū gained access to the corridors of power, which it used to lobby bureaucrats and politicians for favors, negotiate with government over the setting of rice prices, and observe LDP meetings on farm-related matters. And the LDP could count on the countryside to help keep it in power. As rural populations steadily declined in the wake of industrialization and urbanization, the conservative party ignored calls to reapportion lower house electoral districts in farming areas, thus ensuring that the farm vote would continue to significantly outweigh the urban vote.

Redistributive policies had their intended effects on farm incomes. In 1960, the average income earned by farmers was approximately 70 percent that of average incomes earned by workers in manufacturing industries (seizōgyō). The two sides were at rough parity by 1970, but then the income gap reemerged—this time with farmer incomes significantly exceeding those of workers (see chapter 3, esp. figure 3.2). The gap continued until the end of the 1990s despite agricultural productivity indexes that lagged behind those of the manufacturing sector.[78]

High prices and closed markets for rice and other redistributive perquisites contributed to an unnaturally large population of rice farmers, who even today compose fully 70 percent of all farmers.[79] From 1960, Japanese consumer demand for rice began a precipitous, decades-long descent, and yet rice production continued to increase. High prices also incentivized farmers to continue cultivating rice along the sides of mountains and hills and in other inhospitable terrain (chūsankan chiiki). Japan's picturesque, terraced rice paddies (tanada) may be a plus for rural tourism, but they are very costly to cultivate; had more competitive market forces been in effect, they would have been far less common.

Not surprisingly, by 1970 the country was awash in an oversupply of rice. The government could have lowered rice subsidies to correct the problem, but that would have driven many farmers-cum-members-cum-voters out of business. Instead, it resorted to yet another redistributive program, this time to regulate the supply of rice. The rice acreage reduction program—or gentan, as it was commonly known—imposed production quotas on farmers and channeled subsidies via JA to those who fulfilled them.[80] Villages that failed to comply with the directives risked significant penalties.

Gentan was highly unpopular at first. Farmers and JA organizations balked at the notion of producing less rice when prices were so high, while economists criticized the program for further weakening the link between production and consumer demand. Government rewards for fulfilling quotas helped dampen that opposition, especially among part-time farmers—virtually all of whom were rice farmers—with time on their hands for off-farm employment. More competitive farmers were won over by subsidies for switching to alternative crops. It was not until the mid-1990s, when the domestic rice market was partially liberalized, that JA organizations and farmers lined up behind gentan as their best bet for keeping rice prices high,[81] even though high prices stood to weaken long-term consumer demand for rice.[82] But there were still some holdouts. In Akita Prefecture's fertile Ōgata village, for instance, many farmers opted out of gentan by bypassing JA and marketing their high-quality rice via private distributors.[83] The local co-op adapted by all but abandoning its marketing services and concentrating on input sales.[84]

Gentan eliminated the rice glut, but at a hefty price: as government expenditures skyrocketed, part-time farmers found yet another reason to remain on the land, thus further weakening incentives for land consolidation. But since JA's national and prefectural organizations benefited handsomely from gentan and other redistributive policies, they did nothing to oppose them. Gentan justified the top-heavy, bureaucratized JA system, which channeled government subsidies to farmers and, in time, assumed responsibility for the distribution of production quotas. High rice prices and protections from cheaper imports enriched Zennō by enabling it to extract more commissions from farmer-members for its marketing services. All the while, rice price supports, gentan, tariffs, and rural public works projects helped slow the shrinkage of co-op memberships; those memberships were integral to JA's electoral clout and lobbying efforts to preserve the status quo. These were the components of a cycle of exchange between JA and the LDP that continued decade after decade after decade.

To paraphrase Douglass North's ruminations about path dependence, new rules of the game can generate organizations that in turn try to shape the future trajectories of those rules—and in ways that serve the interests (and power) of the organizations themselves.[85] And so it was with JA. Legal reforms introduced during the occupation and the redistributive policies of the rapid growth era helped shape JA's organizational parameters, relationships with its farmer-members, business strategies, and political power. JA's national organizations then used their lobbying and electoral clout to entrench all that in perpetuity. As later chapters elaborate, these efforts proved highly damaging both to the health of Japanese agriculture and to JA's very future.

To be sure, occupation-era reforms to the agricultural sector and the complementary institutional and political developments of subsequent decades gave the Japanese people much to celebrate. After years of food shortages, consumers gained access to a stable—but highly priced—supply of rice and other foodstuffs. Japan's once beleaguered farm households now owned the land they tilled and could count on easy access to a variety of essential services. To the extent the co-op system drastically reduced the economic risks inherent in farming and helped catapult farm households into the middle class, the reforms were a resounding success. But the reforms did little to shield farmers from high-priced farm inputs and hefty co-op commissions. Nor did they democratize farmer participation in the co-ops. The structure of the co-op system ensured that while membership may have been voluntary in theory, it was compulsory in practice; in contrast to their counterparts in virtually every country in the world—with the exceptions of Soviet Russia and Mao's China—the co-ops could boast of membership rates of nearly 100 percent. By no means the locus of co-op sovereignty, those farmer-members were subject to the manipulations of prefectural and national leaders in the JA system. To students of Japan's prewar co-ops, not much had changed beyond the lettering on the signboard (*kanban*) outside the co-op door.[86]

Farmers were not the only ones held captive by the postwar co-op system; local co-ops also chafed at their relative lack of autonomy within the system's hierarchical structure. But the costs of exiting JA were prohibitively high. For as long as JA dominated most farmer services and functioned as the main conduit for the dispensation of government farm subsidies, restless co-ops had no choice but to remain within the network. Even decades later, when deregulation had increased the number of competitors facing JA, co-ops that procured farm inputs from—or marketed farmer product—outside of Zennō and/or the prefectural economic federations faced retaliation in the form of reduced access to credit and other network services. (Zennō and the economic federations got away with all this in part because of their exemptions from, or the weak enforcement of, Anti-Monopoly Law provisions.) For all intents and purposes, the costs of defection had rendered both the co-ops and their farmer-members virtual hostages of JA.

Postwar JA in Organizational and Strategic Perspective

Chapters 4 to 6 analyze why and how local co-op organizations and strategies have been changing over the past generation, while Chapter 7 explores recent reforms at the national level of JA. The purpose of the remainder of this chapter is to establish some baselines for that analysis. What were the strategic and organizational features of postwar (i.e., pre-1990) JA organizations and their farmer-members? How did informal institutions help reinforce postwar agricultural cooperation? What, finally, were some of the postwar precedents for change within JA, and why was change most likely at the local level?

JA at the National Level

Strategically, JA's postwar national service associations behaved primarily as profit-oriented, rent-seeking service providers to local co-ops. For them, the name of the game was cornering markets, and they accomplished this with a leg up from government. JA Bank benefited from a de facto monopoly over the provision of savings and credit to cultivators, its status as an agent of the state in the dispensation of agricultural subsidies, and from government-established interest rates that were always slightly higher than those of commercial banks. Zennō, for its part, could thank its role as state agent under the 1942 Staple Food Control Act for its enormous power over rice transactions.

Zennō also strived for market dominance as a purchasing co-op. For agricultural chemicals, it was cornering 80 percent of the market by the mid-1970s.[87] Its share of the fertilizer market was even greater, increasing from 66 percent in 1955 to a whopping 90 percent in 2003. This extraordinary performance was in part the product of government regulations in effect between 1954 and 1986 that enabled Zennō to export fertilizers at low prices and to charge inflated prices at home—a brazen example of formalized rent seeking.[88] In many areas, the co-ops would contract with small local dealers who sold inputs directly to farmers; Zennō set the base price, and the dealer was free to increase it.[89] But nobody knew exactly how high those base prices were, since Zennō was under no official obligation before 2017 to disclose them. We do know, however, that Zennō was quick to take advantage of its privileged position to devise clever strategies for increasing returns. In one telling example, it refused to standardize the size of cardboard boxes used for the transport of produce, since doing so would have increased the efficiency of production, thereby lowering prices and hence Zennō's income from commissions.[90] As late as 1992, farmers were purchasing approximately 75 percent of their cardboard boxes and other packing materials through Zennō.[91]

Zennō's profit-oriented, market-cornering strategies were complemented by its organizational linkages with private manufacturers. For fertilizers, Zennō stood at the summit of a network of small domestic firms that some critics have likened to a government-sanctioned cartel.[92] Zennō cultivated similar ties with the manufacturers of other farm inputs, including pesticides, farm machinery, and those notorious cardboard boxes. Within JA, Zennō's strategies were enabled by its relationships to other organizations, most notably by its relative lack of accountability to players lower down in the JA hierarchy. Nevertheless, Zennō governed itself as a cooperative insofar as it was nominally headed by a board of directors (rijikai), the members of which were primarily prefectural economic federations and some local co-ops. In short, JA combined the organizational features of cooperatives and investor-owned firms.

Zenchū, a membership organization that also consisted primarily of JA's prefectural federations, worked to preserve the organizations and strategies of the entire JA hierarchy. Zenchū and its prefectural counterparts enforced co-op compliance with JA practices through its auditing, supervisory, and other functions. Zenchū also sought to preserve the institutional conditions for profitable rent seeking among JA's economic service providers by engaging in political lobbying, which was paid for with levies (fukakin) extracted from individual co-ops (and hence farmers), and by using JA's electoral influence to keep sympathetic politicians in power at all levels of government. In sum, Zenchū was part administrative organization and part political interest group.

Like Japan's famed keiretsu, or business conglomerates, JA's national associations developed a large bureaucracy staffed by well-trained employees who enjoyed lifetime employment and lodged that bureaucracy in a gleaming, high-rise office building in the Ōtemachi district of Tokyo—the geographic heart of the country's big business community. And like the keiretsu, the associations were attuned to shifting financial opportunities. To offset shrinking demand caused by the steadily declining farm population, Zennō kept its prices and commissions high, while JA Bank and Zenkyōren expanded their credit and insurance offerings, respectively, to nonfarm associate members. And JA diversified into services that were decidedly unconventional by the standards of traditional agricultural cooperation—think car and tombstone sales—and offered them to members and nonmembers alike.

Strategic and organizational reform at the upper echelons of the JA system during the postwar era took place within the parameters of path dependence. Consider, for instance, its strategic expansion into a panoply of nonagricultural services. This conformed with JA's expansive mandate under the 1947 Co-op Law to supply farmers with basic agricultural and financial services, help govern the agricultural resource commons, and tend to the welfare and daily life needs of farmers and their communities. JA's service expansion also conformed with the spirit of the Co-op Law, which sought to elevate the economic and social status of farmers. And there was nothing incongruent about JA Bank expanding beyond credit and savings to offer nonfarmer members loans and retail services, given the Co-op Law's provisions for associate membership and for JA to offer "services accompanying other services"—a green light, if ever there was one, to diversify and expand.[93] JA, in short, was just being JA. The problem was that these strategies served JA interests more than the material well-being of farmers.

Because of rent seeking, being anything but JA became more and more difficult with each passing decade. As they grew increasingly vested in the status quo, JA's national leadership viewed threats to its rent-seeking opportunities as existential. And for good reason: rice price supports, curbs on imports, opportunities to form virtual cartels with private firms—these and other government favors reduced market competition and expanded JA coffers far beyond what freer markets would have allowed. Not surprisingly, JA's national associations fought tooth and nail against pressures to change and balked at even the suggestion of agricultural market liberalization.

The rents-dependent, market-cornering strategies that JA's upper tier was so intent on preserving in turn necessitated a relatively compliant population of local co-ops and farmers. If the co-ops were to become more like traditionally organized co-ops by increasing their accountability to their farmer-members, Zennō's income would have shrunk in response to farmer expectations for lower transaction costs. But with a few noteworthy exceptions, postwar co-ops and farmers acquiesced to the system—and not only because they were pressured into doing so. Many co-ops fared better financially when subject to the controls of prefectural and national JA organizations. And for as long as the economy was expanding, commodity prices remained high, and JA had few competitors, the farmer's quests for risk reduction and income expansion were better served inside—rather than outside of—JA.

Local Co-ops and Their Farmer-Members

Strategically, as we have seen, the postwar multipurpose co-ops resembled traditionally organized agricultural co-ops in North America and Europe in their emphasis on providing farm inputs to their members and collecting and lightly processing their members' raw product. Unlike their foreign counterparts, however, the vast majority of co-ops handed that raw product not to a wholesaler, processor, or retailer but rather to the next rung in a hierarchy of co-op organizations.

In addition, the co-ops served as agents for the sale of financial and other services that normally fell under the purview of separate co-ops in other countries.

The multipurpose co-ops connected to their farmer-members via diverse networks of grassroots organizations. Each co-op was divided into local branches (*shiten*) that were grafted onto rural communities via one or a few foundational organizations (*kiso soshiki*)—hamlet or village governance organizations, agricultural production committees, and other communitywide or exclusively farmer associations. For the most part, these foundational organizations emerged spontaneously out of traditional social networks and existed independently of the co-op (*gaibu soshiki*); none were accounted for by law.[94] They also varied in terms of their names, size, and functions from co-op to co-op—and even from branch to branch. But they were integral to the effective implementation of co-op functions. The foundational organizations served variably as channels or partners for collecting and fulfilling farmer input orders, monitoring farmer fulfilment of co-op-wide production standards, collecting raw product, disseminating JA and government information, and a variety of other co-op tasks.[95] They also functioned as important forums for communication, deliberation, and consensus building between farmers and their co-op branch,[96] not to mention solidarity organizations through which the norms of agricultural production were reinforced.

The existence of foundational organizations illuminates Ronald Dore's observations about how hard it could be to distinguish early postwar farmer loyalty to the village from loyalty to the co-op and why farmers often failed to develop a strong co-op consciousness;[97] the reason was that a great deal of farmer interaction with the co-op was filtered through these traditional village associations. Be that as it may, the foundational organizations began to shrink or even disappear during the postwar era as farm populations declined and rural communities diversified. Some co-ops tried to fill the void by establishing or strengthening farmer production and women's, youth, and other functionally specific membership associations within the branch bureaucracy itself. But as the co-ops grew to encompass ever-larger geographic spaces following waves of inter-co-op mergers, many branches were themselves scaled down or shuttered.[98] These organizational developments weakened communications between farmers and their co-op branches, thereby stoking a sense of abandonment among cultivators that was only to intensify following the 1990 collapse of the bubble economy. As we illustrate in later chapters, one of the challenges inherent in adapting co-op strategies to changing market conditions was rebuilding or replacing those foundational organizations.

Some foundational organizations were also linked to co-op governance.[99] In many cases, it was through these organizations that farmer-members selected delegates to participate in the general meeting (*sōkai* or *sōtaikai*) of the co-op, which was the forum in which the co-op's all-important board of directors was elected. These boards varied in terms of their size and whether members served full- or part-time, but board members were, for the most part, farmers. Each board included a co-op head (*kumiaichō*), who represented the co-op to prefectural and national JA organizations and who oversaw the co-op's long-term planning and day-to-day affairs. In keeping with the simplicity of postwar co-op strategies, co-op heads and their fellow board members rarely had significant management, technological, or marketing skills.

Given their extraordinary multifunctionality and expanding geographic reach, the co-ops required large staffs and spacious headquarters to accommodate them. But like many agricultural co-ops in the United States and elsewhere,[100] Japanese co-ops have always had a hard time attracting high-quality human resources. In contrast to JA's national or prefectural federations, which, as de facto commercial organizations, were often able to hire well-educated employees, most local co-ops were staffed by personnel with just high school diplomas or a year or two of college. Many co-ops lacked adequate on-the-job training programs and were known to assign their more capable employees to those all-important financial services.[101] Turnover rates, moreover, were high, as employees rebelled against strict quotas for the sale of agricultural, credit, and insurance services or quit their positions for more rewarding jobs in the local commercial sector.[102] Some co-ops practiced more effective management than others, but few had the human resources or esprit de corps to function as more than passive cogs in the JA hierarchy,[103] offering services overseen by prefectural and national federations to local farmers and channeling member product into the JA system.

Individual farm households organized and conducted themselves in ways that both reflected and complemented the structure and strategies of the JA system. For rice-producing farm households in general and part-time farm households in particular, the ubiquity and convenience of JA services encouraged farmers to operate much as they had during the prewar era, when they simply grew rice and then handed it over to their local landlord.[104] With the exception of some larger-scale, full-time farm households, rice farmers had little incentive to run their farms as for-profit businesses by diversifying their products, branding those products, and forging new, more lucrative routes to market. The predominant farmer strategy was to function as passive producers at the base of the food supply chain.

Passive producers have no need for sophisticated organization. Since small-scale, family farmers could count on a stable, long-term income stream by relying on JA and did not require advanced production, processing, and marketing skills or outside labor, they could easily make do within the simple organizational framework of the traditional farm household. The traditional farm household was an unincorporated business that practiced family management (*kazoku keiei*); the family owned the farmland and supplied all the labor needed to till it. And since the overwhelming purpose of this setup was to secure the family's livelihood, the farm household maintained no meaningful distinction between farm-related finances and those of the household itself.[105]

The simple strategies and organizational structure of the typical (rice-producing) farm household neatly complemented the co-ops' relatively passive position within the JA system's top-heavy pecking order. So, too, did the values that composed the household's passive-producer mindset: a commitment to the welfare of the community and to farmer equality, an aversion to both risk taking and excessive profit making, and a view of farmland as an almost sacred family asset rather than a means of production. To be sure, these "non-wealth maximizing values" were influenced by the incentives and constraints of the cooperative system itself, excessive government subsidies, and the legacy of Japan's government-led food-control system.[106] They were also symptomatic of the tightly knit social structure of the early postwar farm hamlet, Japan's relatively brief experience with commercial agriculture and independent—that is, nontenant—farmers, and a raft of geographic, historical, and legal impediments to the expansion of plot size. And they evoked *nōhonshugi* (agricultural fundamentalism), the early Meiji ideology that, among other things, extolled the spiritual values of the countryside and of hard work, frugality, attention to duty, small-scale farming, and so on—a kind of "pastoral idealism" that was deliberately nurtured and manipulated by local and national authorities as they decried the principles of large-scale, capitalist, "Western-style" agriculture.[107] Whatever their origins, these nonmaterial values that inform the passive-producer mindset are often celebrated—even romanticized—by contemporary Japanese popular culture. The problem was that they helped turn farmers into "mere spectators" of co-op affairs by smothering the development of a strong "co-op consciousness"—an awareness that, in principle, traditionally organized agricultural co-ops are meant to be operated by farmers for their own material gain.[108]

The typical postwar cultivator was a far cry from Robert Bates's "rational farmer" who strives for material advancement.[109] But it would be a mistake to conclude that Japanese farmers were inherently "irrational." When given the chance, many cultivators behaved as any other rational farmer would—especially as postwar village norms and social structures deteriorated in the wake of urbanization, depopulation, and social diversification. In the more open and competitive fruit and vegetable markets, for example, cultivators often jumped at the chance to expand their farmland holdings and increase their profits—often outside of JA channels. And there was no shortage of rice farmers who rushed to sell their farmland—that precious family asset—to deep-pocketed real estate developers in the heady days of the 1980s bubble economy. In short, where freer market forces prevailed, there were farmers ready to take advantage of them.

Strategic Innovation among Postwar Co-ops

Japan's local multipurpose co-ops were characterized by a remarkable degree of isomorphism, or organizational and strategic homogeneity. This is hardly surprising given the leading role of the state in the establishment and subsequent development of the JA system, the more-or-less uniform imposition of many of the rules of the cooperative game on the co-ops by either government or prefectural and national JA authorities, the dearth of diversity and competition within the heavily regulated agricultural sector, and the fact that the sector's main asset—farmland—is nonportable. Also contributing to intra-JA homogeneity was the controlling influence of prefectural and national JA organizations that were in turn disincentivized by rent seeking to spearhead reform—especially reforms that could trigger co-op defections from JA's government-sanctioned services. But in our attention to the exogenously imposed rules of the co-op game, we tend to forget that individual co-ops enjoyed significant freedoms to respond flexibly to grassroots conditions.[110] It was at this level that the co-ops generated their own unique operational rules for devising and implementing local production standards and practices, interfacing with various hamlet associations, collecting farmer product, and so on. And it was this grassroots space for independent action that enabled a few local co-ops to generate modest reforms during the postwar era—in some cases within a few short years of their establishment. Noteworthy for our purposes were strategic reforms that addressed the long-term material interests of the co-ops' farmer-members and that served as precedents for the more extensive co-op changes that emerged from the late twentieth century.

The Tamagawa Co-op's Plus Alpha Movement was among the most well-known examples of early postwar strategic reform at the local cooperative level.[111] Although rice and barley remained the Ibaraki Prefecture co-op's core commodities during the 1960s, the movement encouraged farmer-members to spread their risk over several commodities by adding livestock and vegetables ("plus alpha") to their production. Since the multipurpose co-ops were not required to operate as agents of the state in the marketing of nonrice products, the co-op sold vegetables and livestock products directly to urban consumer cooperatives. In so doing, the Tamagawa Co-op was among the first multipurpose co-ops to bypass Zennō, a marketing strategy that gained widespread traction in Japan during the 1980s with the expansion of organic production and the farm-to-table movement. Meanwhile, the locally initiated notion of plus alpha helped set a new national standard for farmer risk minimization through product diversification—a standard that remains influential today.

Iwate Prefecture's Shiwa Co-op also introduced plus alpha strategies as it struggled to respond to the specific needs and capabilities of its farmer-members. Determined to loosen farmer dependence on off-farm employment by boosting farm-related incomes, the co-op went beyond the Tamagawa model by encouraging a much wider scope of product diversification, helping farmers tailor their choices to local soil conditions, the size of their farms, and their labor capabilities, and then diversifying co-op marketing strategies to accommodate the various product lines. In its 1964 guidelines for this initiative, Shiwa described the pitfalls for both farmer incomes and local villages of an overreliance on rice, highlighted the need to help even the smallest of farms achieve living standards comparable to those of workers in other industries, and extolled the virtues of traditional cooperative principles and the benefits of uniting farmers in truly cooperative arrangements.

The Plus Alpha Movement was enabled in part by post-1960 increases in consumer demand for nonrice food products. It was also likely inspired by the strategies embraced by the JA system's special-purpose agricultural cooperatives (*senmon nōkyō*). Less prominent but more numerous than the multipurpose co-ops and free to transcend the administrative jurisdictions of their multipurpose counterparts, the special-purpose co-ops provided purchasing and marketing services for just one or a small class of agricultural product, did not offer credit or insurance services, and focused on full-time—rather than part-time—farmers.[112] (As such, they resembled the North American—or European-style traditionally organized co-ops that SCAP had championed during the occupation.) The fact that their products did not fall under the purview of the 1942 Staple Food Control Act meant that the special-purpose co-ops enjoyed some freedom to experiment with new marketing strategies, unlike the rice-centric multipurpose co-ops, which were required by law to send the bulk of their rice through government-backed channels within the JA system. Many special-purpose co-ops flourished during the 1960s as consumer preferences changed and incomes increased, and some scholars suggest that their successes encouraged otherwise rice-centric co-ops like JA Tamagawa and JA Shiwa to diversify their production and marketing strategies. It is also likely that from the 1970s, the multipurpose co-ops benefited from the acquisition of new experts and marketing know-how in the wake of slower growth and, in time, agricultural trade liberalization, as many special-purpose co-ops—some of which were in financial distress—merged with the multipurpose co-ops.[113]

Most co-op attempts at strategic self-reform were spearheaded by entrepreneurial farmers and/or by progressive co-op leaders who had their fingers on the pulse of emerging farmer discontent. The experiences of Kajiura Yoshimasa are a case in point.[114] Kajiura led Hokkaido's Nakasatsunai Co-op from 1953 until 1984 and later served as managing director of Hokuren, the prefectural economic federation affiliated with Zennō, and of the kyōsairen, JA's prefectural insurance association. These positions gave Kajiura both hands-on experience in co-op management and a bird's-eye view of how financial mismanagement within the JA system negatively affected farmers. Throughout his career, Kajiura argued that the co-ops' primary responsibility was to empower farmers to chart their own course. He made good on his convictions by being among the first co-op leaders to promote the incorporation of farm households, the establishment of grassroots, non-JA co-op organizations for sharing farm inputs and labor, and even the transfer of control over co-op retail stores (A-Co-op) to consumer cooperatives. By the early 1990s, Kajiura accelerated his reform efforts by establishing a local—but short-lived—purchasing co-op outside of the JA system in northern Hokkaido that attracted national attention for directly importing inexpensive fertilizers from South Korea.

Kajiura rebelled against the passive producer mindset that imbued farm communities and was quick to criticize most multipurpose co-ops as out of touch with the interests and needs of farmers. For him, the co-ops and JA more broadly had passed a point of no return during the post-oil-shock recession of the mid-1970s, when they elevated their organizational self-preservation over the interests of farmers. Rice and agricultural prices may have been high, Kajiura observed, but JA's increasing input prices and service commissions were reducing returns to farmers. Attentive to the early signs of aging within the farm population during the 1980s, he also lamented the plight of younger farmers, many of whom were leaving agriculture in opposition to the constraints imposed by subsidy programs like gentan and to the monotony of Japanese-style cultivation. These farmers would have run their farms like businesses, he complained, but government policies and JA orthodoxy were turning them into mere peasants. These were the cultivators, Kajiura concluded, who would soon stand at the forefront of the "So long, JA" phenomenon (JA sayonara genshō).

Herein lies the crux of local co-op reform. Unlike JA's national and prefectural associations, which were separated from local farmer-members by layers of organization and their dependence on rent seeking, the local co-ops had a direct relationship with those members. If local farmers were unhappy about the impact of JA's high prices on their bottom line, the co-ops heard about it first. If, for whatever reason, those farmers decided to say sayonara to JA and risk going it alone, the volume of co-op transactions invariably decreased. No amount of auditing and management supervision by Zenchū and its prefectural counter-parts could alter the fact that the fate of the local co-op ultimately depended on its relationship with its members. Of course, co-ops could always compensate for their declining agricultural profits by increasing their nonfarm offerings to associate members—and even to nonmembers. Indeed, this is precisely what many—if not most—co-ops eventually did. But to co-op leaders like Kajiura who prioritized farmers over co-op interests and for whom the principles of agricul-tural cooperation mattered, this was not enough. To them, the survival of the co-op—and indeed of local agriculture itself—meant adapting co-op strategies and organization to the changing needs of local cultivators. As the next chapter explains, changes in farmer needs were only to accelerate by the end of the twen-tieth century.

Postwar Legacies and the Challenges of Reform

Although Japanese agriculture would not erupt into full-blown demographic and economic crisis until after the 1990 collapse of the economic bubble, entrepre-neurial farmers and co-op leaders like Kajiura, progressive policy makers, and agricultural economists saw the writing on the wall long before that.[115] Rural communities were struggling as the farm population shrank from about two-fifths of the overall working population during the mid-1950s to just one-tenth by the late 1980s,[116] and the average age of farmers crept steadily upward. Pro-duction costs were rising, and farm-related inefficiencies were becoming more and more glaring. Farmland regulations, subsidies, protectionism, and a host of other policies were to blame for many of these developments. And so was the JA system.

Even during the 1980s, when it was at the peak of its influence, JA clearly needed to change. In keeping with the basic principles of agricultural coopera-tion, it needed to be more farmer-centric. And it needed to pay far more atten-tion to the needs of larger-scale, full-time farmers, since it was they, rather than part-time producers, who were best positioned to adapt to changing conditions and thus to secure the future of Japanese agriculture. JA needed to devise new agricultural production and marketing strategies that would boost returns to farmers—and that, in turn, meant diversifying away from rice production and JA's one-size-fits-all marketing schemes and addressing the goals, needs, and ca-pabilities of individual farmers. Finally, the system's component organizations—and particularly the local co-ops—needed to do more to systematically connect with their farmer-members, many of whom were increasingly disgruntled with

JA as their local co-ops grew larger through mergers and extracted more and more fees, commissions, and levies from them. JA, in short, needed to behave more like a traditionally organized agriculture co-op.

But strategic and organizational change was easier said than done. Reform was hindered at the national and prefectural levels by rent seeking and at the local co-op level by the controlling influence of national and prefectural JA organizations and passive mindsets within the farming population. And as even JA insiders would admit, skilled, change-oriented leaders were in short supply.[117] Also problematic was the fact that JA had become far more than a co-op over the years. After crowding out many of its competitors, JA was for many small rural communities the only source of farm inputs and rice distribution, not to mention basic financial services. As those communities began to feel the effects of population and economic decline, moreover, JA was often the sole provider of gasoline, groceries, and other basic consumer services. Finally, as community cohesiveness weakened, local governments shrank as villages were folded into ever larger municipalities, and basic social welfare services like elder care dwindled—trends that were only to accelerate after 1990—it was often up to the local co-op to fill the vacuum. Theorists of agricultural cooperation have long maintained that co-ops should serve the social as well as economic needs of farmers and their immediate communities, but the economic and social reach of JA was internationally unprecedented. For many struggling communities, JA had become the only game in town.

If becoming more like a co-op meant focusing on core co-op principles and helping farm households increase profits, JA would have to reconsider its extraordinary multifunctionality and focus on the basics. But that, in turn, could sound a death knell for some rural communities. The challenge for JA moving forward, then, was to strike a balance between serving the material interests of farmers and preserving one of rural Japan's last remaining social safety nets.

3

JAPAN'S CHANGING AGRICULTURAL LANDSCAPE

1990–2018

Otsu Takamitsu is a veteran family farmer based in the outskirts of Kumamoto City in Kyushu. In 1996, Otsu responded to the deteriorating agricultural conditions of his locality by founding Agri Tomoai, a hamlet-based farm association (*shūraku einō*) that includes all but a few households in his community. Now an incorporated farm enterprise (*nōgyō hōjin*), Agri Tomoai provides a variety of low-cost services to its 140 member households, from the provision of extra farmhands to marketing services. For households that lack successors, the corporation leases their farmland and cultivates it directly. Although hardly a cure-all for the farm sector's many problems, ventures like Agri Tomoai are attracting national attention for helping aging, small-scale farmers cut production costs, slow the spread of abandoned farmland, and enable struggling farm hamlets to survive.

Since its establishment, Agri Tomoai has nurtured an arm's-length relationship with JA. It zealously guards its autonomy by keeping JA Kumamoto City, the local multipurpose co-op, out of its managerial affairs, and it negotiates independent contracts with food-related firms. But Agri Tomoai also accepts investment funds from the co-op and relies on it for access to farm inputs and to market a portion of its rice and other raw product. Without this essential support, Otsu explains, Agri Tomoai could very well go under.[1]

On the other side of town, Shimada Toshio runs Nakata Onshitsu, an incorporated family farm that produces hothouse parsley, *shiso* (beefsteak leaves), and tomatoes. Established the same year as Agri Tomoai, Nakata Onshitsu has a second farm at nearby Mount Aso, employs several full- and part-time workers and a few agricultural trainees from Vietnam, processes much of its produce on-site, and negotiates directly with buyers in advance of the growing season to set both output and prices. Thanks in part to Nakata Onshitsu's profitability, Shimada has lined up a successor; when he retires, one of his four children—a daughter—will take over the family business.

A member of two multipurpose co-ops, Shimada is quick to acknowledge JA's many contributions to postwar agricultural development and to the recovery of local farms following the devastating Kumamoto earthquake of April 2016.[2] But in a classic example of defection from the co-op network, he refuses to make full use of JA's services:

> What's the point of selling your produce to JA? JA offers a uniform price to its farmer-members, and there's no telling what that price will be until after the growing season has ended. . . . JA has got its members over a barrel! I'm not against the idea of JA, per se, but it does a poor job these days of serving farmers. JA is lazy. Irresponsible! . . . . I'm making a much better living shouldering the risks of farming on my own than if I had remained an active member of JA.[3]

Two entrepreneurial farmers, two very different relationships with JA. While Otsu oversees a venture that cooperates with JA as it addresses the needs of traditional farm households, Shimada is a businessman who bypasses the co-op system in his efforts to establish a foothold in niche consumer markets. But both men might still be traditional family farmers operating exclusively under the JA umbrella were it not for a raft of structural—demographic and economic—challenges and institutional changes since the early 1990s that have incentivized producers to transform the way they run their farms and connect to the market. What are these changes? What role has government played in their introduction? And what are their implications for the future of JA?

In addressing these questions, this chapter emphasizes three main points. First, we spotlight demographic trends. Scholars and journalists have long commented on the rapid decline and aging of the farm population, but our aim in this chapter is to understand how these trends are combining with other developments to change farmer behavior. Second, while recognizing the failures of government policy to fix all that is wrong with Japanese agriculture—the small plots, the spread of abandoned farmland, declining farm household incomes, the farm successor shortage—we demonstrate how a gradual shift in policy priorities over the past three decades from *redistribution* to productivity-boosting *structural reform* has triggered some significant changes in the way farmers manage their farms and think about their roles and responsibilities as farmers. Which brings us to our final point: the fundamental role of farmers in the story of institutional change inside JA. As membership-based economic enterprises, local co-ops cannot expect their strategic and other institutional reforms to gain traction if those reforms do not resonate with the changing needs and expectations of the co-ops' farmer-members. In an effort to understand those needs and expectations, this chapter allows farmers like Otsu Takamitsu and Shimada Toshio to speak for themselves.

Japanese Agriculture in Crisis

The tiny, picturesque rice-farming village of Kanakura in Wajima City is nestled deep in the mountains of the Noto Peninsula, just a few kilometers inland from the spectacular Shiroyone Senmaida ("1,000 terraced rice paddies") that ascend precipitously from the peninsula's northwestern coastline. Surrounded by verdant mountains and rice paddies, Kanakura is at the heart of Ishikawa Prefecture's famed *satoyama*, or mountainous ecosystem. In 2011, the Food and Agriculture Organization of the United Nations designated this and surrounding areas a Geographically Important Agricultural Heritage System (GIAHS) in recognition of their agricultural, ecological, historical, and cultural significance. The distinction is a source of immense pride for communities like Kanakura but also a reminder of the region's fragility.

Kanakura is in the throes of demographic and economic decline. With 104 households at its postwar peak,[4] its population in 2015 stood at just 44 households.[5] Since the hamlet suffers from an acute successor shortage, further shrinkage is all but inevitable. While sipping cold tea on a hot day in late July 2015, Ishizaki Hidezumi, the village head, described the problem in stark terms:

> This is serious business. For more than fifteen years we've been talking about how to preserve our farmland and our hamlet's five temples. . . . We've created data sets to track changing conditions in the hamlet— the ages of farmers and the land they cultivate, the scope of abandoned farmland, even plant life in the area—and we reach out to the media to draw attention to our plight. We're trying to improve the quality and appeal of our rice by using fewer chemicals during the growing process. We're mobilizing grannies [obāchan] to help make local products, including that tea you're drinking, which is made from wild plants that grow nearby. . . . People from the outside are full of praise for what we're doing, and teachers, professors, and other folks from the cities show up from time to time to help out and offer advice. But it's been tough. And it can be really hard to motivate our neighbors to get involved.[6]

Ishizaki, whose boundless energy defies his advancing years, went on to describe what can happen to a hamlet when its population dwindles and nature encroaches on abandoned fields. One concern has been the growing population of wild boars (*inoshishi*) in the area. The animals wreak havoc on the land and are a danger to elderly residents. Kanakura now has a budget to build an electric fence around parts of the community to keep the animals at bay. But Ishizaki was clearly bothered by the unwelcome intrusion.

Kanakura is a fairly typical example of rural villages in contemporary Japan that are struggling with a deepening agricultural crisis.[7] Talk of "crisis" is certainly nothing new in the farm sector. As we observed in chapter 2, until the early postwar era, Japan faced the specter or reality of severe food shortages, a threat that necessitated aggressive government intervention to increase and stabilize the food supply. No sooner did Japan get a handle on that issue than another big problem loomed: signs of a growing income gap between the countryside and the cities during the early stages of postwar rapid industrialization and urbanization. Determined to secure the electoral allegiance of farmers, the LDP government (1955–1993) averted a full-blown crisis by introducing a string of redistributive policies, including new forms of agricultural price supports and tax breaks for farmers. But socioeconomic parity between rural and urban areas was purchased at the price of gross structural inefficiencies, not least small average plot size and the growing preponderance of part-time farmers. By the mid- to late 1980s, as agricultural production first peaked and then began its long-term decline, the future looked ominous: both agriculture and Japan's costly redistributive policy regime had become unsustainable.[8]

In the 1990s, deepening demographic challenges and new economic developments combined to dramatically exacerbate agriculture's inherent vulnerabilities. Of particular note has been a steady drop in the farm population. As table 3.1 highlights, in 1995 Japan counted approximately 2.65 million commercial farm households (*hanbai nōka*; family farms that produce for sale); by 2020, that number had fallen to just 1.03 million. To be sure, all advanced industrialized economies experience shrinking farm populations; to the extent that technological advances make farming more efficient, we should view this as a positive development. The problem in the Japanese case is that there is no end in sight to the decline. There are two main reasons for this. First, Japanese farmers are rapidly aging—and at a rate much faster than that of the general population. As figure 3.1 shows, the percentage of the general population age 65 or older increased from 12 percent in 1990 to 28.7 percent in 2020, while the corresponding figures for the farm population more than doubled, from 33.1 percent in 1990 to an astonishing 68 percent in 2020. As of 2020, the average age of farmers was 67.8[9]—significantly

TABLE 3.1 Commercial farm households and farm successors, 1995–2020

YEAR	TOTAL NUMBER COMMERCIAL FARM HOUSEHOLDS (1,000S) (% CHANGE)	% HOUSEHOLDS W/SUCCESSORS RESIDING IN SAME HOUSEHOLD (% CHANGE)	% HOUSEHOLDS W/SUCCESSORS (% CHANGE)
1995	2,651	–	–
2000	2,337 (Δ11.8)	57.3	70.4
2005	1,963 (Δ16.0)	44.2 (Δ22.9)	54.6 (Δ22.4)
2010	1,631 (Δ16.9)	41.4 (Δ6.3)	59.4 (8.8)
2015	1,330 (Δ18.5)	29.9 (Δ27.8)	48.7 (Δ18.0)
2020	1,028 (Δ22.7)	NA	24.4*

Source: MAFF, "Census of Agriculture and Forestry," various years.
*The 2020 data reflects those who have secured a successor for within the next five years.

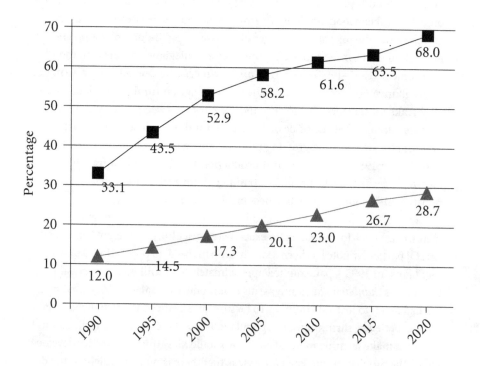

FIGURE 3.1. Percentages of the general population and farm population over the age of sixty-five in five-year increments, from 1990 to 2020.

Sources: MIC, Statistical Handbook of Japan: 2016; MAFF, "Statistical Yearbook of the Ministry of Agriculture, Forestry and Fisheries," various years; MIC, "Tōkei kara mita waga kuni no kōreisha"; "Ninaite kōreika susumu."

higher than the corresponding figures for the United States (57.5, as of 2017)[10] and the United Kingdom (59, as of 2019).[11]

Second, and more ominously, Japan is facing an acute shortage of farm successors (kōkeisha). As table 3.1 reveals, between 2000, the year the MAFF started collecting data on this issue in its quinquennial agricultural censuses, and 2015, the percentage of commercial farm households with known farm successors decreased from 70.4 percent to just 48.7 percent. The situation has drastically worsened since then; as of 2020, only 24.4 percent of farmers have secured successors for within the next five years.

What exactly is causing the successor shortage? The answer is complex. At one level, a tightening of the supply of farm successors—along with the agricultural labor force more generally—is to be expected as an economy moves through the various stages of industrial and postindustrial development and the offspring of farming families pursue alternative employment opportunities. Governmental redistributive policies that effectively compensate farmers who remain on the land no doubt prevented this trend from spiraling out of control in postwar Japan. But conditions have changed in recent years. First, farming is no longer as attractive as it once was because rice prices are declining. As we elaborate in chapter 6, this reflects the gradual deregulation of the rice market since the mid-1990s. Second, the demand for food—and especially for rice—is shrinking. As economic growth accelerated during the 1960s, consumer tastes rapidly diversified, and rice consumption began to slip; between 1962 and 2012, annual per capita rice consumption fell from a peak of 118.3 kilograms to just 56.3 kilograms.[12] And demand will continue to shrink now that the size of the general population is contracting and individuals age sixty-five or older compose an increasing proportion of the whole. As Noda Takeshi, a long-term lower house Diet member from Kumamoto Prefecture, put it, "Japan's aging population is a real problem for the demand for food. Old people eat less!"[13]

Third, redistributive policy supports for farmers are being dismantled. As a later section further explains, Japanese governments have been slowly moving away from the postwar practice of offering income supports to all farmers, regardless of their productivity levels, toward a system in which cultivators with more "viable" farm enterprises receive the lion's share of assistance. Even gentan, the controversial rice acreage adjustment program implemented in 1971 to help stabilize rural incomes, was put on the chopping block in 2013. Finally, public works spending has declined after peaking during the mid-1990s, thus diminishing opportunities for off-farm employment—an important source of income for Japan's many part-time farmers. Farmers continue to enjoy some noteworthy privileges, such as reduced property taxes for certain types of agricultural lands, the indefinite postponement of inheritance taxes for heirs who continue to work the soil,[14] a lax income tax withholding system (only 30 percent of taxes on farmer earnings are withheld at their source, in contrast to 100 percent for urban salarymen), and reduced electricity and water rates.[15] But these privileges are not enough to offset the financial losses incurred from reduced government subsidies and, more importantly, declining prices and consumer demand.

Farming, in short, is losing its financial allure. As Agri Tomoai's Otsu Takamitsu remarked, by the late 1990s "fewer and fewer people were prepared to put out [ganbarō] for farming, claiming they just didn't have it in them to do the job [yaruki ga nai]."[16] And as figure 3.2 shows, long-term income data reveal that the situation has only worsened since then. For decades after 1970, commercial farm household income, which includes income from both farming and non-farming pursuits, pension benefits, and other sources, outpaced that of worker households in the manufacturing sector by significant margins before hitting its postwar peak in 1995, just as rice markets were cracking open; since then, farm household incomes have been shrinking at a faster rate than those of their manufacturing counterparts. By the end of the first decade of this century, the socioeconomic challenge that governments had worked so hard to prevent during the rapid growth era had come to pass; many farm households were now making considerably less than worker households. Small wonder, then, that farmers are having so much trouble attracting young blood to the soil.

To be sure, the farm sector is grappling with a litany of other problems, from a decreasing national food self-sufficiency rate, which now stands at just 37 percent in calorie terms,[17] to the spread of abandoned farmland. But as our discussions with dozens of farmers and agricultural experts underscore, no other issue keeps farmers—and policy makers—awake at night quite like the successor shortage and its underlying causes.

The ongoing struggles of Ishikawa Prefecture's "1,000 terraced rice paddies" are a telling illustration of the severity of the shortage for small farm households and their surrounding communities. Some no bigger than a typical parking space, the paddies are officially trademarked as "sacred land of Japanese agriculture" (Nihon nōgyō no seichi). In the past, twenty farm households tilled the soil while holding second jobs in local public works projects, stone quarries, and a charcoal manufacturing plant. Now that most of those employment opportunities have disappeared, just one farm household remains. To preserve the site, in 2007 Wajima City launched a terraced rice paddy owner (tanada ōnā) program in which city dwellers from around the country pay an annual fee of 20,000 JPY to the city to temporarily "own" (in the figurative sense) the land; in return for occasionally working the paddies with help from local volunteers, participants receive a portion of the harvest. Thanks to the recent opening of a new Shinkansen line from Tokyo to

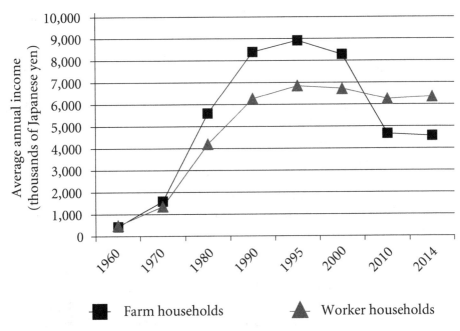

FIGURE 3.2. Average annual income of workers' households and farm households from 1960 to 2014 in thousands of Japanese yen.

Sources: OECD, Evaluation of Agricultural Policy Reforms, 24; MIC, Statistical Handbook of Japan, various years.

Ishikawa Prefecture and NHK's sympathetic portrayal of the Noto Peninsula in *Mare*, a popular television series, the number of program participants reached 175 in 2015.[18] But while programs like these help broadcast the plight of Japanese agriculture, bridge the psychological divide between city and countryside, and provide an attractive outlet for the expression of urban nostalgia toward traditional farm villages, they are, at best, a stopgap solution. To attract long-term successors, Japanese agriculture needs radical change. As we elaborate below, modest but significant progress has been made in that direction.

The Changing Context of Family Farming
The Political Context

Today, more and more Japanese farmers are concluding that the survival of agriculture depends on the introduction of new, more market-conforming production and sales strategies—strategies, in other words, that respond directly to consumer demand and increase farm household profits. Skeptical that this can be achieved solely through JA, entrepreneurial farmers like Shimada Toshio and Otsu Takamitsu of Kumamoto City are, to varying degrees, charting their own paths forward. That these farmers have achieved a measure of success is due in no small part to government efforts to change the legal and regulatory context—the formal rules of the game—of farming.

Japanese agricultural reforms over the years have been frustratingly slow and narrow—particularly when assessed on a case-by-case basis. Never has the government moved to sweep away postwar restrictions on, say, land consolidation or the participation of nonfarm corporations (e.g., construction firms, food processors, retail chains) in agriculture; often, it just tinkers with those restrictions at the margins. Be that as it may, the cumulative effects of small-scale agricultural reforms over the course of two to three decades have been deeply significant, if not transformative. Now, more than ever, entrepreneurial producers are finding it easier to expand their farms and access routes to markets outside of JA. These developments are fueling momentum for further reform within the farm sector. And they are putting JA on the defensive.

The reforms are ultimately enabled by shifts in the political context of agriculture. As we saw in chapter 2, for much of the postwar period, the LDP partnered with MAFF bureaucrats and JA representatives to privilege the interests of small, inefficient part-time farmers, showering them with market-defying subsidies and other favors in exchange for their electoral support. The bargain was, at root, a Faustian one insofar as the price paid for LDP dominance was economic inefficiency in the countryside. More recently, however, advocates of market-oriented farm reform have been gaining a foothold in the political world.[19]

One reason for this is that the organized farm vote has been losing electoral influence in the wake of a declining farm population, the reform of electoral rules in both houses of the Diet, and the partial reapportionment of rural electoral districts.[20] Gone are the days when JA could mobilize upward of one million voters behind its sponsored candidates in upper house elections; nor does the farm vote carry as much weight in the post-1994 mixed-member district lower house electoral system as it did under the old single nontransferable vote multimember district system (SNTV/MMD). The decline of the farm vote has in turn altered the career trajectories of sympathetic LDP politicians. As Ellis Krauss and Robert Pekkanen explain, candidates for the lower house can no longer assume victory simply by appealing to one or a few special interest groups; they must instead cast their nets broadly to attract as wide a cross-section of voters as possible, relying increasingly on programmatic policy appeals to urban voters.[21] Moreover, candidates who overidentify with special interests like JA enjoy far fewer opportunities for career advancement within the LDP than they once did. Yamada Toshio is a good case in point. JA's sponsored candidate in the upper house since 2007, Yamada received only minor appointments in the party over the years and played no meaningful role in the Abe Shinzō government's early agricultural reform efforts. That he managed to gain elected office at all—not once but three times, as of this writing—is likely the result of concerted support not from JA's farmer-members but rather from its staff.[22]

Regardless of whether the farm vote reflects the wishes of farmers or JA staff, it is not about to completely disappear. It still matters, for example, in the winner-takes-all single-member districts (SMD) of the lower house, where the loss of a small percentage of the electorate as represented by a local multipurpose co-op can spell defeat for a candidate.[23] And as the 2014 general election underscored, candidates from all parties will still go the distance to secure JA's electoral endorsement.[24] Finally, JA continues to play an important electoral role at the prefectural and local levels. The resounding loss of the LDP's Hiwatashi Keisuke to the independent candidate Yamaguchi Yoshinori in the January 2015 gubernatorial election in Saga Prefecture, for example, is widely attributed to Hiwatashi's failure to secure the support of the prefecture's farmers' political league (nōseiren), JA's de facto electoral arm.[25] That said, the anti-reformist farm vote is facing strong and effective challenges from reformist elements in the party system as personalism cedes ground to more programmatic appeals in national elections.

Changes are also afoot within the MAFF. As former administrative vice minister of agriculture Takagi Yūki explains, agricultural policy in the past was invariably at the mercy of "politics." Efforts by far-sighted policy makers to initiate reforms without the LDP's prior approval, for example, would elicit howls of protest from members of the LDP farm tribe (nōrin zoku), who feared estrangement from JA and the farm vote.[26] But these constraints are now weakening. To be sure, many officials remain stalwart defenders of the status quo. But more and more voices are pushing for change. The Management Bureau (Keieikyoku), for example, a traditionally conservative unit that oversees JA, is doing more to help entrepreneurial farmers, while the Production Bureau (Seisankyoku) is actively promoting market-oriented agricultural reforms.[27]

Meanwhile, the MAFF's informal ties to JA are weakening as reformist elements within the ministry grow more emboldened. The turning point came with the liberalization of rice pricing during the mid-1990s (see below), which all but eliminated an important source of cooperation between the two sides. This, in turn, helps explain why the MAFF no longer plays a big role in elections. In the past, those upper house sponsored candidates backed by JA were often former MAFF bureaucrats who had been carefully selected by their superiors. But 2001 was the last time the ministry put forward such a candidate.[28] And since the parties now have fewer incentives to recruit one of their own to run in a farm bureaucrat's stead, JA has had to sift through its own administrative ranks for potential candidates. Yamada Toshio, a former Zenchū official, is one such candidate.[29] As even Zenchū officials will admit, the MAFF's retreat from electoral politics has only deepened pro-JA and anti-JA divisions with the ministry and hence ministerial conflict with top JA officials.[30]

As the incentives that once shaped postwar cooperation among bureaucrats, politicians, and JA on behalf of generous redistributive policies and other dimensions of the postwar agricultural status quo weaken or disappear, political and bureaucratic momentum behind market-oriented reform has gathered steam. What follows is an overview of key reforms that have encouraged greater levels of entrepreneurship among producers while chipping away at the supremacy of part-time farmers and JA in the agricultural sector.

Market Openings

Among the more dramatic developments over the past generation that have enhanced competitive forces within the agricultural sector and diminished JA's influence has been the gradual liberalization of farm imports. Postwar Japanese agriculture is no stranger to imports; from 1960, five years after the country joined the General Agreement on Tariffs and Trade (GATT), Tokyo slowly loosened controls over the importation of a long list of relatively minor food items.[31] But by the end of the bubble years, more politically sensitive items were winding their way onto the liberalization docket. In 1988, Japan reluctantly opened its markets for beef and oranges in response to US pressure. And in 1994, upon joining the Uruguay Round's Agreement on Agriculture, Japan pledged to loosen import restrictions on twenty-eight commodities, including rice. For twenty-seven of those commodities, the government agreed to gradually replace its quotas with tariffs; rice imports, by contrast, were subjected first to "minimum access quotas" and then, after 2000, to tariffication.[32] For JA, Honma Masayoshi observes, these changes were tantamount to the second coming of Commodore Perry's "black ships."[33]

JA was justified in viewing these developments with trepidation, for no sooner was the ink dry on the Agreement on Agriculture than the Japanese government moved to knock down the legislative foundations of JA's dominance in the postwar rice market. In 1995, the Diet repealed the 1942 Staple Food Control Act (Shokuryō kanri hō), which had authorized the government to purchase rice (seifumai, or government rice) at high prices from domestic producers via JA and then sell it through licensed vendors to consumers at reduced prices. Necessitated by the pending increases in food imports, which would undermine government efforts to keep prices high,[34] the law's repeal and replacement by the more liberal

Staple Food Act freed rice farmers to sell all their rice through private wholesalers or directly to retailers—a major blow to JA. Rice retailers, for their part, no longer required government licenses to enter the market. As a result of these changes, rice prices began to decline; while the continuation of quotas, tariffs, and lobbying by JA and LDP politicians ensured that prices remained above freer market levels, they were now more responsive to supply and demand.[35]

The partial liberalization of the rice market proved distressing to small-scale, struggling rice farmers. It also, as Aurelia George Mulgan notes, weakened JA's historically powerful position as a "corporatist intermediary" between farmers and the government.[36] But for others, it opened long-awaited opportunities. Rice retailing has diversified; consumers can now purchase bags of rice not only from specialized rice vendors but also from their neighborhood grocery store. And entrepreneurial rice farmers are taking steps to produce and market products that conform more closely to consumer demand—and not necessarily in concert with JA.

Not all farmers are equipped to adapt to changing market signals, as we discovered for ourselves during a July 2015 conversation with a group of about twenty farmers outside Shiga Prefecture's Minami Kusatsu City. "Rockie" Nakai, a gregarious full-time farmer who had spent time as a young man studying agriculture at the University of Nebraska, was one of the few success stories in the group. Nakai has lowered his production costs by fertilizing his rice seedlings with inexpensive pellets made from discarded fragments of processed rice kernels; the natural fertilizer, along with his use of nonsynthetic pesticides and herbicides, positions Nakai to advertise his rice as "chemical free." Like a growing number of JA defectors who have lost their tolerance for Zennō's high prices and commissions, Nakai purchases pesticides, herbicides, and other farm supplies from big-box home improvement and garden centers that have proliferated following the deregulation of the Japanese retail sector. Although Nakai admits that turning a profit can be a chore, he has gained a modest foothold in the local market with his brand of high-fiber rice, which he proudly markets as a health and beauty product for women.

Others in the group spoke of very different experiences. While Nakai oversees a large—by Japanese standards—farm of nearly thirty hectares, the others manage microfarms. One cultivator, whose tiny rice paddy is inconveniently located on the side of a hill, complained about his failed attempts to expand. Another confessed to his weak grasp of the finer points of marketing; Nakai responded by sharing some nuggets of hard-earned wisdom, only to be met, for the most part, with resigned shrugs. Nakai's colleagues are representative of the kinds of farmers who continue to lean heavily on JA.

Prioritizing Efficient Farmers

Since the 1960s, the state has professed a commitment to encouraging more efficient, larger-scale farmers like Rockie Nakai. As we saw in chapter 2, the 1961 Agricultural Basic Law (ABL)—Japan's agricultural "constitution"—championed the modernization of agriculture by improving, among other things, the structure and management of farms.[37] Japan took a few steps toward that goal by introducing, for example, government-led structural improvement (*hojō seibi*) projects to rezone farmland into more evenly sized and contiguous plots and reconfiguring irrigational and other supporting infrastructure. But in its zeal to narrow the emerging income gap between farmers and city dwellers, the government compromised its pledge to rationalize agriculture by dragging its feet on measures to promote farm consolidation and introducing a slew of protectionist measures and other market-distorting farm supports.

Market principles received a noteworthy boost in 1999, when the Diet replaced the old ABL with the Basic Law on Food, Agriculture and Rural Areas (Shokuryō・nōgyō・nōson kihon hō, or New Basic Law). Enacted in part to reflect the changes introduced to the domestic market following Japan's endorsement of the Uruguay Round's Agreement on Agriculture, the New Basic Law by no means heralded a total victory of market principles over government intervention in the agricultural sector;[38] indeed, it would be unreasonable to expect any country to go to such lengths. What the statute did do was endorse the introduction of more market-conforming agricultural strategies while justifying continuing government intervention on behalf of the public interest. The law thus encouraged government to support production strategies that were attentive to consumer demand (art. 30.1) while taking necessary steps to ensure a "stable supply of good-quality food at reasonable prices" (art. 2.1) and to promote the global "competitiveness of domestic farm products" (art. 18.2) as it guarded against the "adverse effects" of competition from imports (art. 18.1).[39] As such, the stipulations constituted a nod to the public's—and particularly JA's—deep ambivalence about competition in the agricultural sector, which is to be expected for as long as JA and its sympathizers have a political voice. But when all is said and done, the New Basic Law marked both an important departure from postwar Japan's highly protectionist, JA-centric approach to agricultural production and a step toward a more diverse and competitive system.[40]

The government's Basic Plans for Food, Agriculture and Rural Areas gave concrete expression to the principles of the New Basic Law by identifying specific targets and objectives for the agricultural sector and strategies for fulfilling them. The plans spotlighted objectives that spoke to the ongoing farm crisis, from increasing agricultural output to stemming the spread of abandoned farmland and boosting farm household incomes. Once justified from the perspective of redistributive principles, these objectives were increasingly portrayed as key to enhancing the competitive capacity of farmers in freer, more open markets.

One prominent strategy for achieving these objectives since the late 1990s has been the promotion of *ninaite* (lit., agricultural "carriers" or "bearers"), or core farmers. The core farmer is a rather vague category that includes full-time commercial farm households and other types of farm enterprises that operate, or are expected to operate, "effective and stable" farms.[41] The MAFF now helps coordinate the provision of promotional services to various types of core farmers, including through national and prefectural organizations known as comprehensive support councils for the promotion of core farmers (*ninaite ikusei sōgō shien kyōgikai*). Advertised as "one-stop support offices" and administered with help from bureaucrats, JA, and local agricultural committees (nōgyō iinkai), the councils provide training assistance, financial support for the acquisition of farm machinery, advice on effective farm management, and the like.[42]

Among the more prominent core farmers nowadays are certified farmers (*nintei nōgyōsha*), or farm enterprises that have received official designation as larger-scale, stable farms by their local governments in accordance with the 1993 Agricultural Management Infrastructure Enforcement Act (Nōgyō keiei kiban kyōka sokushin hō).[43] Certified farmers are singled out for special support— start-up grants, tax breaks, preferential access to loans and leased land, and other subsidies. The prioritization of core farmers in general and certified farmers in particular signifies a deliberate shift from an emphasis on redistributive policy supports for all farmers toward measures designed to promote more productive, market-conforming structural reforms of agriculture.

The promotion of certified farmers is not, however, producing the intended results. There are many reasons for this, including bureaucratic red tape and varying levels of commitment to the initiative among local governments. And as we discovered through numerous interviews, some eligible farmers refrain from applying for the designation for fear of losing subsidies connected to other agricultural programs (see chapter 5). Finally, the fact that the national government itself has wavered on the initiative has not helped matters. After the Democratic Party of Japan's (DPJ) coalition government came to power in 2009, for instance, it made good on a campaign promise to extend income-support subsidies to all farmers, regardless of their viability. Not surprisingly, and as figure 3.3 shows, the total number of certified farm enterprises significantly decreased from 249,369 to 231,101 between 2010 and 2014. But in response to renewed efforts to promote structural reform in the agricultural sector during the early years of the Abe administration, that number increased to 246,085 by

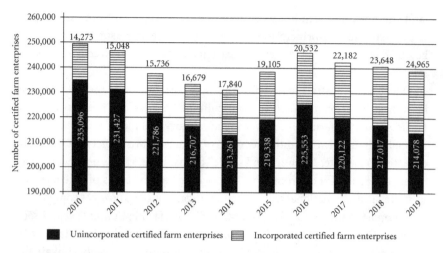

FIGURE 3.3.   Number of certified farm enterprises between 2010 and 2019.

Source: MAFF, "Nintei nōgyōsha no nintei jōkyō."

2016, only to start shrinking once again; as of 2019, the total stands at 239,043. This trend reflects in part the decline and aging of the overall farm population.

Nor is the promotion of certified farm enterprises sufficient to attract younger people to farming. If it were, we should expect to see increases in the number of farm enterprises owned by younger individuals and a corresponding decrease in those owned by elderly Japanese. But the reverse has been the case. For example, between 2011 and 2014 alone the proportion of certified farm enterprises owned by cultivators under the age of fifty slipped from 25.1 percent to 22.6 percent, while the proportion held by those age sixty-five and over increased quite significantly, from 17.5 percent to 26.7 percent.[44]

In sum, the promotion of certified and other core farmers has produced mixed results. Nevertheless, the hope remains that when combined with the reforms outlined below, these new types of farmers will increase their adaptability to market signals, secure higher incomes, and thus stand a greater chance of attracting successors.

The Push for Land Consolidation

The state of Japanese farmland reflects agriculture's demographic crisis in at least two ways. First, the rapid aging of the farm population and acute shortage of farm successors is accelerating the spread of abandoned farmland, since farms that lack successors run a higher risker of literally "going to seed." Between 1985 and 2015, total abandoned farmland increased from 131,000 hectares to a whopping 423,000 hectares[45]—an area slightly larger than Fukui Prefecture. Second, at roughly 2 hectares, the average Japanese farm remains very small—too small to significantly reduce production costs to levels that would make farming more attractive to potential newcomers. For the MAFF, the magic number for rice cultivators is 15 hectares; farms of that size or greater shoulder 30 percent lower costs than the average-sized farm enterprise. Mindful of that correlation and of the connections between farm size and the successor shortage, the Abe government announced in 2014 that it aspired to increase the core farmer population's share of total farmland from 50 percent to 80 percent by 2023.[46]

The promotion of larger farms via farmland consolidation was on the government's radar long before the demographic crisis fully problematized it. Building on the spirit of the 1961 Agricultural Basic Law, which championed larger-scale farming, the MAFF first tackled the issue during the early 1960s by seeking to ease restrictions on the purchase, sale, and leasing of farmland by special types of corporations. But the move was roundly rebuffed by JA and both LDP and Japan Socialist Party politicians, all of whom opposed nonfarm corporate participation in agriculture on principle.[47] The government then set its sights on relaxing the 1952 Agricultural Land Act's (ALA) restrictions on farmland leasing, which, as chapter 2 explains, had effectively removed the circulation of farmland from the free market in an effort to preclude the rebirth of the prewar landlord class and protect the rights of small-scale owner-cultivators.[48] In 1970, the Diet amended the ALA to loosen some of the restrictions on both the leasing and ownership of farmland, ended farmland rent controls, and introduced a local agricultural landholding rationalization system (*nōchi hoyū gōrika jigyō*) for matching farmland owners with potential leasers.[49] These and related changes marked a weakening commitment to the early postwar principle of owner-cultivatorism (*jisakunōshugi*) in favor of a system that recognized more diverse farmland rights, including those of tenants.[50]

The impact of these initiatives on farm size was disappointingly small; between 1990 and 2005, the average farm grew from 1.1 hectares to just 1.3 hectares.[51] Since 2005, however, the average farm size has expanded to approximately 2 hectares. More significantly, the proportion of farmland owned by core farmers has increased—from just 27.8 percent in 2001 to 50.3 percent in 2015.[52] While the government still has further to go before reaching its 2023 target of 80 percent, the trend is certainly on the uptick. We can attribute these increases to several policy initiatives, most notably the 2009 amendment of the ALA to authorize nonfarm corporations to lease farmland; although construction, processing, retail, and other food-related firms are still prohibited from directly owning farmland, the amendments mark a significant weakening of one of postwar Japan's most enduring agriculture taboos.[53] More recently, the Abe government instructed rural municipal governments to craft agricultural master plans for promoting certified farmers and strategies for optimal farmland usage and increased subsidies for both certified farmers who expand their holdings through leasing and the owners of that leased farmland.[54] It also legislated a plan to replace the agricultural land-holding rationalization system with more influential farmland consolidation banks (FLCB, *nōchi chūkan kanri kikō*) in all forty-seven prefectures,[55] a target that was fulfilled by late 2014. In fiscal year (FY) 2014, the farmland consolidation banks orchestrated the leasing or subleasing of 53,000 hectares.[56] (We revisit this topic in chapter 7.)

There is reason to be cautiously optimistic about the future of farmland consolidation. Declining land prices are weakening pressures for the conversion of farmland for commercial or residential purposes; this explains at least in part why the rate of farmland conversion has decreased somewhat since 1995.[57] And while declining land prices can function as an impediment to the sale of farmland to core farmers, they may very well encourage leasing. These material incentives for land consolidation via leasing are reinforced by demographic trends; as Honma observes, elderly, part-time farmers without successors are likely to lease their precious land to core farmers—providing, of course, that those core farmers are deemed sufficiently trustworthy.[58]

On their own, these upward trends in land consolidation cannot resolve Japan's multifaceted agricultural crisis. However, the slow but inexorable expansion of Japanese farm size is contributing to the decline of part-time farming—a major source of agricultural inefficiency and a cornerstone of JA's influence. As table 3.2 illustrates, while the number of both full-time and part-time commercial farm households is declining, part-time households have been disappearing at a rate much faster than their full-time counterparts, although the data for 2018 suggest that the latter trend may be slowing.

The Diversification of Farm Enterprises

As family farms grapple with the challenges of rapid aging and lower agricultural prices, some are taking advantage of past government reforms to promote new business management models that enhance productivity and profitability. The resulting diversification of farm enterprises is incentivizing many farmer-members to rethink their relationship to JA services.

Recent changes in farm management extend to the very foundations of modern Japanese agriculture: the traditional farm household (nōka). As we noted in

TABLE 3.2   Full-time vs. part-time commercial farm households, 1990–2018

YEAR	TOTAL (1,000s)	FULL-TIME	PART-TIME	PT:FT
1990	2,971	473	2,497	5.28:1
1995	2,651	428	2,224	5.20:1
2000	2,337	426	1,911	4.49:1
2005	1,963	443	1,520	3.43:1
2010	1,631	451	1,180	2.62:1
2015	1,330	443	887	2.00:1
2018	1,164	375	789	2.10:1

Sources: MAFF, "Statistical Yearbook," various years; MAFF, "Report on the Results"; and MIC, *Dai69 Nihon*.

chapter 2, the traditional farm household embraces a form of family management (kazoku keiei) in which the household owns all farm-related assets and is the sole source of farm labor[59] and in which farmland ownership is transferred via inheritance. Family management continues to be the dominant approach to farming today. But some households are choosing to change their management structure by incorporating themselves.[60] Incorporation has been an option for family farms for decades, but it was not until the 1992 release of the Direction of New Policies for Food, Agriculture and Rural Villages (Atarashii shokuryō · nōgyō · nōson seisaku no hōkō) that its promotion became official government policy.[61] The government's rationale was that incorporated farm enterprises (nōgyō hōjin) would be better suited to meeting the challenges of market liberalization than the traditional nōka.[62]

Incorporation does indeed have several advantages. It simplifies and clarifies bookkeeping by separating farm and household finances. It provides for the expansion of the farm's labor pool by authorizing the chief company officer—normally the head of the farm household—to hire both family members and outsiders as contracted employees. This capacity to hire from outside the family in turn enables the enterprise to increase its pool of agricultural, managerial, and financial expertise. As the number of skilled employees grows, so, too, does the enterprise's creditworthiness. And the larger and more creditworthy the enterprise, the greater its eligibility for certified farmer status and its accompanying benefits,[63] and the greater the likelihood that the farm household can expand by purchasing and/or leasing extra farmland. Finally, incorporation can alleviate the challenge of succession. Whereas the traditional family farm faces extinction when there are no blood relations on the horizon to serve as successors, incorporated family farms can tap their nonfamily employees to eventually run their farms.[64] More to the point, to the extent that a farm household can translate its incorporated status into other benefits that boost its long-term income stream, it stands a greater chance of finding any kind of successor.

But incorporation also has some drawbacks. Many farmers complain of the red tape surrounding the incorporation process, although the Abe government took steps to alleviate this problem. And farmers worry about the financial strain associated with putting outside labor on the payroll. Full-time employees require benefits and, in some cases, training, the costs of which can eat into the family's net income.[65] What is more, incorporated family farm enterprises confronting short-term capital shortages—a common occurrence before the harvest comes in and farmers are paid for their produce—are sometimes reduced to having one of their officers take out loans (*yakuin kariirekin*); since eligible officers are usually family members, the loans can prove catastrophic for the family if agricultural prices drop before repayment is due.[66]

For many farmers—and especially part-time farmers—incorporation may be more trouble than it is worth. Together with the steady decline in the overall farm population, this helps explain why the overall number of incorporated farms has decreased in recent years. Between 2005 and 2015, as the total number of farm households dropped precipitously from nearly 2 million to just over 1.3 million, the number of incorporated households slipped from approximately 5,000 to 4,000. But the important takeaway here is that the *proportion* of such households has increased slightly, from roughly 0.25 percent to 0.30 percent.[67] Perhaps more significantly, given their status as core—that is, viable—farmers, certified farmers are pursuing incorporation at higher rates; as figure 3.3 illustrates, while the overall numbers of certified farm enterprises dropped by more than 10,000 between 2010 and 2019, the proportion of incorporated certified farm enterprises increased from less than 6 percent of the total to just over 10 percent.

There is still much to be learned about the exact impact of incorporation on the performance and productivity of family farms. At least one study has found that incorporated farms are correlated with higher revenues,[68] but farm size—incorporated family farms tend to be larger than average—may be the key driver here. Nevertheless, it is reasonable to conclude that incorporated family farms are more likely than traditional farm households to acquire the resources needed to adapt quickly and profitably to shifting price and other market signals. Judging from its expansion of official programs designed to help farm households navigate the incorporation process, the Abe administration clearly agreed.

Anecdotal evidence strongly suggests that incorporated family farms are less likely than traditional family farms to lean heavily on JA. Shimada Toshio, the full-time vegetable producer from the outskirts of Kumamoto City, exemplifies why this is so. Between himself and his employees—several of them family members—Shimada has both the manpower and the management expertise to negotiate directly with buyers, run his own processing facilities, and arrange for the transport of his finished products. The costs incurred from taking care of these tasks in-house, he claims, are less than if his local co-op were to do the job.[69] Other farmers point out that by hiring staff to take care of the enterprise's paperwork, they avoid having to rely on JA's services;[70] this, in turn, can lessen the chances of unwanted interference from their local co-op. The anti-JA preferences of farmers like Shimada help explain why JA traditionally viewed incorporated farm enterprises as changelings (*onikko*)[71]—unnatural, disruptive participants in Japan's traditional agricultural hierarchy.

In its efforts to encourage more efficient farm management and farmland consolidation, the MAFF has also promoted the establishment of hamlet-based farm associations (*shūraku einō soshiki*, or, more simply, shūraku einō: HBFAs). These resemble agricultural production co-ops (see chapter 2) found in Israel, Russia, and Central and South Asia in that they compose entire—or large portions of—farm communities and facilitate the sharing of (often jointly owned) farm implements, but farmland is privately, rather than collectively, owned. HB-FAs, which have roots in the Meiji era,[72] grew popular during the 1960s along with ad hoc labor-pooling associations of (mostly) part-time farmers who needed help in the paddies while they worked in nearby factories or other off-farm jobs. By the 1970s, HBFAs were coordinating the joint use of sophisticated—and expensive—farm machinery and, by the 1980s, member crop rotations under gentan.[73] As their numbers and functions increased, many HBFAs introduced centralized management systems. Today, they are found mostly in rice-producing areas and normally encompass all or a large majority of farm households within a hamlet or small group of hamlets. By the 1980s, the HBFAs were significant participants in the implementation of crop rotation and other programs connected to gentan.[74]

Agricultural experts have praised the HBFAs for alleviating economic and demographic pressures on farmers. Most notably, they help compensate for the many barriers to consolidating farmland ownership by consolidating farmland management. In keeping with the spirit and provisions of the New Basic Law, which encourages efficient forms of farm management, governments during the 2000s aggressively promoted them as core farmers and encouraged their incorporation. Like incorporated farm households, incorporated HBFAs are positioned to accumulate capital, hire outside labor, and thus to respond more nimbly to price and other market signals. And like incorporated farm households, incorporated HBFAs are qualified to receive local government approval as certified farmers and, subsequently, more government largesse.[75] The government's

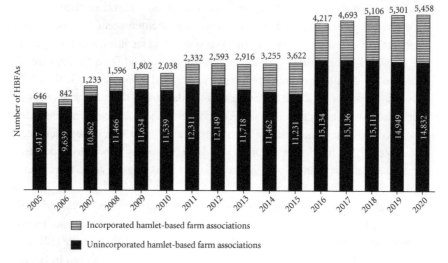

FIGURE 3.4. Annual number of hamlet-based farm associations, from 2005 to 2020.

Source: MAFF, "Shūraku einō jittai chōsa gaiyō."

promotion of HBFAs has borne some fruit; between 2005 and 2017, the total number of hamlet-based farm associations grew steadily from 10,063 to 15,136; between 2017 and 2020, the total gradually declined to 14,832, no doubt in response to the rapid shrinkage and aging of the farm population. Significantly for our purposes, the proportion of incorporated associations increased from 6.4 percent in 2005 to a noteworthy 37 percent in 2020, with the largest year-to-year increases registering during the Abe administration (see figure 3.4).

Today, hamlet-based farm associations help farmers—particularly part-time rice farmers—in a number of ways. Some households join an association to gain access to jointly owned, and hence lower-cost, farm equipment. Others turn to it for seasonal labor. Those who are too old to till the soil themselves, or who are retiring and lack successors, may lease their land to the incorporated HBFA, thus securing an income stream for themselves and their heirs and the long-term preservation of their most precious family asset. This latter trend has been gaining traction as a partial solution to the successor shortage.[76]

HBFAs are by no means devoid of problems. Agri Tomoai's Otsu Takamitsu points out that these enterprises can only become vehicles for de facto farmland consolidation when all—or nearly all—farm households in a community participate. (This can be hard to achieve in communities populated by farmers with traditional mindsets who do not want to change the way they manage their farms.) Full participation is also more cost effective for the HBFA, since it enables farmers to easily transfer heavy machinery to their neighbors, assuming, of course, that farms are (relatively) contiguous; otherwise, the association must shoulder the costs of loading that equipment onto trucks and transporting it from member to member over longer distances.[77] Meanwhile, some HBFAs are formed solely to gain access to government subsidies,[78] which helps explain why local (JA) co-ops are often so eager to support them. Lastly, these ventures do little to discourage inefficient part-time farmers from remaining on the land; in fact, they do the opposite.[79]

Hamlet-based farm associations have varying relationships with JA. Some completely divorce themselves from the traditional JA network and assume all functions relating to the planting, harvesting, and marketing of member output. Many more nurture close relationships with JA. Still others, like Agri Tomoai, rely on JA for limited assistance, including investment capital. At first, JA sought majority ownership of Agri Tomoai to ensure that its products were channeled through JA networks. But Otsu restricted JA's investment share to less than 50 percent, so he could be free to negotiate with non-JA buyers and suppliers, thus maximizing potential returns on member output. Nevertheless, a JA representative sits on Agri Tomoai's board, and the cooperative is headquartered within a branch office of JA Kumamoto City. The co-op benefits from this arrangement in that a portion of Agri Tomoai's produce is distributed through its networks; it also receives a small return on its investments. Agri Tomoai, for its own part, can count on a stable financial base.[80]

In some ways, Agri Tomoai protects traditional family farms and local communities while alleviating some of the challenges posed by the successor shortage. Although the enterprise struggles to make a profit, it offers aging, small-scale farmers who lack successors an opportunity to keep their farms and protect their farmland. And while it by no means poses an existential threat to part-time farmers or to JA, Agri Tomoai incentivizes the local multipurpose co-op to break with tradition and experiment with new kinds of partnerships with local farmers, a topic we explore further in later chapters. Viewed in this way, Otsu's venture challenges the JA Group's highly centralized, top-down management model by encouraging greater levels of co-op responsiveness to local farmer needs.

Nonfarm Corporate Entry into Agriculture

Far more troubling to JA has been the recent entry of nonfarm corporations into agriculture. Historically, JA and farm households opposed the participation of construction, manufacturing, technology, or other firms in agricultural production as threats to the owner-cultivator principle—namely, that farmland ownership rights should lie exclusively with the cultivator. Not coincidentally, this principle legitimized the (inefficient) small-scale farm households that formed the nucleus of JA's regular membership base. Others criticized nonfarm corporate entry for fear it would lead to the mismanagement of farmland and land speculation. By the late twentieth century, however, the liberalization of nonfarm corporate entry was widely touted as a solution to the rapid spread of abandoned farmland and shortage of farm successors and backed by both Keidanren (Japan Business Federation) and government proponents of deregulation.[81]

The history of nonfarm corporate participation in the agricultural sector extends to the early 1960s. In 1962, amendments to the ALA to loosen the rule that only farmers—that is, individuals who were actively engaged in farming for a minimum of 150 days per year—be permitted to own farmland paved the way for the establishment of agricultural production corporations (*nōgyō seisan hōjin*, or APCs), incorporated farm enterprises in which a minority portion of shares could be owned by nonfarm firms.[82] (Amendments to the ALA have gradually increased the total proportion of APC shares owned by nonfarm firms to just under 50 percent, as of 2015.) In response to corporate pressure, the ALA was amended again in 2001 to permit APCs to commit up to half of their total sales to nonagricultural business and to accept modest investments from food processors and retailers.[83] The number of APCs grew slowly at first, from 2,740 in 1970 to 4,150 in 1995, but then picked up speed; by 2014, the total reached 14,333.[84] Were it not for the stipulation that farmers constitute the majority of APC shareholders and members of boards of directors, this number would likely have been higher.

Other types of nonfarm enterprises have entered the agricultural sector as well in recent years. During the early 2000s, the government launched pilot projects to allow nonfarm, non-APC corporations to lease farmland; the 2009 round of ALA amendments formalized these changes. This means that firms in construction, food retail, and other industries are now free to set up agricultural subsidiaries for leasing farmland and engaging in production for niche consumer markets. In many, if not most, cases, the parent company serves as the primary investor.

When all is said and done, continuing restrictions on the ownership, leasing, and transfer of farmland, lingering distrust of nonfarm corporations in the agricultural sector, and the discontiguity of arable land in Japan will ensure that agribusinesses on the scale of Cargill, Archer Daniels Midland, or Monsanto will be slow to develop in Japan—if ever. For the foreseeable future, at least, the family farm will remain the dominant player on the Japanese agricultural landscape. Be that as it may, incremental changes to the legal foundations of farmland usage have facilitated a modest diversification of farm enterprises and a concomitant weakening of small-scale farm households. As the next section explains, these trends are further enabled by structural changes in the broader food industry.

Japan's Changing Food Supply Chains

The economic and demographic pressures plaguing the agricultural sector are important motivators behind the government's gradual relaxation of rules governing who can farm and how. But crisis is not the only driving force behind reform. Opportunities also matter—most notably those generated by the gradual transformation of Japanese food supply chains in the context of stepped-up economic liberalization since the early 1990s. By food supply chains, we mean the networks of agricultural producers, food processors, and retailers—and of the wholesalers, transport companies, and other intermediaries that connect these three main groups to one another—through which food products wind their way from farm to table. The liberalization of farmland, the legal diversification of farm management structures, and other regulatory reforms have enabled entrepreneurial farmers over the past generation to adapt to these changes by expanding into food processing and retailing and/or collaborating with downstream firms. And as farmers add value to their raw product, they stand a better chance of making a good living outside of JA networks.

Changes in consumer demand lie at the heart of Japan's evolving food supply chains. Households continue to insist on safe, high-quality foods—preferably those that have been grown and processed domestically—and are willing to pay relatively high prices for them.[85] Many are also gravitating toward organic foods, which the JA Group has been slow to promote given its heavy reliance on proceeds from the sale of agricultural chemicals. They are developing loyalties toward niche brands that reflect geographic origin, culinary specialties, health and safety benefits, and even beauty benefits, as Rockie Nakai understood when he developed his varietal of high-fiber rice. Meanwhile, younger consumers continue to frequent fast-food outlets, thus generating corporate demand for lower-quality ingredients, while the growing popularity of gourmet restaurants is expanding demand for high-end foods. Together, these structural developments are broadening opportunities for producers to change what they grow and how they grow it.

Kumamoto Prefecture's Shimada Toshio is a prime example of how entrepreneurial farmers can respond effectively to changes in consumer demand by developing new business strategies and partnerships outside of JA's controlling embrace. Shimada has acquired the technology to manufacture jams, sauces, and snacks for direct sale to discriminating end-use consumers. The bulk of his income, however, is derived from the sale of raw product to commercial consumers like food processors and local restaurants. Shimada communicates directly with his corporate customers to decide what and how much parsley or shiso to produce and at what price. This is *contract farming* (*keiyaku nōgyō*)—and in a stable market, both parties win. Unlike the postwar JA farmer-members who learned the price of their raw product only after the harvest, the savvy, independent farmer can lock in a good price before planting even begins. The buyer, meanwhile, cuts costs by dealing directly with the producer and gains a degree of control over the exact quantity and quality of the finished product.

Farmers engaged in contract farming for corporate consumers incur numerous risks, some of which underscore the advantages of relying on JA. Although JA has been known to pressure farmer-members into marketing their raw product through the its multitiered distribution system, or keitō, members nevertheless do have the option of selling on the open market. Contract farmers enjoy no such option, which means that when market prices increase after a contract has been concluded, the farmer's potential profit margin shrinks. (Of course, it is the corporate buyer who loses when prices decrease.) And while JA typically purchases whatever its members have managed to produce during the growing season, contract farmers are obligated to fulfill the terms of their contracts by a predetermined time regardless of growing conditions. Shimazaki Hideki, the founder of Nagano Prefecture's well-known Top River (a limited liability APC), learned this the hard way. When Top River fell short of its contracted lettuce production targets during the early 2000s, it had to cover the shortfall by purchasing (expensive) lettuce from unaffiliated farms.[86] Contract farmers also face increased transaction costs associated with the yearly or biennial renegotiation of contracts. There are no such costs associated with working through JA. Finally, stories abound of powerful commercial buyers that, in their zeal to reduce costs, impose too many production risks on farmers or arbitrarily change contract terms. These and related risks are anathema to Japan's small-scale, part-time passive producers. But for well-informed, entrepreneurial farmers like Shimada who want to increase profits, they are well worth taking.

While Shimada's relatively modest enterprise relies heavily on partnerships with firms elsewhere in the food supply chain, other entrepreneurial farmers are more focused on developing in-house processing and retail capacities. Rokusei, a Kanazawa-based agricultural production corporation, has expanded gradually downstream since the late 1970s to become Ishikawa Prefecture's largest—and, arguably, most famous—food corporation.[87] Originally a family-operated rice farm, Rokusei eventually incorporated itself and then expanded its scope by either contracting with or leasing the land of neighboring farms. Today, the firm oversees 140 hectares of rice paddies as well as broad swaths of farmland for vegetable production.[88] Rokusei also ventured into the manufacturing of omochi, or rice cakes, and osechi ryōri, traditional New Year's foods served in special stacked boxes. The firm struggled to gain a foothold in the osechi market, in part because of inconsistencies in the quality of the raw product supplied by its vast networks of farmer suppliers. But it soon learned how to produce a consistently high-quality brand by forging close, contracted relationships with only the most reliable local cultivators. Rokusei's osechi and other products are sold over the internet and in retail shops that are owned and directly managed by the firm (chokueiten), as well as at independent supermarkets and department stores.[89] Rokusei has established something of a national reach, but like most entrepreneurial farm enterprises, it is primarily focused on nurturing a consumer base at the regional level.[90]

Another successful—and unusually flamboyant—example of farmer expansion down the value-added chain is Mokumoku Tezukuri Farm,[91] an independent pig farm outside Iga City in Mie Prefecture that has learned how to combine production, processing, and retailing functions in ways that appeal to far more than the consumer's taste buds. The farm's founder is Kimura Osamu, a farmer-businessman now in his midsixties who acquired a deep understanding of Japanese food supply chains while working as an official in the meat division of JA's prefectural economic federation (keizairen). In the early 1980s, Kimura quit his JA job to establish a pig farm that he hoped would succeed where JA was failing—by carefully differentiating prices on the basis of product quality, negotiating with retailers for prices that are favorable to producers, and responding nimbly to regional niche demand. Over time, Mokumoku expanded beyond pork to produce rice, shiitake mushrooms, berries, and several other fruits and vegetables, which it sells to end-use consumers through its own distribution channels. The enterprise also established in-house processing facilities to prepare hams, sausages and other pork products, Japanese sweets, breads, tofu, and beer, and it built exclusive retail outlets and farm-to-table restaurants (Mokumoku nōjō resutoran) in Tokyo and other major cities. But what really sets Mokumoku apart are its theme park, petting zoo, outdoor theater, and educational programs that inform children about agriculture, the environment, food, and nutrition. And then there are its on-site restaurants, one of which—Buubuu Hausu, lit. "Oink Oink House"—serves high-grade barbecue pork dishes as fat pigs roam the lawns outside.[92] Mokumoku may be an extreme example of Japanese farm multifunctionality and marketing ingenuity, but it underscores a key point in Japan's changing agricultural landscape: farmers who wish to think outside the box now have more opportunities to do so.

Many contemporary farm enterprises that venture downstream secure loans from regional banks.[93] Although still in its infancy, the trend reflects the diversification of commercial banks' loan portfolios in an age of increasing financial competition. Ironically, it is also testament to JA Bank's often stringent rules for lending to farmers, its growing prioritization of more lucrative, nonfarm investment opportunities, and its reluctance to assist—through lending and the provision of supporting information—farmers who might very well secure their inputs and market their products outside of JA channels. Nevertheless, growing competition in agricultural financial services should, in theory, incentivize JA to embrace institutional change. We explore this topic further in the next chapter.

Japanese processors are also diversifying their stakes in food supply chains and in ways that can benefit producers. Japan has no shortage of large food processors with internationally recognized brands—think Ajinomoto, Kikkoman, and Kirin Brewery. But in their efforts to cut costs, many are relying on cheap food imports for their ingredients.[94] Some smaller processors, by contrast, are figuring out how to source their ingredients from domestic producers. Hamada Shōyu, a family-operated soy sauce manufacturer located not too far from Shimada's hothouses in Kumamoto City, is a case in point. Established in 1818, the firm produces a brand of high-quality soy sauce that, true to Kumamoto custom, is slightly sweeter than Japan's mass-marketed alternatives. A generation ago, Hamada set out to diversify its offerings to include beautifully packaged miso, sauces, dressings, bean paste buns, crackers, sweets, and a variety of other products. The firm now bypasses costly wholesalers by directly contracting with local soybean growers, and it goes to great lengths to ensure that those growers deliver a top-notch product. It brands and prices its products to appeal to different regional and urban markets, sells directly to local sushi shops and other restaurants, and conducts internet sales. And it transformed its plant into a stylish tourist attraction by adding contemporary touches to its Tokugawa-era architecture; building a posh, on-site coffee shop that serves gourmet coffees and uniquely flavored (e.g., soy sauce) ice creams; and merging its storefront into its processing facility so that shoppers can inspect the firm's massive vats of fermenting soy sauces. As Hamada's owner-manager explained, this expansion up and down the supply chain is driven by necessity; given cut-throat competition in the area, exacting consumer standards, and declining demand for traditional Japanese foods, a trend the national government tries to offset by exempting soy sauce from consumption taxes, the firm has had no choice but to diversify.[95]

Perhaps the biggest story in the transformation of Japan's food supply chains has been the increasing concentration and diversification of food retailers. The standout players in this regard have been large convenience store (konbini), fast food, and supermarket chains. Take, for instance, Lawson, the convenience store chain. Recognizing the growing demand among working mothers, young men living alone, and seniors for fresh, prepackaged foods, the firm established a subsidiary called Lawson Farms, an agricultural production corporation, in 2010.[96] The subsidiary contracts directly with incorporated family farms to grow fruits and vegetables, which it then transfers to Lawson's regional processing centers using Lawson trucks. The raw product is cut and assembled into packaged meals or single servings stored in plastic cups and then distributed to Natural Lawson and Lawson Store 100 outlets. By 2016, Lawson Farms had twenty-three locations around the country that produced thirty-seven types of fruits and vegetables and was supplying 7 percent of the foods sold in Lawson stores.[97] Those farms provide opportunities for local farmers to sell some or all of their products outside of JA.

While Lawson depends on contracted relationships with independent farm enterprises, other food retailers are engaged more directly in cultivation. Aeon Agri Create, established in 2009 as a farming subsidiary of Japan's mammoth supermarket chain Aeon, now leases farmland in several prefectures to grow rice and vegetables.[98] Many of the subsidiary's products are used as ingredients in Aeon's private brand, Topvalu.

Participation by Lawson and Aeon in agricultural production—either directly via leasing or in partnership with local growers—would be impossible were it not for the deregulation of farmland. Other deregulatory measures have further enabled large retailers to transform food supply chains to their advantage. Supermarkets and convenience stores now dwarf Japan's small-scale food retailers, thanks in part to the gradual loosening of the infamous Large-Sale Retail Store Law during the 1990s in response to US trade pressure and its replacement in 2000 by the more liberal Large-Scale Retail Location Law. Later measures opened the food retail sector to a wider variety of enterprises, including pharmacies. As a result, food retailing has become increasingly concentrated in a handful of large chains, which has far-reaching implications for how food travels from farm to table. The small, local vendors of fruits, vegetables, and lightly processed foods that dominated postwar Japan's neighborhood shopping districts (shōtengai) lack the resources and know-how to control the way they acquire their raw product; today, those that have not succumbed to competition tend to remain heavily dependent on costly networks of wholesalers and transporters in which JA plays an important part.[99] Large retailers, by contrast, are spared these dependencies, as Lawson's experiences illustrate. Owners of networks of warehouses, brick-and-mortar stores, and a large fleet of trucks, Lawson and its agricultural subsidiary can grow, transport, process, store, and market food without turning to outsiders for help. This gives the chain a clear cost advantage that small retailers, many of which struggle with rising transportation costs,[100] have no hope of matching. Other food retailers, including large discount stores like Ito-Yokado, and department stores with food basements (depachika), like Sogo and Seibu, enjoy similar cost advantages, as do MOS Burger, Yoshinoya, and other chains that proliferated in recent decades in response to rising consumer demand for fast foods.[101]

The government now has a slogan to capture the ongoing transformation of national food supply chains: the "sixth industrialization" (*rokuji sangyōka*)—or the vertical integration of the primary (farming), secondary (food processing), and tertiary (retail) sectors $(1 + 2 + 3 = 6)$. The concept first appeared during the mid-1990s, when market openings jumpstarted a series of MAFF-sponsored policy discussions about the future of rural villages and the structural reform of agriculture.[102] Since then, "sixth industrialization" has become a catchphrase for value-added agricultural production and the promotion of synergies among various market players. Less well known—but equally revealing—slogans articulated by officialdom include the MAFF's "food industry clusters" (*shokuryō kurasutā*), a play on Michael Porter's concept of "industry clusters," and the Ministry of Economy, Trade and Industry's (METI) "food, commerce, and industry coordination" (*nōshōkō renkei*).

Some analysts justifiably dismiss these initiatives as empty sloganeering. Few food industry clusters have gained traction, while the best practices of those that have done so are not easily diffused to other agricultural areas.[103] Meanwhile, relatively few farmers are venturing down the value-added path. This is not surprising. As we saw in the case of herbal teas produced by the tiny farm households of Kanakura, most farmers lack the manufacturing, branding, and marketing skills to process more than rudimentary products composed of easily accessed local ingredients. Those who do have these skills, including the managers of Rokusei and Mokumoku, know all too well that their finished products will succeed only if they incorporate high-quality, tasty ingredients. ("If it's not delicious," one of our interviewees reminded us, "it just won't sell."[104] And it is the customer who decides if it is delicious.[105]) And as Rokusei's experiences illustrate, it can take years to master the fine art of food processing, especially when it involves traditional food products for which consumer demand is low but expectations high. In keeping with the Japanese adage that "rice cakes should be made by rice cake makers" (*mochi wa mochiya*), many farmers who venture into the risky world of food processing abandon their dreams, ceding the task to the experts.[106]

These caveats notwithstanding, the vertical integration of the Japanese food system—whether via the sixth industrialization of individual farm enterprises like Rokusei or through the pursuit of Lawson-style farmer, commerce, industry coordination—has become a widely held priority. In 2008, the Diet passed the Law to Promote the Coordination of Food, Commerce and Industry (Nōshōkō renkei sokushin hō), and government has taken numerous steps since then to help things along. The MAFF and METI—long-standing bureaucratic rivals—have cooperated to promote the vertical integration of food supply chains by providing technical assistance to interested firms, as well as information and consultation services to encourage appropriate matchups.[107] Finally, private and semiprivate organizations are cropping up at the national, prefectural, and local levels to assist farm enterprises as they strive to expand downstream.

Few observers would disagree that the expansion of intersector synergies within Japanese food supply chains is still in its infancy. But the writing on the wall is clear: an alternative, more competitive agricultural universe is slowly taking shape outside of JA.

Entrepreneurship, Changing Mindsets, and the Future of JA

Japanese farmers are diversifying. Although the majority of farmers today resemble Ishizaki Hidezumi from Kanakura, a small but growing number are breaking away from Japan's traditional, JA-centric system of production to introduce a variety of different business strategies and complementary organizations and management systems. From the incorporated family farms owned by Rockie Nakai or Shimada Toshio to regional powerhouses like Rokusei and Mokumoku Tezukuri Farm, more and more farm enterprises are being run just like any other profit-oriented business that adapts its strategies and organization to changing market conditions.

Farmers are diversifying because they must. Over the past generation, Japanese agriculture has been in the midst of an existential crisis driven by a confluence of demographic and economic trends. Shrinking domestic demand caused by the simultaneous decline and aging of the general population has combined with decreasing agricultural prices resulting from market liberalizations and governmental deregulatory measures to send farm household incomes into a downward trajectory over the past two decades. And for as long as farm incomes shrink, Japan's aging producers will struggle to find successors. In an era when government is losing its capacity to shield agriculture from competition, a consensus is rapidly emerging among farmers, scholars, and policy makers alike that Japan's agricultural crisis can only be alleviated if farming becomes more profitable.

Farmers are also diversifying because they can. For decades—and particularly since the early 1990s—governments have been introducing legal and regulatory reforms that have gradually transformed the institutional foundations of agriculture. The operative word here is "gradually." Unlike the financial reforms of the late 1990s, there has been no deregulatory "big bang" in the farm sector; change has instead come in bits and pieces and in ways that have frustrated—even exasperated—critics. Few would disagree that far more work needs to be done to put agriculture on more solid ground. But when taken together, the slow liberalization of farmland rights and the legal diversification of farm enterprises in the context of diversifying food supply chains—supply chains that are themselves responding to governmental deregulatory measures—are expanding the menu of choices for farmers as they figure out how best to structure their enterprises and market their products.

Organizational and strategic changes among farm households reflect—and contribute to—broad shifts in farmer mindsets. As we noted in chapter 2, postwar farmers embedded in hamlet-level social networks and a food supply chain dominated by JA tended to embrace the values and objectives of passive producers. Against this backdrop, talk of entrepreneurship or profit was considered not only unnecessary but also selfish and unseemly—an affront to the collective norms and spirit of the hamlet and the valuation of farmland as a near sacred family and community asset. And why should farmers think otherwise for as long as the postwar agricultural "regime" provided them with generous incomes and lowered their risks to near zero?

Growing entrepreneurship among farmers reflects new, alternative norms that began to take root during the postwar era as new generations of Japanese took over their family farms. Many farmers in these and subsequent generations have been better educated, less willing to take orders and farm the way their parents did, more willing to question the practices of their co-op, and more in tune with the needs of consumers.[108] Many see themselves not only as producers but also as farm managers (nōgyō keieisha) whose job it is to acquire a mix of skills—technological, administrative, branding, marketing—that businesspeople in other economic sectors have long taken for granted.[109] Put simply, these farmers are not "prepping to be peasants"; they are looking for business opportunities.[110]

While some farmers resist this emerging—and still amorphous—entrepreneurial mindset, others are working hard to promote it. Bookstores are now stacked with magazines and how-to books on agricultural entrepreneurship, farm incorporation, hamlet-based farm associations, and agricultural branding strategies. Successful farmers are publishing memoirs that are as much a clarion call to other entrepreneurial farmers to adopt business-oriented farm strategies as they are personal histories. In one such book—appropriately titled *Profitable Agriculture* (*Mōkaru nōgyō*)—Top River's Shimazaki Hideki calls on traditional farmers to shed their "herd mentality" and misplaced sense of equality and on entrepreneurial farmers to take more leadership in their communities, trumpets the virtues of helping new farm entrants apprentice with successful farmers, urges incorporated farm enterprises to hire employees who are skilled in innovative production and marketing strategies, and advises farmers on how to minimize costs and listen to consumers.[111] Shimazaki and other entrepreneurial farmers are achieving minor celebrity status in business circles as the media showcases their achievements as examples of what makes for effective farming in today's changing agricultural marketplace.[112]

Some successful farmers, like Kimura Osamu of Mokumoku Tezukuri Farms, have even attracted social acclaim in their local communities. It helps, Kimura confessed, that Mokumoku has received a string of awards for agricultural and entrepreneurial excellence from both the government and private-sector organizations.[113] To that we might add Kimura's environmental sensitivities and strong community spirit and the many employment opportunities offered by his enterprise—all of which put him in good stead with the surrounding communities that have long been struggling with depopulation and deindustrialization. Kimura's experiences, and those of others like him, strongly suggest that if entrepreneurial farmers implement new ideas about agricultural production in ways that complement rather than defy long-standing community needs, those ideas stand a greater chance of being translated into norms—taken-for-granted behaviors acquired through social learning. And this, in turn, is likely to raise expectations for further market-conforming change in the future.

These and related changes are unlikely to result in JA's demise. JA will not be displaced any time soon by the kinds of large-scale agribusinesses that dominate the North American agricultural input and market sectors; a host of lingering legal, geographical, cultural, and political impediments will see to that. And for as long as traditional family farms dominate the agricultural landscape, most will continue to look to JA rather than to supermarket or convenience store chains to secure their incomes and mitigate risk.

But the crises and accelerating market changes chronicled above do threaten JA's long-term dominance. Put simply, the diversification of the food supply chain, the rise of more entrepreneurial farmer mindsets, and the selective defection of less risk-averse producers from JA services are shrinking JA's market share and challenging the legitimacy of JA's traditional business model. For JA to remain broadly relevant, it must do more to prioritize the interests of farmers—particularly entrepreneurial farmers—by helping them to lower their production costs and increase their incomes, and in ways that mitigate risk. JA must, in other words, reform its business strategies and organizational relationships with farmers. In the next three chapters, we explore the conditions and processes in which reform unfolds—particularly at the local co-op level.

PUTTING FARMERS FIRST
The Post-1990 Era of JA Reform

What makes a co-op a good co-op? Inspired by the universal principles of agricultural cooperation, Japan's 1947 Agricultural Cooperative Law defines a good co-op as one that elevates the economic and social status of its farmer-members. By any measure, the postwar era brought prosperity to Japanese farmers, but the reasons for this had as much—if not more—to do with high economic growth rates, inflated government-guaranteed rice prices, and closed rice markets as it did with the actions of JA. In fact, some of the very conditions that helped catapult farmers into the middle class also positioned JA organizations to operate as extractive, self-interested players in the food supply chain.

Things changed for JA following the 1990 collapse of the economic bubble. As the conditions of postwar farmer prosperity deteriorated and the farm sector's demographic challenges intensified, JA organizations were increasingly pressured to put farmers first by increasing their incomes. Doing so stood to benefit not just farmers but also the future of Japanese agriculture, for only by operating as price makers—value-generating agents of the farmer interest—could JA increase farmers' chances of securing those all-important successors. Putting farmers first was also the co-op's best hope for securing farmer loyalties as competition against JA began to intensify.

Increasing farmer incomes can be accomplished via a range of strategies. JA organizations can lower service commissions and the price of farm inputs. They can help farmers achieve greater economies of scale by facilitating farmland consolidation. Even more importantly in today's agricultural economy, they can add value to co-op products via new production techniques, processing, branding, and marketing. And they can negotiate more effectively with buyers for higher prices. At the individual co-op level, these strategies are rooted in a raft of "operational rules"—fine-grained, context-specific rules and operating procedures that are endogenously generated within the co-op itself.[1]

Not all JA organizations jumped onto the reform bandwagon during the 1990s. JA's national service and administrative organizations were quick to champion self-reform (jiko kaikaku), but in their determination to preserve the powers and basic organizational parameters of the JA Group, they avoided major changes that would put farmers first. At the local level, some co-ops embraced reform, while others did not. Our purpose in this chapter is to explain these variations, both between JA tiers and especially among local co-ops. In so doing, we make the case that effective strategic change depends, at minimum, on three sets of conditions: favorable growing conditions and corresponding market opportunities; the presence of entrepreneurial agents of change; and enduring organizational linkages between co-ops and farmers.

To put our story in comparative perspective, this chapter begins with an analysis of how agricultural cooperation has changed in recent decades, using North American and European co-ops as examples. We then explore the limited and deeply path-dependent responses of JA's national organizations to post-1990 pressures for change. The subsequent section focuses on strategic reform at the local level by engaging in data analysis to identify some of the objective conditions for change. To conclude, we set the stage for the case studies in chapters 5 and 6 by outlining a general blueprint for the processes and successes of value-generating—price-making—strategic changes, underscoring the importance of resource, agency, and organizational variables.

Agricultural Cooperatives in International Context

With an eye to identifying what is distinctive about Japanese agricultural co-ops, this section briefly explores some of the key strategic and organizational responses of European and North American co-ops to the rapid transformation of food supply chains and other structural changes. Along the way, we assess some of the implications of those responses for the principles and functions of traditional agricultural cooperation.[2]

To a significant degree, the context of co-op reform in Europe and North America resembles that of Japan (see chapter 3). Farm populations are aging, and successors are in increasingly short supply, although these challenges are not nearly as severe as they are in Japan. Food is no longer an undifferentiated commodity, in part because of the increasing sophistication and segmentation of consumer demand. Food supply chains have been transformed as large-scale food processing and retail firms consolidate and increase their economic influence. Thanks to economic liberalization and globalization, including market integration among the member countries of the European Union and the North American Free Trade Agreement, processors and retailers now have many more opportunities to source their raw product from countries where production costs are lower.[3]

Unlike Japan, North America and many EU countries have witnessed the rapid rise of massive agribusinesses, many of which integrate production, processing, marketing, and even food retail functions. These enterprises are often large enough to manipulate consumer demand for food and to control supply by concluding production contracts with family farms, which remain by far the most common form of farm organization. Some family farmers in the United States regard the industrialization of agriculture as a welcome, profit-making opportunity. But for many of those steeped in the traditional values of American agrarianism, the rise of "factory farming" violates the long-standing supremacy and independence of the family farm and represents a slippery slope toward virtual "serfdom."[4] Welcome or not, these and other changes to food supply chains are pressuring family farms to acquire more sophisticated financial and marketing skills as they seek to reverse their declining share of the "consumer's food dollar."[5] For better or worse, farming is becoming just another business—"a profession" like any other.[6]

To be sure, structural pressures on farmers are attenuated by government-initiated protectionist measures and various forms of subsidies. From the European Union's Common Agricultural Policy (CAP) to the US farm bill and Canada's famous dairy subsidies, all countries take steps to shield farmers from risk and to supplement their incomes. One indicator of this is the Producer Support Estimate, or PSE, which measures the percentage of gross farm receipts obtained from government transfers. According to the Organisation for Economic Co-operation and Development (OECD), the 2018 PSE scores for Canada, the United States, and the European Union were 7.52 percent, 10.55 percent, and 19.66 percent, respectively. (Japan's score, by contrast, was 41.25 percent—significantly less than the 55.75 percent recorded in 2000 but still far higher than European levels.)[7]

Agricultural cooperatives can also help alleviate these structural pressures on farmers. In fact, co-ops may be no less relevant in today's industrializing and globalizing agricultural markets than they were when food was undifferentiated, farmers were relatively homogenous and consumers less discriminating, and food supply chains less complex. Purchasing and marketing co-ops can still help farmers overcome information asymmetries and collectively represent them to increasingly concentrated input manufacturers, processors, and retailers, as well as integrated agribusinesses. And they can still reduce farmer risk by all but guaranteeing growers payment for their raw product over the long term. Where today's co-ops face the biggest challenges, however, is in meeting the growing expectations of business-savvy farmers to maximize farmer incomes by capturing "a larger share of the marketing profits generated between the farmgate and consumers."[8]

And to do that, co-ops often have no choice but to adapt their strategies to the realities of industrialized and globalized agriculture.[9] For marketing co-ops, this means adding value to member product through processing, by targeting markets where there is segmentation and product differentiation,[10] and via branding and aggressive marketing. As the United States' Land O'Lakes and Farmland Industries demonstrate, it can mean growing larger and more vertically integrated—just like their large, vertically integrated competitors and buyers. And like any other market-driven economic enterprise, it means doing more to address the needs of consumers, as well as producers, and to make a good profit.[11]

As co-ops strive to adapt to the realities of changing food supply chains in their efforts to add value to member product, many are changing the ways they organize themselves. To reduce costs and enhance their capacity to compete against large agribusinesses and other market players, many local co-ops are increasing their size through mergers. And in their quest to increase the equity needed for processing and marketing purposes, some co-ops are transitioning into investor-owned firms (IOFs) or co-op–IOF hybrids, relying completely or in part on nonfarmer member investments.[12] Also significant is the appearance of new-generation co-ops (NGCs), which were first established in the US Midwest in the 1990s and then spread to different parts of North America and Europe. NGCs differ from traditionally organized co-ops in several respects. While both types are owned by the farmers they serve, farmer-members invest only small amounts in traditional co-ops and have unrestricted delivery rights—they are free, in other words, to sell to the co-op whatever portion of their raw product they choose, and the co-op is obligated to purchase it. In the NGC, farmer-members acquire delivery shares in proportion to the amount of tradeable equity shares they purchase in the co-op. (Those who fail to fill their quotas must make up the difference through either a cash payment to the co-op or by purchasing additional product from other growers.) The two types of co-ops also differ in terms of how profits are returned to farmer-members. In traditional co-ops, farmers are normally paid market prices at the time of delivery. In NGCs, where contract production is the norm, producer prices are determined in advance of the growing season. (Some traditional co-ops are doing this as well.) While these guaranteed prices boost the grower's income security, there is always the risk that the guaranteed producer price will fall short of market prices. Finally, scholars note that NGCs may be a more suitable "home" for progressive, business-savvy, creative farmers—farmers who understand the demands of marketing in today's economy and who expect their co-ops to react accordingly.[13]

Strategic and organizational adaptation to the industrialization of agriculture can lead to violations of traditional cooperative principles. For example, reformist co-ops may do a better job of maximizing farmer incomes in today's markets, but they often do so at the expense of farmer sovereignty. Recall from earlier chapters that traditionally organized agricultural co-ops are owned and controlled by their users/beneficiaries—that is, their farmer-members.[14] Focusing on the needs of consumers, however, can ultimately weaken farmer voices, as can the expanding size of many co-ops and efforts among increasingly professional co-op managers to establish autonomy from rank-and-file members.[15] Farmer voices can also be diluted in co-ops that increase their equity by granting ownership rights—and perhaps even decision-making rights—to nonfarmers.

Co-op reform can also threaten the long-standing—and, as some would have it, outmoded—principle of farmer equality. In North America and Europe, some co-ops are implementing or considering new systems in which decision-making rights are weighted according to a farmer's equity stake or degree of co-op patronage. This marks a major shift away from the vaunted rule of one farmer, one vote.

Some reformist co-ops are also distancing themselves from their origins as populist solutions to distinctly local needs. Many European and North American co-ops are expanding beyond not only local and regional borders but also national borders by reinventing themselves as transnational co-ops, which acquire members in foreign countries, or international co-ops, which, like Land O'Lakes, the large dairy co-op, are establishing nonmembership subsidiaries and joint ventures around the globe.[16]

To sum up, changes in agricultural markets present both economic opportunities and intellectual and cultural challenges to agricultural cooperatives. On the one hand, changing market conditions offer co-ops a broader menu of strategic options for serving farmers.[17] On the other hand, those same market forces can drive co-ops to acquire the corporate orientation and global reach of proprietary firms. In the final analysis, these changes can help co-ops increase farmer returns and reduce farmer risk but at the price of weaker democratic mechanisms of farmer control over their co-ops—the hallmark of traditional agricultural cooperation.

JA's Postbubble Organizational Reforms

While the 1990s marked a turning point in the history of JA, the decade by no means amounted to a critical juncture comparable to the immediate postwar years, when US occupying authorities and the Japanese government single-handedly transformed the context and rules of agricultural cooperation. To borrow T. J. Pempel's terminology, the institutional foundations, policies, and political alliances that made up Japan's postwar agricultural regime may have been shaken by the bubble's collapse and the political and economic events that followed, but that regime failed to undergo a radical "shift" over the next two decades.[18] The JA-LDP electoral exchange relationship had survived, albeit in weakened form (see chapter 3). And thanks to the suppression of nonfarm corporate participation in agriculture and a deeply illiberal agricultural economy, JA faced virtually no competition at home from large, vertically integrated agribusinesses that had been such a spur to co-op reform in North America and Europe. So, for as long as JA and the LDP continued to rely on each other and JA remained Japan's dominant agricultural player, JA would have significant control over its own institutional reform agenda. Not surprisingly, JA's self-reform choices during the 1990s and 2000s were deeply path dependent and narrow in scope—designed, in a word, to *preserve* rather than transform the JA hierarchy's basic organizational and power structure, and not always in ways that facilitated effective adaption to the changes that were occurring in the agricultural economy. In this section, we explore some of those reforms.

There was no shortage of incentives for JA organizations to take self-reform seriously after 1990. Farmers were aging more rapidly, and the successor shortage was becoming more acute. Although Japanese food supply chains were much slower to change than their North American and European counterparts, they were nevertheless becoming more integrated by the early 1990s. Many farmers and local co-ops had been thrown into financial distress following the collapse of the economic bubble. And the LDP was wavering in its commitment to some of the policy mainstays of JA's economic power. As early as 1986, for example, the Nakasone government's (1982–1987) landmark Maekawa report had issued a strong recommendation for the liberalization of agricultural imports and a reduction in agricultural price supports.[19] That same year, Japan had joined the Uruguay Round of GATT trade negotiations, which prioritized the liberalization of trade in agricultural goods among member countries. These trends culminated by the mid-1990s in the partial liberalization of Japanese rice markets (see chapters 3 and 6).

All the while, there were signs of deepening farmer discontent with the JA system. Hokkaido JA's Kajiura Yoshimasa, a frequent commentator on farmer dissatisfaction with prevailing agricultural conditions and the costs incurred by working within the keitō (Zennō's distribution networks), predicted in 1995 an uptick in farmer defections from JA.[20] To be sure, entrepreneurial farmers were not about to give up their JA memberships. Membership was cheap—just a few thousand yen per year (less than 100 US dollars)—and it gave farmers automatic access to a range of convenient services. Co-op membership was also a well-established norm that accorded farmers a sense of belonging in hamlet society, much like church membership serves as a source of social integration in the rural United States. Instead, farmers were becoming more selective in their use of JA services in that they were buying more of their inputs and/or selling more of their product outside of JA channels.

JA organizations prioritized steps to either prevent these selective farmer defections—"going out" (*autosuru*), as insiders called them—or compensate for projected lost income. For example, before the Japan Fair Trade Commission stepped up its monitoring of JA from the 2000s, many co-ops openly flaunted Anti-Monopoly Law rules and the principles of voluntarism by withholding essential services from farmers who sought to loosen their dependence on JA, and JA's national and prefectural organizations levied similar penalties on co-ops that strayed from the keitō.[21] JA's national leaders also fought hard against market liberalization policies that narrowed opportunities for rent seeking and aggressively expanded its credit and insurance services for nonfarmer associate members (jun kumiaiin). The problem was that neither of these measures served the interests of farmers.

JA knew it had to do more. As the examples of co-op reform in North America and Europe showed, curbing farmer defections from agricultural cooperatives ultimately depended on putting more money in farmers' pockets by lowering farmer production and transaction costs and adding value to farmer product. But at the national level, JA's efforts often ran counter to these goals. Most conspicuously, JA Zennō kept production costs high by charging inflated prices for its fertilizer, pesticide, machinery, and other farm inputs and hefty commissions for its input and marketing services. Although a few co-ops lowered their input prices in response to increasing competition from private retail outlets during the late 1980s and early 1990s,[22] Zennō, for the most part, got away with these practices for as long as it could exert credible threats against potential defectors, and JA organizations were under no legal obligation to disclose their input prices and commission rates.[23]

JA's national authorities did, however, take steps to lower the transaction costs associated with working through JA by restructuring the JA system's three-tiered organizational hierarchy. The idea was first floated in 1988 during JA's eighteenth triennial national convention, just a few years after Zennō earnings had passed their postwar peak;[24] at the 1991 convention, Zenchū's restructuring proposals were adopted as official JA policy.[25] The leadership then proceeded to streamline the JA hierarchy and orchestrate the largest wave of co-op mergers since the early 1950s.

Knocking out the hierarchy's second tier by merging prefectural, service-specific federations with their national counterparts was step one in the reorganization of JA. The initiative met with mixed success. The regional credit federations, or shinren, refused to play along; there were thirty-five such federations before the initiative was launched, and there are thirty-five of them today. By contrast, in 2000 all forty-seven regional insurance federations (kyōsairen) merged with JA's national insurance organization (Zenkyōren).[26] The most important second-tier organizations for our purposes were the prefectural economic federations (keizairen) connected to Zennō that acted as middlemen in the provision of farm inputs to farmers and the marketing of farmer product. Of the forty-eight federations—Yamagata Prefecture had two of them—forty merged with Zennō between 1998 and 2007.[27] The mergers transformed what were once the headquarters of the prefectural economic federations into Zennō's main branch offices in the prefectures. And for a brief time after 2002, at least, they appeared to help boost Zennō's earnings; those gains, however, proved short-lived.[28]

The economic federations of eight prefectures—Aichi, Fukui, Hokkaido, Kagoshima, Kumamoto, Miyazaki, Shizuoka, and Wakayama—opted to remain independent. And they could do so because of several inherent advantages. All tend to operate in prefectures with relatively strong agricultural sectors. With the exception of Fukui, which produces mostly rice, all have fairly diverse product lines. And several of the prefectures have developed distinctive agricultural identities; Kagoshima is known for its high-quality pork and beef, while Hokkaido stands out for its beef and dairy products. Finally, the local multipurpose co-ops in these prefectures had long relied heavily on their prefectural economic federation to market their raw product and, to a lesser extent, to procure farm inputs;[29] the federations, for their part, had histories of successfully bypassing Zennō and going straight to market. In sum, these federations were strong enough to go it alone—and in defiance of Zennō.

Those who value efficiency for efficiency's sake found little to criticize in the keizairen-Zennō mergers, for they eliminated a layer of transaction costs and helped boost Zennō's earnings, at least for a time. But the claim that mergers would motivate Zennō to become a more aggressive price maker for farmers was weak, since the association was simultaneously increasing its commissions.[30] For all intents and purposes, the mergers were meant to increase the profitability of the keitō.[31] Nor did the mergers do anything to enhance co-op accountability to farmers or Zennō accountability to the co-ops. Now that most co-ops were linked directly to powerful Zennō, the reforms likely did the opposite.

The other major component in the reorganization of JA's organizational hierarchy was the aggressive promotion of local co-op mergers. For decades, co-op mergers tended to follow municipal mergers at the village, town, and city level and were designed to achieve greater levels of administrative efficiency. For a time, the general standard was one co-op per municipality; today, there is one co-op for every three municipalities. But today's mergers are often carried out for reasons that have little to do with adaptation to local administration—or, for that matter, with the interests of farmers. The first reason is financial. After the bubble burst, when many local co-ops were falling on hard economic times, Zenchū and its corresponding prefectural unions (chūōkai) assumed that creating larger economies of scale through mergers would position co-ops to avoid the huge infusions of government funds that the beleaguered commercial banks were experiencing during the 1990s.[32]

Second, JA's national and prefectural leadership looked to co-op mergers as a vehicle for creating greater economies of scale for the network's credit and insurance services. The reasoning here was simple: as co-op boundaries expanded to include more towns and cities, so, too, would the pool of potential nonfarmer associate members who could purchase home, educational, and other loans and various types of insurance. JA's national leadership championed these services as key to the network's long-term financial viability in the wake of farm/rural population decline. Sure enough, by 2009 total JA revenue from its credit and insurance services exceeded that generated by its agricultural purchasing and marketing services, and many former co-op headquarters had been transformed into mere branches of JA Bank.[33] The problem was that these organizational reforms did virtually nothing to advance the interests of farmers.

The third motivation behind co-op mergers does speak to the interests of farmers, and it continues to motivate JA reform today. Briefly stated, by generating more farmer-members per co-op and hence larger input orders and product deliveries into the keitō, mergers increase the potential returns to farmers by lowering transaction costs. At the same time, however, JA at the national level had yet to fully embrace the lessons learned by many North American and European co-ops, which were combining greater economies of scale with new, more sophisticated processing and marketing strategies for adding value to member products. While some local co-ops had begun to expand their processing and even retailing capabilities and Zennō, as we note below, was developing similar capacities in some of its subsidiaries, Zennō was doing not nearly enough to lay the foundations to increase the percentage of the consumer's food dollar that accrued to farmers. By neglect or by choice, JA at the national level was still at the early stages of its strategic learning curve.

The amount of effort put into the merger process varied across co-ops. Some co-ops merged too hastily, inviting all sorts of long-term problems. Others approached the task more carefully and methodically. In Kagoshima Prefecture, local co-op bankruptcies from the late 1980s built momentum behind co-op mergers, which were implemented slowly over the course of several years and after careful planning and extensive farmer-member input. Kagoshima had ninety local multipurpose co-ops at the time of the bubble's collapse; by 2012, it had only fifteen.[34] Other local co-ops either refused to merge or dragged their feet. These co-ops were in good financial shape or feared damage to the reputation of their brands, were loyal to their tightly knit villages,[35] or, like Tokushima Prefecture co-ops, wanted to experiment with their own self-reform ideas before melding with neighboring co-ops.[36] Whatever the co-op's decision, the voices of farmers were essential to the decision-making process—especially when farmers were well organized.[37] During interviews conducted in 2018 in Nagano Prefecture, we learned of ambitious farmers who abhorred the very idea of co-op mergers, since the addition of "less talented" producers threatened to reduce household incomes by violating product standards and lowering prices. It was only after their co-op painstakingly installed quality-control procedures and promised to retain essential co-op personnel that these naysayers were won over to the cause.[38] Still other co-ops found ways to achieve the goals of mergers without giving up their independence. In Hokkaido, for instance, a number of co-ops established product-specific networks of inter-co-op collaboration in their efforts to cut costs and increase returns to farmers.[39]

As Tashiro Yōichi illustrates in a recent study, whether a co-op merger can be deemed "successful" depends on what is to be achieved.[40] If the aim is to simply reduce the number of local multipurpose co-ops, mergers have been a resounding success; the total shrank from 2,635 in 1995 to just 708 co-ops in 2015.[41] (By April 1, 2020, the total had slipped to 584 and continues to shrink.)[42] If the goal is to reduce transaction costs, bigger is indeed better—but more so for JA's credit and insurance services than for its traditional agricultural services. As for changing a co-op's agricultural strategies, there is no evidence that mergers have triggered significant reforms.[43] Finally, if the goal is to increase farmer incomes, the jury is still out. Tashiro argues that larger economies of scale do not necessarily translate into more returns to farmers from the sale of crops and livestock. (Co-ops with smaller memberships tend to perform better in this regard, he observes, although this correlation appears to hold more for Hokkaido—Japan's agricultural powerhouse—than for other prefectures.) Nor is there a direct, positive correlation between a co-op's membership size and the rate of land consolidation, which is an important determinant of farm efficiency and profitability.

Nor do mergers do much to advance the principles of traditional agricultural cooperation. To the contrary, Tashiro asserts, they tend to work at cross-purposes to the identity of co-ops as democratic, "mutual aid" associations by shutting down many co-op branches and dramatically increasing the number of farmer-members per co-op and co-op employee.[44] (Between 2003 and 2017 alone, the average number of regular members per co-op increased from 5,384 to 6,520.)[45] These challenges are most worrisome in areas with deteriorating foundational organizations (kiso soshiki)—those autonomous hamlet organizations and grassroots producers' associations that have traditionally linked farmers to their co-ops (see chapter 2). And they are particularly pronounced in Kagawa, Nara, Okinawa, Yamaguchi, Fukui, and Shimane Prefectures, where the merger process has culminated in the establishment of a single, prefecturewide co-op. These and other large-scale co-ops are taking steps to narrow the yawning gaps between co-ops and their members. The Kagawa co-op, for instance, is establishing branch-level steering committees (shiten un'ei iinkai) consisting of members from different hamlets; in addition to keeping communications open between co-ops and farmers, the steering committees sometimes assume the functions of declining foundational organizations, including the selection of delegates to the co-op's all-important general assembly (sōkai).[46]

Among other organizational reforms introduced to the JA hierarchy to streamline the implementation of co-op functions, some resemble those of proprietary firms—and of business-oriented co-ops in North America and Europe. For example, in their efforts to increase profits, JA organizations at all levels of the hierarchy have been establishing incorporated subsidiaries, many of which perform essential business functions. Zennō, which long had a network of incorporated subsidiaries, stepped up its reliance on these entities during the 1990s and early 2000s by transferring, among other things, its animal-processing tasks to them.[47] With 121 subsidiaries by 2012,[48] Zennō had come to resemble a well-entrenched vertical conglomerate (keiretsu). Other JA organizations at the national level have been busy establishing subsidiaries as well; Yamashita Kazuhito estimates that the combined total reached 683 by 2010.[49]

As later chapters further illustrate, local co-ops also devoted more attention to establishing subsidiaries from the 1990s. Fukui Prefecture's JA Echizen Takefu, for example, set up several incorporated subsidiaries to more efficiently market co-op rice, manufacture or procure farm inputs, and perform a host of other co-op functions.[50] But many—if not most—subsidiaries at this level take the form of JA-invested agricultural corporations (JA shusshigata nōgyō hōjin),[51] which are partially or wholly co-op-owned incorporated farm enterprises. Unlike most subsidiaries at JA's national level, profit is not the main concern of these enterprises. And unlike their North American or European counterparts, they are not established to extend co-op operations to other regions or abroad. Instead, the purpose of these JA-invested corporations is to offer labor or management support to struggling local farm households and other agricultural enterprises. Kumamoto City's Agri Tomoai, the hamlet-based agricultural association that we introduced in chapter 3, is one such enterprise. Some, finally, can be viewed as a variation of production cooperatives (see chapter 2) in that they engage directly in agricultural production.

JA also parts company from many Western co-ops in its refusal to consider the incorporation (*hōjinka*) of cooperatives and the other main organizations of the JA Group. Some JA insiders argue that incorporation would weaken basic co-op principles, including the co-op's formal nonprofit orientation and the distribution of co-op returns on the basis of farmer patronage of co-op services rather than shares owned; a more cynical observer would point out that these steps would undercut JA's firm adherence to the one-farmer-one-vote principle that has long empowered the part-time farmers who lie at the heart of JA power. Incorporation would also deprive the co-ops of certain rent-seeking opportunities by abolishing their many exemptions under the Anti-Monopoly Law. Ceteris paribus, the loss of those antimonopoly exemptions would weaken JA's share of the agricultural inputs, marketing, credit, and insurance sectors and force the network to work harder.

Japanese co-ops are very sensitive to the broader social ramifications of their organizational reforms. Consider, for instance, co-op subsidiaries, many of which are as much a response to the distinctly social and demographic needs of struggling rural communities as they are an effort to become more corporate. Many JA-invested agricultural corporations, including Agri Tomoai, are set up to counter local labor shortages and other challenges caused by shrinking and aging farm populations. And some co-op subsidiaries are assuming social-welfare functions outsourced by merging municipalities with disintegrating administrative roots at the hamlet level; these functions include daycare centers, homes for senior citizens, and funeral services. To be sure, this outsourcing and the employment opportunities it generates positions many co-ops to contribute to the cohesion of rural communities. But they can also place a heavy burden on the co-ops. As we discovered during our travels through numerous farming areas, as rural populations continue to shrink, many daycare centers and seniors' facilities are either under- or unoccupied and/or in the red. Ironically, these challenges are interpreted by some JA authorities as yet another rationale for more co-op mergers.

Although most of the organizational reforms of the 1990s and early 2000s fall under the category of JA self-reform, a few were the handiwork of government.

Among the most significant of those reforms were new co-op governance measures for helping co-ops adapt to the new realities of increasing competition within changing food supply chains. In 1992, the national government revised the 1947 Co-op Law to give co-ops the option to expand the proportion of non-farmer professionals on their governing board of directors (rijikai) from a maximum of one-quarter to one-third.[52] (The Abe government's 2015 amendments made it mandatory for at least one-third of board members to be management professionals. See chapter 7.) And amendments introduced in 1996 and 2001 allowed co-ops to establish management committees (*keiei kanri iinkai*) alongside their boards of directors. Consisting of elected regular members, the committees are in charge of broad co-op planning and of selecting the members of the board of directors, which oversees the co-op's day-to-day operations. Based on the German model of corporate governance, the division of labor was supposed to professionalize the co-ops by expanding their management skills.[53] But the scheme did not live up to expectations. Only a few co-ops have successfully introduced these bifurcated governance systems, and some, like the famous Takefu, tried and failed;[54] one of Tomita Takashi's first acts upon assuming the co-op's top leadership position was to abolish the management committee, which he viewed as a drag on the exercise of strong co-op leadership.[55]

Measures to professionalize boards of directors and establish management committees were ultimately meant to help co-ops acquire the skills for adding value to member product. But in the wake of waves of co-op mergers, these measures met with pushback from rank-and-file co-op members on the grounds that they defied co-op principles of farmer sovereignty and democratic decision making. The co-ops, they argued, were losing their "co-op-ness" (*nōkyōrashisa*) and becoming too much like corporations.[56] Such sentiments were also among the reasons why proposals to change the rules of equity accumulation that characterize some proprietary firms and NGCs in other countries never gained traction inside JA. In this regard, all JA stakeholders seemed to be of a single voice—that co-ops were meant to be owned by the farmers they served and that linking user rights with equity shares or allowing nonfarmer investment in the co-op would violate the principles of farmer sovereignty and equality. Left unsaid was the fact that such innovations would trigger the loss of JA's antimonopoly exemptions. JA may have had a history of undercutting the principles of traditional agricultural cooperation, but when those principles served the status quo, JA organizations were among their staunchest defenders.

What is the ideal size for a local multipurpose cooperative? The answer is that it depends on the needs of the co-op. Like co-ops everywhere, Japanese co-ops in today's increasingly concentrated and integrated food supply chains must strike their own balance between expanding their economy of scale and maintaining close ties to their farmer-members. Be that as it may, JA's national leaders continue to push for more mergers in the name of economic efficiency, and many prefectures—including Niigata, Japan's biggest and most successful rice-producing region—are in near constant dialogue about the merits of further mergers, including the movement toward just one prefecturewide co-op.[57] It is worth noting, however, who has final say on these decisions: the farmers.

To sum up, JA has followed the lead of European and North American co-ops in its pursuit of a more corporate organizational style, but not nearly to the same degree. For reasons specific to Japan's distinctive political-economic context, JA organizations continue to embrace certain core cooperative principles, such as the retention of the one-farmer-one-vote rule, while rejecting the outright incorporation of local co-ops. To be sure, JA introduced organizational reforms, but these steps were far more preservative than transformative. They reflected, in other words, a deep-seated determination to protect the essence of the JA Group's top-heavy organizational hierarchy.

Assessing Strategic Reform at the Local Co-op Level

While chapter 7 revisits the question of institutional reform at the national level of JA over the past decade or so, the remainder of this chapter explores variations of reform at the local co-op level. In this section, we engage in data analysis to identify three measures of a co-op's strategic performance and the potential reasons for variations along those measures across local co-ops. We focus on strategies that prioritize the improvement of farmer incomes. To be sure, and as later chapters elaborate, farmers have other concerns besides how much they earn. They also care about risk minimization—so much so that they are often willing to forgo some income for the sake of lower risk. Farmers also think about the reputation of the foods they cultivate, the integrity of their farmland, their place in hamlet communities, and a host of other economic and noneconomic issues, many of which influence a co-op's strategic choices. But when all is said and done, an increasing number of Japanese farmers in today's challenging economic and demographic environment now define a good co-op mostly in income-related terms—as one that works hard to increase, or at least stabilize, their bank accounts. This point is borne out in surveys; in one survey conducted by the MAFF every five years since 2003, JA's farmer-members consistently ranked the strengthening of product sales and reduction of input prices as the two most important issues for JA to address.[58] The point was also drummed into us in our interviews with a variety of stakeholders over the years, from farmers to co-op employees to government officials, and Zennō now openly acknowledges it as a priority in its publications and on its websites.[59] And why should it be otherwise? For decades, Japanese farmers have occupied positions in the middle class; it is natural for them to want to remain there. Farmers are also well aware that income levels hold the key to their farm's long-term survival, for, as we know, prosperous farmers are more likely to secure successors.

Measuring what it means for a farmer to be prosperous is not an exact science, not least because farm household accounting often does not clarify who in the household is earning the farm-related income and who is pulling in a paycheck from off-farm employment. What we do know on the basis of our interviews, however, is that farmers—particularly full-time farmers—tend to think of themselves as prosperous when their total household income exceeds that of the typical urban salaryman with a desk job. For a number of our interviewees, this translates into a gross annual household income of approximately 20 to 30 million yen, or 200,000 to 300,000 US dollars.[60]

Measuring how individual co-ops contribute to farmer incomes is also challenging, since the co-ops do not normally release income-related data about their members. We do, however, have access to aggregate-level data for each JA service that can give us a general idea of how JA as a whole has performed over the years—including in ways that contribute to farmer incomes. Of course, one of the most striking takeaways of JA's aggregate performance has been its overall decline since the mid-1980s and early 1990s (see table 4.1).

To get a sense of which co-ops are doing more to serve the economic interests of farmers, as well as how and why they are doing so, we have collected a variety of demographic, economic, and other indicators from local co-ops in six prefectures—a total of 105 co-ops. Since few co-ops post more than their most recent indicators on the internet, our data are confined to a single point in time: March 2018 (the end of FY 2017).[61] While this limits our scope for comparison, it is a useful data point for understanding in general terms where local co-ops have landed nearly thirty years—or a generation—after the end of JA's long postwar era (1945–1990), when JA organizations, especially at the national level, often prioritized their own organizational and financial interests over the financial well-being of their farmer-members. It also enables us to identify which co-ops appear to be more strategically in tune with the interests of farmers today and why that may be the case.

We selected six prefectures with diverse product lines and variations in both population density and geographic location.[62] Two of them—Shizuoka and Chiba—are periurban prefectures that feed the metropolitan Tokyo area with a diverse array of agricultural products. Kumamoto and Nagano, by contrast, are largely rural

TABLE 4.1   Aggregate handling volumes of major JA services for all co-ops, 1980–2015

YEAR	UNITS	1980	1985	1990	1995	2000	2005	2010	2015
Sales of daily necessities	Trillion JPY	1.5	1.9	2.0	1.9	1.5	1.1	1.0	0.7
Sales of agricultural inputs to member farmers	Trillion JPY	3.2	3.4	3.2	3.0	2.7	2.4	2.0	1.9
Sales of agricultural products for member farmers	Trillion JPY	5.4	6.6	6.3	5.8	4.8	4.4	4.1	4.4
% of total national production handled by JA	%	52	56	55	55	53	52	50	50
Sales of rice for member farmers	Trillion JPY	1.9	2.5	1.9	1.9	1.2	1.0	0.8	0.8
% of national rice production handled by JA	%	63	66	61	60	50	51	52	50

Source: MAFF, "Nōkyō ni tsuite," November 2017, 5, 6, 8.

prefectures known mostly as fruit and vegetable producers. Kumamoto is located along the western side of Kyushu, far from major metropolitan areas, and Nagano, while mountainous, has some access to the Tokyo market. Yamagata and Niigata, finally, are rural prefectures that produce high volumes of rice.[63]

Three Strategic Performance Indicators of Reformist Co-ops

One measure of a co-op that strives to put money in the pockets of its members is the value of agricultural product per farmer that a co-op sends to market (see table 4.2).[64] This is in keeping with the conventional wisdom among scholars that the sale of member product (*hanbai*) is the most important service performed by co-ops today.[65] We calculate our measure by dividing the co-op's amount marketed and handled (*hanbai toriatsukai daka*, or AMH)—that is, the yen value of all output collected from farmers and sold by the co-op through the keitō, at farmers' markets and other co-op retail outlets, and directly to buyers—by the number of its regular farmer-members (sei kumiaiin).[66]

The AMH per regular member may be the most obvious and reliable indicator of a co-op that works hard for its farmers; ceteris paribus, the more product

TABLE 4.2 Three strategic performance indicators of co-ops, FY 2017–2018

FY 2017–2018 NUMBER OF CO-OPS SURVEYED: 105	AVERAGE	MIN.	MAX.
Amount marketed and handled per regular member (1,000 JPY)	1,123	19	8,724
Co-op profits from agricultural sales per regular member (1,000 JPY)	35.4	1.68	217
Agricultural loans % of total loans	16.7	0.21	43.2

Source: Annual disclosure documents of each JA co-op for FY 2017–2018.

a co-op sells, the more money in the pockets of its members.[67] But three caveats are in order. First, the AMH is a monetary measure and thus sensitive to market prices, which fluctuate not only over the course of a year but also at different product-specific rates. Since a co-op may be advantaged (or disadvantaged) by short-term changes in prices that are beyond its control, it is not always the case that the higher the AMH, the more hardworking the co-op. We must also be mindful that co-ops specializing in rice production have been subject to long-term declines in consumer demand and rice prices and may thus appear to be underperforming when evaluated on the basis of their AMH alone. Second, the AMH indicator does not tell us whether the co-op—or Zennō or prefectural economic federation (keizairen), if the co-op is relying on the keitō—is functioning as a full-fledged price maker by securing the maximum possible prices from wholesalers and other buyers; nor does it tell us exactly what proportion of those earnings is returned to farmers. Third, the AMH measure does not reflect the fact that farmers are often willing to sacrifice some of their potential income in return for risk mitigation. These latter two points are addressed in part through the specific methods the co-op uses to collect and pay for member product—methods that are not revealed in co-op disclosure documents.

In general, co-ops can follow one or both of two methods for collecting raw product and paying farmers, each of which presents to the farmer a distinctive mix of financial benefits (measured in terms of returns and income stability) and risk minimization. Under the unconditional consignment sales (*mujōken itaku hanbai*) method, which is by far the most common of the two, especially for rice, farmers entrust their raw product to the co-op and have no say over when and to whom the co-op subsequently sells that product and at what price. The co-op provides the farmer with a temporary payment at the point of collection and then adjusts that payment after it sells the product to wholesalers or other buyers. It is customary for co-ops that follow the consignment sales method to calculate their final payments to farmers on the basis of what is known as the joint calculation (*kyōdō keisan hanbai*) system. Typically, the co-op sells collected raw product over a set period, knowing that the product's market price will vary from day to day. The co-op then calculates the average price received during that period and pays that price to all participating farmers. Co-ops benefit from consignment sales and the joint calculation payment method in that they can pool raw product at the co-op level and then capture market share. For the farmer, the advantages and disadvantages are mixed. Since the farmers effectively own their raw product while it is under the co-op's management, they must bear at least some of the costs incurred should that product be damaged before final sale or if it fails to sell;[68] the advantage, however, is that those risks are dispersed among all participating farmers. In terms of financial benefits, farmers forgo the potentially higher returns that can be earned by, say, selling crops directly to market—a much riskier strategy that depends on good timing and a great deal of luck; in return, they secure a stable income, which for many participants is the joint system's biggest advantage.

The second sales method is known as buy-up sales (*kaitori hanbai*). Here, the co-op purchases farmer output outright, providing the producer with a one-time, final payment at the point of collection. In many cases, purchase prices are settled via contract before planting even begins. The buy-up method has a long history among co-ops that have special, direct relationships with retailers or end users, such as restaurant chains. And although it is taking root in vegetable production (see the JA Saku Asama case study in chapter 5), it is most commonly and most easily practiced vis-à-vis rice (see the JA Uonuma Minami case study in chapter 6). Rice is harvested at roughly the same time—give or take a few weeks—nationwide but is sold at different times throughout the year; this incentivizes co-ops to time their sales for when demand, and hence prices, are expected to be high. For co-ops, the advantage of this method is that it allows the co-op to more effectively calibrate supply to variations in consumer demand, which in turn can boost prices. But the method also entails more work for the co-op, while contract production tailored to a corporate consumer's specifications curbs product pooling. The advantages to farmers of the buy-up method include lower risk, since the co-op, as owner of the product, must cover the costs associated with product damages or low sales. The method can also be financially advantageous for farmers—particularly if market prices drop after the co-op purchases their product. But the reverse is also true; when market prices increase after they get paid, farmers have missed out on an opportunity to earn higher returns, while the co-op itself gains. In sum, the buy-up method translates into less risk for farmers and potentially higher prices but less income stability. In 2013, only 3.7 percent of all agricultural product sold through the JA keitō was purchased via this buy-up method.[69] Since then, Zennō has come to view the method as integral to responding effectively to niche consumer demand and boosting farmer incomes; in FY 2020, it fulfilled its goal to sell 40 percent of its rice using the method.[70]

Support for one method over the other tends to vary. While Zennō, the Abe government, and many co-ops that sell relatively small amounts of rice wedded themselves to the buy-up method, co-ops with many large-scale rice farmers are less enthusiastic, since these farmers often prefer to assess various market options before selling off their product.[71] As for the typical farmer, how he or she assesses the relative advantages and disadvantages of the buy-up versus consignment sales methods depends on how he or she prefers to balance risks against financial benefits. No matter what the method, many co-ops have been criticized for failing to clinch the best possible prices for their farmers. (But one argument in the co-ops' defense is that they have always done a good job reducing risk, especially for their smaller, part-time farmer-members.)

The second measure of a profarmer co-op we explore is the amount of co-op profits earned from the sale of agricultural product per regular member. Co-op profits are calculated by subtracting the transaction costs of member-product sales (shipping, labor, etc.) from the total revenue (including commission paid by the farmer to the co-op) earned from those sales. Co-ops can increase profits by expanding the volume of member-product sales, decreasing the transaction costs associated with those sales, and/or negotiating higher wholesale or retail prices. Ceteris paribus, the higher the co-op profits, the higher the returns to farmers in the form of both higher prices paid to them and increased year-end dividends.[72] However, profits as a measure of a co-op's strategic performance are subject to several caveats: like the AMH measure, they are affected by fluctuating market prices; nor do profits tell us whether the co-op has secured the highest possible prices from their buyers.

Our third and final indicator of a profarmer co-op is the value of JA Bank loans for agricultural purposes issued per regular farmer-member. Farmers often rely on credit to purchase expensive machinery, to acquire new land, and, in the case of (rice) farmers who are awaiting final payment for their previous year's harvest, to buy seeds. For years, lending and other banking services have been money makers for the co-ops; in FY 2015, 669 of 686 co-ops surveyed were profitable in banking.[73] But JA Bank's lending rate is quite low; only 20 percent of its deposits are earmarked for loans, and the remaining 80 percent is invested, both at home and abroad. And just 10 percent of the funds reserved for loans (or 2 percent of total deposits) is lent to agricultural enterprises. This surprisingly low agricultural lending rate from a bank that was established to assist farmers has attracted intense criticism from scholars and politicians over the years,[74] as has JA's tendency in the past to tie its loans to the purchase of inputs through Zennō. And yet JA's market share for agricultural loans has been shrinking— from 68 percent to 56 percent between 2011 and 2017 alone[75]—thanks in part to increasing competition; in their efforts to diversify their customer base since the 1990s and especially after the 2008 global financial crisis, regional banks have begun lending to farm enterprises, most notably incorporated farm enterprises. Nevertheless, JA Bank remains the country's largest agricultural lender. And it repeatedly claims that it is committed to increasing its lending to agricultural entities as part of its current self-reform campaign; to wit, even as its share of the market continued to shrink—from 56 percent to 54 percent between 2017 and 2018—by 2018 JA Bank had increased the absolute amount of its agricultural loans for three consecutive years.[76] We have ample reason, in other words, to view a co-op's agricultural lending as a measure of its commitment to the farmer's financial welfare.

Explanatory Variables and Hypotheses

What are the potential drivers of a co-op's strategic efforts to improve farmer income? The data disclosed by the co-ops position us to analyze four of them, the details of which are outlined in table 4.3.

First, we consider the relationship between the size of a co-op as measured by the absolute number of regular members and co-op performance. Building on the conventional wisdom that the size of the regular membership affects the quality of communications between farmers and co-op personnel, we test the proposition that the smaller the number of regular members per co-op, the more likely the coop will work harder for the farmer. Our findings on this measure in turn position us to comment on the impact of co-op mergers on co-op performance.

Second, we consider the ratio of regular (farmer) members (sei kumiaiin) to associate members (jun kumiaiin). Here, we build on a common critique of JA's expansion of its nonagricultural financial (credit and insurance) services from the early 1990s; since these services speak to the needs of associate members as much as, if not more than, regular members, it makes sense to hypothesize that co-ops with greater ratios of regular members to associate members will be more likely to push profarmer strategic reforms. It is also important to note that we have yet to come upon an example in our interviews and archival research of a co-op that is actively seeking to expand its regular membership; indeed, since the number of regular co-op members often exceeds that of actual farmers in some areas, it is safe to assume that virtually all active farmers in Japan are

TABLE 4.3 Summary of explanatory variables by prefecture, FY 2017–2018

UNITS: JPY PER REGULAR CO-OP MEMBER FOR FY 2017–2018	YAMAGATA	NIIGATA	NAGANO	CHIBA	SHIZUOKA	KUMAMOTO
Location type	Rural	Rural	Rural	Urban	Urban	Rural
Main products	Rice +α	Rice	Fruits and vegetables	Rice +α	Fruits and vegetables	Fruits and vegetables
Total arable land (sq km)	1,194	1,713	1,080	1,263	671	1,120
Arable land per farmer (sq km)	0.024	0.027	0.011	0.017	0.01	0.015
Number of farmers	49,962	62,886	94,010	75,479	65,030	72,728
Average age of farmers (national average 66.4)	65.8	66.6	67.9	65.6	67.2	64.2
% of farmers over 65 years old (2015)	59.8	66.2	69.5	60.8	64.1	56.8
Number of co-ops (March 2018)	15	24	16	19	17	14
Regular co-op members (March 2016)	98,333	159,258	183,114	139,411	143,305	90,852
Associate co-op members (March 2016)	51,629	156,331	136,021	128,926	295,054	69,898
Ratio of regular to associate members	1.90	1.02	1.35	1.08	0.49	1.30
Ratio of full-time to part-time farmers	0.32	0.25	0.50	0.44	0.45	0.73

Sources: MAFF, "Census of Agriculture and Forestry"; MAFF, "Nōkyō ni tsuite," November 2017.

already regular co-op members. Thus, a lower ratio of regular to associate members suggests that the co-op faces greater incentives to enrich itself over the farmer.

Third, we assess the impact of the age of farmers on profarmer co-op strategies. Our 105 co-ops do not release data on the average age of their member farmers, so we assume that this feature of the farming population mimics the age spread of the general population in a co-op's jurisdiction. Specifically, we take the percentage of the general population over the age of sixty-five as a proxy measure of the aging farming population. Since we know that farmers in general are older than the general population, our observations about the potential impact of this variable on a co-op's commitment to farmers will be conservative. We also know that regular JA members are on average older than associate members, placing the direction of bias in our favor.[77] Assuming that younger farmers are more market friendly, we hypothesize that co-ops will be more reform oriented the lower the average age of their farmers.

Finally, we explore the relationship between the ratio of full-time farmers to part-time farmers and a co-op's performance. Given the conventional wisdom that full-time farmers are more willing and able to defect from co-op services, we hypothesize that the higher the ratio, the more reformist the co-op. Since the data released by individual co-ops on their full-time and part-time farmers are inconsistent across co-ops,[78] we rely on prefectural data as a proxy.[79] And we remain mindful of two important caveats. First, not all full-time farmers are alike in their relationship with their co-op; some rely completely on JA services, while others pick and choose. Unfortunately, data on these distinctions is unavailable. Second, we should not assume that all co-ops pay more attention to their full-time members than to their part-time members. Yes, the co-ops worry about farmer defections, and yes, it is reasonable to assume that those defections will be more likely among larger-scale, full-time farmers than among small-scale cultivators who are often too busy with their off-farm jobs to contemplate navigating agricultural markets on their own. These caveats notwithstanding, we anticipate that the findings on this measure should provide greater insight into whether full-time farmers matter to the local co-ops.

Analysis

JA is no longer the powerhouse it once was. As table 4.4 illustrates, its lending service has declined steadily between FY 2008 and FY 2017 and its insurance service at an even faster rate. Even more pronounced has been its steadily decreasing sales of agricultural inputs—by 9.7 percent in 2014 alone. Only JA's bank deposits have done well, registering small but consistent increases since 2008. That said, table 4.4 highlights a subtle but significant trend; despite marked variation

TABLE 4.4   Changes in the handling volumes of major JA activities (annual % change), 2008–2017

YEAR	2008	2009	2010	2011	2012	2013	2014	2015	2016	2017
Deposits	1.5	1.5	1.5	2.8	1.9	1.9	2.3	2.4	2.6	2.9
Outstanding loans	4.4	2.7	−0.7	−1.2	−1.7	−0.9	−1.3	−1.4	−2.6	0.1
Long-term insurance	−3.2	−1.8	−3.1	−2.4	−2.2	−2.5	−2.8	−2.7	−2.4	−2.7
Agricultural inputs supplied and handled	0.7	−5.5	−1.1	−0.5	−0.1	3.4	−9.7	−5	−4.3	0.6
Agricultural products marketed and handled	0.2	−3.4	−0.5	−1.7	3.2	1.4	−1.3	5.2	2.9	−0.03

Source: "Jigyō rieki no genshō tsutsuku."

from year to year, JA's AMH has increased by an average of 0.6 percent per year between 2008 and 2017.

Also noteworthy is the fact that rice is steadily decreasing in importance for JA. Table 4.1 reveals that the total value of rice marketed by JA for its farmer-members decreased from 2.5 trillion yen in 1985 to 800 billion yen in 2015. As we further explain in chapter 6, these figures reflect three important points. First, the demand for rice and hence the price of rice are declining, which translates into a rapid decline in the yen value of rice produced, marketed, and handled. Second, rice is becoming less important to JA's bottom line insofar as its agricultural marketing services are concerned; in any given year, JA markets far more vegetables than rice.[80] Third, despite these trends, JA remains the most important player in the Japanese rice market.

Which co-ops in our population of 105 co-ops in six prefectures had the highest AMH and profits per regular member? The answer, at first glance, and as table 4.5 summarizes, is co-ops with higher ratios of regular members to associate members and lower ratios of populations over the age of sixty-five; co-ops with higher ratios of full-time farmers to part-time farmers also had higher AMH per regular member. To the extent that more than just fortuitous price increases are at work, these may be the kinds of co-ops that are driving the small increases in the overall AMH within the JA network.

The correlations between the ratio of regular members to associate members, on the one hand, and AMH and profit per regular member, on the other hand, were statistically significant. This supports our hypothesis that co-ops with

TABLE 4.5 Correlation between strategic performance indicators and co-op characteristics, FY 2017–2018

FY 2017–2018 NUMBER OF CO-OPS SURVEYED: 105	NUMBER OF REGULAR JA MEMBERS	RATIO OF REGULAR TO ASSOCIATE MEMBERS	% OF POPULATION OVER 65 YEARS OLD	RATIO OF FULL-TIME TO PART-TIME WORKERS
Amount marketed and handled per regular member	Insignificant	Positive	Negative	Positive
Co-op profits from agricultural sales per regular member	Insignificant	Positive	Negative	Insignificant
Agricultural loans per regular member	Insignificant	Insignificant	Insignificant	Insignificant

Source: Annual disclosure documents of each JA co-op for FY 2017–2018.

higher ratios of farmer to nonfarmer members are more likely to work hard on behalf of farmers. Also statistically significant was the important finding that more profitable co-ops had much higher levels of AMH per member than co-ops that were in the red, which suggests that the future of the co-ops lies in the expansion of their agricultural marketing services rather than their nonagricultural financial pursuits.[81]

Our other findings were less robust. For instance, the absolute numbers of regular members per co-op was not significantly correlated with AMH or profit per regular member. We cannot definitively say, therefore, that the smaller the number of regular members in a co-op, the more money the co-op puts in each farmer's pocket. There are several potential reasons for this. A co-op's marketing efforts may be suboptimal from the perspective of local entrepreneurial farmers or current market conditions. Or, as we illustrate in our Nagano case study in chapter 5, a co-op's diligent marketing efforts may be undercut by those of a neighboring co-op that produces similar products.

Nor, for that matter, can we definitely say that co-ops with larger numbers of regular members do worse by their farmers. This point hints at some of the conflicting pressures faced by today's co-ops. On the one hand, co-ops are well aware that one way to boost their AMH is to increase the absolute volume of agricultural product in their marketing channels.[82] This can be accomplished by simply expanding the ranks of their farmer-members: ceteris paribus, the more members, the more product handled, and the more product handled, the lower the transaction costs and the greater co-op returns. But as Tashiro Yōichi's findings noted above remind us, and a 2007 MAFF study further underscores,[83] co-ops that achieve a larger economy of scale do not necessarily perform better in terms of increasing member-farmer incomes. One reason for this, of course, is that many co-ops with large farmer memberships are the product of mergers of smaller co-ops that were themselves inherently incapable of boosting farmer incomes. We also know that the risk of communicative disconnect between farmers and co-op personnel is higher in larger co-ops; this in turn can incentivize entrepreneurial farmers to market their products elsewhere. While it bears repeating that the jury is still out on the proposition that smaller is better, these observations should thus give pause to those who push mergers as a solution to the economic and demographic challenges currently confronting the co-ops.

The correlations between the average age of farmers and AMH and profits per regular member were also statistically insignificant. This is no doubt because there is little variation among co-ops in our population in terms of age; Japanese farmers, in other words, are aging everywhere. Also insignificant were the correlations between the ratio of full-time versus part-time farmers and the co-op's AMH and profits per regular member.

Our interviews offer some additional insights into how, if at all, age and full-time versus part-time farmer status might influence co-op reform. For starters, we observed that age appears to matter only at the extreme ends—when farmers are very young or very old. But what matters even more is whether farmers are entrepreneurial—a variable that cannot be measured given existing government or co-op-disclosure data. Entrepreneurship knows no age limits; we found it among farmers both young and old. (To be sure, older farmers do not suddenly become entrepreneurial when they are nearing retirement age; they have been that way for a while.) Nor was age a clear predictor of whether those top farmers will defect from their co-op. Some young farmers certainly have turned their backs on JA, but many others have not. And for every Shimada Toshio of Kumamoto Prefecture, the sixty-something entrepreneurial vegetable farmer we met in chapter 3 who is a JA member in name only, there is an entrepreneurial farmer of the same generation like Inayoshi Masahiro, the founder of the innovative tomato-producing Sun Farms in Shizuoka Prefecture that has expanded abroad and that relies completely on JA to market its prized tomatoes in Japan.[84] We can make similar, albeit tentative, conclusions about the relationship between the proportion of full-time farmers in a co-op and co-op reform; the point here is not whether these farmers earn all of their income from agriculture but whether they possess promarket, entrepreneurial mindsets. What is more, while this mindset is likely more common among full-time farmers, it may also be present among some part-time farmers, particularly those designated core farmers, or ninaite. (Our analysis in chapter 6 of farmers in Niigata Prefecture's JA Uonuma Minami corroborates this point.) It is these farmers—entrepreneurial producers both

young and old, full-time and even part-time—who are key to understanding a
co-op's reformist stance. These are the farmers, we believe, who are most likely to
defect from JA and who are nudging responsive co-ops to change their old ways.

A surprising, statistically significant finding that emerged from our analysis
of 105 co-ops is that the higher the AMH per regular co-op member, the greater
the co-op's per-member revenue from input sales. By the early to mid-1990s, JA
was under fire for paying more attention to its input sales than to selling farmer
product, the implication being that JA was only out for itself. The fact that Zennō
has overcharged farmers for fertilizers, tractors, and other farm inputs strongly
supports this claim. But our discovery suggests that "working for JA" and "working for the farmer" are not necessarily incompatible goals. We corroborate this
observation in the next chapter with our analysis of JA in Nagano Prefecture,
where Zennō has cooperated with local co-ops on behalf of "production adjustment" schemes for vegetables that are designed to snare higher prices; in return,
farmers must adhere to strict standards on the use of fertilizers, pesticides, and
herbicides—virtually all of which, of course, are supplied by Zennō.[85]

As for agricultural lending, our final co-op performance indicator, figure 4.1
illustrates that JA Bank's share of total agricultural loans has actually decreased

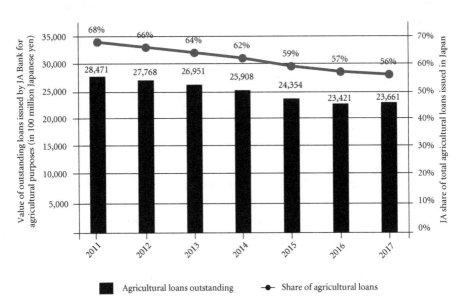

FIGURE 4.1.   Yen value of loans outstanding issued by JA Bank for agricultural
purposes between 2011 and 2017 and their percentage share of total agricultural loans issued in Japan.

Source: "JA Banku zentai."

in recent years. More importantly for our purposes, we found no significant correlation between our independent variables and the amount of loans issued by JA for agricultural purposes. We attribute these findings to two things. First, and as noted earlier, only a tiny share (2 percent) of JA Bank deposits have been channeled into agricultural loans over the years; it is not surprising, therefore, that variations in agricultural lending across co-ops should be miniscule as well. Second, the largest share of agricultural lending goes to the producers of cattle, pork, and dairy products, which are much more expensive to operate than rice or vegetable farms. But there are few of these farms in our six prefectures.

Summary

To sum up, we know for certain that some co-ops do better than others in terms of putting more money in the pockets of farmers. And we can tentatively conclude that greater numbers of regular members relative to associate members is one indicator of this. After all, regular members are farmers, and farmers are most likely to push for profarmer strategies. But it is not clear from our data that those farmers must be full-time or younger cultivators for a co-op to be reformist. Based on our interviews, we suspect that a stronger motivation for strategic reform among co-ops is whether farmers are entrepreneurial, for these are the farmers most likely to defect from a co-op if that co-op does not do well by them.

Although the overall trend for JA is largely one of decline or, at best, near stagnation, small, aggregate increases in AMH over the past decade and our finding that the most profitable co-ops overall tend to be those with high AMH per regular member suggest that the future of JA as a viable network of cooperatives depends precisely on its commitment to improving the financial lot of farmers. JA appears to agree. Our data do not fully reveal, however, what a good co-op might do to further increase its AMH per regular member over the long haul. Given Japan's shrinking population and the declining demand for food, the solution is not to simply increase the volume of agricultural products marketed, although this would make sense if Japan were to significantly increase its agricultural exports. Instead, the co-ops should change the ways they collect raw product from their farmer-members, market it, and pay them for it. For many co-ops, this should include adopting the buy-up sales (kaitori hanbai) method, whereby co-ops purchase member product immediately after the harvest and at competitive prices and then strive to secure good market prices for themselves; this forces co-ops to work harder and to respond more effectively to variations in price and consumer demand. As evidenced by its 2017 pledge to promote the buy-up method and to increase its contractual relationships with farmers, Zennō concurs.

The Conditions for Strategic Reform

What else explains variations in profarmer strategic reform among local co-ops? To answer this question, it is helpful to pinpoint some of the reasons why many co-ops do not reform, even when faced with compelling economic and demographic incentives to do so. For some co-ops, the challenge is insurmountable; nature has prevented them from growing the kinds of products that can earn good prices in today's markets. Others may face such severe demographic and other challenges that they simply give up. And some co-ops may conclude that reform is unnecessary because their associate members so outnumber their regular (farmer) members that they can count on revenue from their financial and other nonagricultural services to keep them afloat.

Some co-ops have a leadership deficit. Co-op employees may be out of touch with farmer expectations or incapable of convincing their superiors of what needs to be done. Or the co-op's board of directors (rijikai) may be at fault. After years—decades—of following directions from prefectural and national leaders in the JA system, some directors simply do not know what it means to manage or lead a co-op on behalf of farmers.[86] The board may be too internally divided to approve strategic changes, or full-time directors at the end of their terms may opt to kick the can down the road.[87] Perhaps the leadership is divided between a board of directors and a management committee that cannot agree on a new strategic game plan. These and related coordination problems help explain why some co-ops cannot commit to the painstaking processes involved in introducing the many operational rules that enable new production and marketing strategies. They explain, in short, why entrepreneurial farmers in some co-ops frequently lament that "no matter what we say, nothing changes."[88]

In some cases, the biggest impediment to reform may be the farmers themselves. Farmers with passive-producer mindsets may refuse to support strategic reforms if they deem them too difficult, risky, or at odds with their values. Or perhaps they do not trust the co-op to do well by them. Finally, in today's increasingly diversified agricultural sector, a community of farmers may be too divided to organize behind strategic change.

Successfully reformist co-ops, by contrast, have three things in common. First, they are blessed with good natural resources and corresponding market opportunities to earn good prices. Second, they have good leaders in their midst— agents of change who identify opportunities in contingent events, help stakeholders recognize the value in existing incentives for change, and resolve collective action and coordination problems.[89] In Fukui Prefecture's JA Echizen Takefu, it was the head of the co-op, Tomita Takashi, who pinpointed opportunities inherent in the prefecture's product lines as his co-op faced mounting economic and demographic pressures and who subsequently rallied the co-op's staff and farmer-members behind the strategic changes that arguably distinguish Takefu as Japan's most radically reformist co-op. But agency need not originate at the top of the co-op hierarchy; as chapter 5 illustrates, it can also emanate from among staff at the co-op branch level.

Third, since co-ops are membership organizations that are only as good as the farmers they serve, successfully reformist co-ops have farmer-members who are supportive of and organized behind new strategies. How farmers are organized depends on both farmer mindsets and the nature of agency inside the co-op. If farmers are staunchly conservative and distrusting of markets, reform will depend on the capacity of co-op leaders to dissuade them of their biases and effectively organize them. These processes can take years. If farmers are entrepreneurial, they themselves may become agents of change. This does not negate the need for strong co-op leadership, however, since even the most entrepreneurial farmers usually lack the time and skills needed to play more than an auxiliary role in strategic co-op reform. We suspect that in most cases, farmer agency emanates primarily from among those most likely to defect from co-op services and that it takes the form of enhanced pressure on the co-op to work harder on farmers' behalf and/or grassroots initiatives for farmers to (re)organize themselves.

The importance of effective farmer organization cannot be overstated. For new, value-added marketing strategies to work, the most effective organization is usually the product-specific production committee (*seisan bukai* or *seisan kumiai*) or its equivalent. Today, the structure and functions of production committees—and other foundational organizations—vary not only across co-ops but also within them, thanks to the diversification of farm enterprises and waves of postwar mergers that have combined co-ops with different organizational traditions. In some hamlets, co-op branches will simply partner with preexisting production committees. Where grassroots production committees have weakened or disintegrated, co-op branches may orchestrate their renewal or even oversee the establishment of new ones.[90] As a result, it can be hard to tell whether a product-specific production committee has been established by farmers, by the co-op, or via a partnership between the two sides. We should also note that the business of organizing farmers into production committees can be conducted by middlemen—a local farm enterprise, for instance, that partners with a co-op on behalf of new strategic initiatives. As we illustrate in chapter 5, the intermediating farm enterprise can itself function as a kind of foundational organization of the co-op. Whatever their profile, these bridging entities must facilitate day-to-day communications between co-op representatives and farmers, as well as the articulation and reinforcement of strategy-specific operational rules.

Not all production committees and other foundational organizations live up to expectations. We learned through our interviews, for example, that if the boundaries of co-op branches do not overlap with the natural boundaries of hamlet or other foundational organizations, trouble can ensue. This was the case in one mountainous but highly fertile area of JA Kamimashiki in Kumamoto Prefecture, where past mergers had produced a disconnect between a co-op branch and its participating hamlets. The resulting conflict among farmer-members at the branch level impeded co-op efforts to introduce new value-added strategies.[91] This example forces us to question the conventional wisdom that rural areas have experienced an irrevocable decline of community. As Hanno Jentzsch deftly reminds us, social networks remain integral to rural Japan, not least to the effective functioning of co-ops.[92]

Building and maintaining these important organizational points of contact between farmers and multipurpose co-ops was a straightforward affair when rural communities were thriving, farm enterprises were relatively homogeneous, and most producers were fixated on (lucrative) rice production. This is no longer the case. Those all-important production committees, for instance, can be internally divided in ways that reflect the steady diversification of local farm populations: full-time farmers versus part-time farmers; younger, progressive farmers versus more numerous—and usually conservative—older farmers; certified farmers (nintei nōgyōsha) versus non-certified farmers; farmers who have successors versus those who do not; producers with big farms versus those with small ones; incorporated farm households versus the more ubiquitous traditional farm households; and the list goes on.[93] In short, it is at the level of the local production committee and other foundational organizations that demographic and economic change meet the Japanese cooperative system, exerting all manner of influence over the reform process.

Reformist co-op leaders determined to add value to member product tend to follow a common script: identify a new or revised product that speaks to consumer demand and that can earn good—or at least decent—prices; remove or sidestep impediments to change within the co-op bureaucracy; persuade farmers to accept the new product and accompanying strategic reforms and then (re)organize them behind the reforms; introduce or revise the many fine-grained rules that operationalize co-op strategies; muster up the necessary financial resources; and then strive to secure high prices for the new value-added product in negotiations with product buyers and, in so doing, earn the trust and loyalty of farmer-members. In keeping with the co-op's social mission, reformist co-op leaders must also ensure that every farmer is fairly served and, as Kitade Toshiaki notes, that smooth relations between the co-op and the broader community are maintained.[94]

Exactly how—and how quickly—these steps are carried out depends on the timing of co-op decision making in response to incentives (and disincentives) generated by a wide gamut of formal and informal institutional developments and interactions, as well as on a range of factors and unforeseen developments, many of them specific to the co-op in question. The point is that while three sets of variables—resource endowments and corresponding market opportunities, leadership, and organization—are key to the success of co-op-level strategic reform, no two reformist co-ops are alike in terms of how reform unfolds. We illustrate these points in the next two chapters.

A TALE OF TWO CO-OPS
The Processes of Strategic Adaptation

What does a good co-op look like—one that boosts farmer incomes by adapting its strategies to changing prices and other market signals? More specifically, how does a good co-op transform ideas about new strategies into reality?

In illustrating the drivers of strategic reform, we build on the arguments of previous chapters. A good co-op knows that strategic reforms that increase the farmer's share of each consumer food dollar are its best hope for preventing capable farmer-members from defecting from co-op services and for alleviating the farm successor crisis. A good co-op has trustworthy agents of change in its midst who can translate ideas into action while navigating the particular mix of opportunities and constraints—many of them local—facing their co-op. And a good co-op recognizes that if new strategies are to stick, farmer-members must be organized into appropriate foundational organizations (kiso soshiki). Of course, not all hardworking co-ops can become really good co-ops; some, for example, suffer from natural resource handicaps that prevent them from growing the kinds of products that secure the best prices.

In this chapter, we demonstrate how these variables can present themselves during the strategic reform process and in the context of dynamic interactions among different types of institutions: relevant laws and regulations; a co-op's operational rules; organizations at various levels of the JA hierarchy; regional, national, and international markets; and a host of related co-op and farmer strategies. Timing, sequencing, and historical contingency can condition how these institutional interactions shape the speed, patterns, and even the scope of reform outcomes. And so can farmer mindsets.

To accomplish our objectives, we tell the story of two co-ops that have strived to do well by their farmers: JA Kamimashiki in Kumamoto Prefecture and Nagano Prefecture's JA Saku Asama. The Kumamoto case recounts how a local co-op employee and then independent farm organizer almost single-handedly mobilized one branch's deeply conservative rice farmers behind new production strategies that included diversification into vegetable production and the corresponding reconfiguration of farmland. The story of JA Saku Asama in Nagano Prefecture, by contrast, is one of cooperation between entrepreneurial vegetable farmers and responsive co-op leaders in the implementation of production and collection strategies that add value to member product.

Our analysis also touches on a number of subthemes. First, we illustrate how an aging farm population can both motivate and constrain strategic reform. Few co-ops will disagree that the adoption of market-driven strategies is now the ticket to attracting younger Japanese to farming. But as our first case study illustrates, it can be difficult for reformist co-op leaders to sell new strategies to older farmer-members who are set in their ways. As our second case study shows, moreover, agents of change often face intergenerational and other conflicts among farmers that can divide the co-op's foundational organizations and weaken farmer compliance with the many operational rules that enable co-op strategies. Good co-ops that survive into the future do not ignore these challenges; they accommodate or resolve them.

Second, we look at the evolving relationship between co-ops and incorporated farm enterprises. The presence of some types of incorporated farm enterprises in a co-op's jurisdiction can motivate farmers to defect from co-op services. But as our cases reveal, they can also goad co-ops into doing more for their members (Nagano) or serve as co-ops' de facto foundational organizations (Kumamoto). While some co-ops may still view large, incorporated farm enterprises as a competitive threat, our findings suggest that many co-ops are coming to terms—and even cooperating—with them.

Third, we illustrate how co-op reform is a social as well as economic process. Good co-ops may put more money in the pockets of their farmer-members, but they are also expected to accommodate local societal norms and fulfill basic cooperative principles, such as the distribution of co-op benefits on the basis of member equality. Adherence to this principle may produce deeply path-dependent reforms that pander to inefficient part-time farmers and prevent the creation of larger-scale, more profitable farms. But for many farmers and co-op leaders even today, good co-ops leave no farmer behind.

Finally, we demonstrate how it takes a village to build and maintain a good co-op. Agency rarely succeeds in a vacuum; it depends on the strategic support of key community leaders and/or local and national politicians and bureaucrats and sometimes on exogenous incentives like government subsidies. Surprisingly, that "village" can even include Zennō when the conditions are right.

Case Selection

Our objectives in this chapter are to explore not only what drives effective strategic co-op reform but also how those reforms unfold. To do this, we selected cases of reformist, well-organized co-ops with the following criteria in mind. First, we chose co-ops in agricultural prefectures—those that rank among the top fifteen of forty-seven prefectures in terms of total agricultural output in FY 2017.[1] (See table 4.3 for a summary of the basic features of co-ops in Kumamoto and Nagano.) In keeping with our findings of chapter 4, these reformist co-ops have relatively high ratios of regular (farmer) members to associate members: JA Kamimashiki has 6,329 regular and 3,379 associate members (1.87), and JA Saku Asama 19,684 regular and 10,753 associate members (1.83).[2] In both cases, these ratios were higher than the relevant prefectural averages. And in keeping with our findings that the higher this ratio, the more likely co-ops are inherently motivated to serve farmers, both co-ops have performed quite well in terms of serving the financial needs of farmers. In 2018, JA Kamimashiki's amount marketed and handled (hanbai toriatsukai daka, or AMH—see chapter 4) per regular member was 1.099 million yen, while the corresponding total for JA Saku Asama was 1 million yen. This performance was quite close to that of JA Uonuma Minami, the rice-centric co-op we address in chapter 6 that is widely viewed as one of Japan's top-performing co-ops. In terms of AMH profits per regular member, the two co-ops performed similarly: 23,750 yen for JA Kamimashiki and 24,440 yen for JA Saku Asama; this was significantly lower, however, than the 44,530 yen for JA Uonuma Minami.

Second, we focus in this chapter on prefectures (and hence co-ops) with diversified product lines, reserving our analysis of rice-centric co-ops for the next chapter. While both Kumamoto and Nagano grow some rice, as do all agricultural regions of Japan—including those in Hokkaido and Okinawa—they are better known for their fruits and vegetables. These subsectors serve as prime laboratories for the study of strategic co-op reform because they have been relatively unfettered by the sorts of government controls over land use, product distribution, and trade that have long slowed reform in major rice-producing areas. They operate, in other words, in relatively free markets. As we observed in earlier chapters, the freer the market, the more likely economic actors will respond to price signals and other market incentives. We see these dynamics at play even in the Kashima branch of JA Kamimashiki, a historically rice-centric area that took its cue from more diversified agricultural regions of the co-op to move into vegetable production many years before the notion of co-op reform had become a national concern.

Third, to better understand the complexity of contemporary Japanese agriculture and the limits of, as well opportunities for, strategic reform, we selected co-ops in prefectures with different natural resource endowments and other geographic conditions, and hence product lines. Located in the temperate climate of southern Kyushu, Kumamoto Prefecture grows watermelons, a citrus fruit known as *dekopon* (tangelo), and *buntan* (similar to the pomelo) in its coastal areas and flowers, tomatoes, cucumbers, and other vegetables further inland. Compared to rice and other grains, these products can earn high prices, especially in urban areas. But the prefecture's distance from the Tokyo metropolitan area poses distribution and marketing challenges for co-op employees determined to add value to local product. Many fruits and vegetables have a short shelf life outside of climate-controlled containers and are hence difficult—and expensive—to transport. Kumamoto's warm climate helps make up for its higher-than-average transport costs by enabling off-season production of everything from strawberries to lettuce.[3] And although the prefecture has yet to take full advantage of this opportunity, its easy ocean access facilitates exports to points throughout East and Southeast Asia.

Nagano's mountainous terrain and cold, snowy winters present a much different set of constraints and opportunities. As one of Japan's few landlocked prefectures, Nagano finds it harder to export. And harsh winters limit the growing season, although the prefecture compensates for this by investing in hothouse production. At the same time, Nagano's warm summer days and cool nights give it a distinct edge over hotter prefectures when it comes to growing high-quality lettuce, cabbage, and other leafy vegetables, as well as fruits like apples, prunes, and grapes. Nagano also enjoys closer proximity to the Tokyo market than Kumamoto, which helps bring down transport costs, although it is not nearly as well situated as, say, Ibaraki Prefecture.

Our fourth case-selection criterion relates to the co-op's linkages with the JA keitō, the distribution network that connects local co-ops to either an independent prefectural economic federation (keizairen) or to Zennō. Since by our reckoning most reformist co-ops introduce changes within the keitō's purview, we focus on co-ops in prefectures that have a close relationship with Zennō or its regional counterparts. JA Kamimashiki distributes the bulk of its products through Kumamoto Prefecture's economic federation, one of only eight left in the country, while Nagano Prefecture's JA Saku Asama relies heavily—and directly—on Zennō. These relationships contradict an apparent assumption within the former Abe government (2012–2020) that a degree of co-op independence from Zennō should be a prerequisite for effective reform. To be sure, a few reformist co-ops, like Fukui Prefecture's JA Echizen Takefu (see chapter 1), have all but abandoned Zennō; Niigata Prefecture's JA Uonuma Minami, which we explore in chapter 6, has followed a similar route. But co-ops like these are exceptions to the norm.

Fifth, we chose cases that represent different styles of agency and hence relationships between co-ops and farmers. In the JA Kamimashiki case, reform was a top-down affair led largely by a proactive local co-op employee, while in JA Saku Asama, the reform process reflected pressures from farmers as well as co-op initiatives. These discrepancies reflect, in part, contrasting farmer mindsets that are in turn the result of different historical trajectories and local conditions. In the Kashima branch of JA Kamimashiki, farmers have it good. The descendants of many generations of rice farmers, local producers have been blessed, as we have seen, with excellent geographic and climatic conditions that facilitate year-round production and double cropping. And yet elements of the old passive-producer mindset that had its heyday under the traditional JA system still have a foothold in Kashima. It would seem, in short, that area farmers suffer from a "curse of abundance."[4] Without the efforts of an indefatigable leader to mobilize lukewarm farmers behind strategic reform, this part of JA Kamimashiki could have easily slipped into rapid economic decline.

Farmers in JA Saku Asama, by contrast, tend to be scrappier and more entrepreneurial, thanks in part to their history of struggle. Like their counterparts throughout Nagano, these farmers have long battled rugged terrain, volcanic soils, and cold temperatures that confine the growing season to just a few months of each year. But with the arrival of the Shinkansen and new highway routes in the leadup to the 1998 Winter Olympics in Nagano, area cultivators recognized new opportunities in the now accessible—and rapidly changing—consumer markets of nearby Tokyo. With the assistance of government subsidies, moreover, local soils have been upgraded. Now, those "poor Nagano farmers" attract national acclaim for their hard work, resourcefulness, and entrepreneurial spirit, and prefectural multipurpose co-ops are widely praised for being among the best in the country.[5] This is in spite of the fact that at an average age of 67.9 in 2015, Nagano farmers are the oldest in our data set of farmers and co-ops in six prefectures (see table 4.3). These findings support our observations in chapter 4 that average farmer age has little, if any, bearing on farmer entrepreneurship—or, for that matter, on co-op reform.

Finally, a caveat: our case selection is complicated by the fact that Japanese co-ops today are extremely diverse. Waves of co-op mergers over the years have produced very large co-ops, each of which can experience enormous internal variations in soil conditions, microclimates, and hence product lines. As a result,

a co-op's capacity to introduce profarmer changes can vary markedly from locale to locale. We take this into account particularly in our Kumamoto case by
exploring how reforms unfolded in just one branch of JA Kamimashiki, a subject
to which we now turn.

Conservative Farmers and Proactive Co-op Leaders: JA Kamimashiki and S. Mega-Farm

Inside the sparkling clean interior of the branch office of JA Kamimashiki in the
town of Kashima, a few kilometers south of Kumamoto City, the employees seated
behind the counter oversee a variety of savings, credit, and insurance services.[6]
Were it not for the JA logo that adorns the smart blue employee uniforms and the
posters on the walls, the office could pass for a commercial bank. It is only outside
that one finds evidence of farming. There, men in blue overalls tend to their business in a large barn-like building that houses a multipurpose combine and other
farm implements and in a number of modest, prefabricated structures.

One of those structures serves as the headquarters of S. Mega-Farm (S. kōiki
nōjō), an incorporated agricultural association (nōji kumiai hōjin). The cramped
space accommodates some shelves stuffed with files, a small conference table,
and three desks, the largest of which is occupied by Kodama Kōyō, the enterprise's founder and president (daihyō riji, lit., representative director). Now nearing seventy, Kodama's tan, weathered face and a missing fingertip suggest a life
spent in the surrounding fields.

JA has long had a reputation for simmering hostility toward incorporated farm
enterprises, which are more likely than traditional farm households to loosen their
dependence on JA services. But JA Kamimashiki is different. S. Mega-Farm is the
co-op's largest customer, composing fully 80 percent of co-op-wide demand for its
inputs and distribution services. This partnership between co-op and corporation
is also at the root of a sweeping product diversification and land reconfiguration
scheme that transformed Kashima into one of Kumamoto Prefecture's most productive agricultural regions, as evidenced by a "rate of arable land use" of an astonishing 170 percent, 60 percent more than the prefectural average.[7] Finally, the
story of JA Kamimashiki illustrates not only how co-ops can partner with incorporated farm enterprises in mutually beneficial ways but also how those enterprises can operate as effective organizational linkages between farmers and their
co-ops.

The partnership is all the more significant given the mindset of Kashima
farmers. Most are part-time cultivators who oversee tiny plots of land inherited

from their rice-farming ancestors. Their land is flat, highly fertile, and served by a plentiful water supply and a temperate climate. But as one high-level prefectural agricultural official observes, abundance has had its drawbacks. Farmers in this area are a little too comfortable—confident in the bounty of the land and satisfied with things the way they are.[8] Scrappy, business-oriented farmers like Shimada Toshio, whom we met in chapter 3, are somewhat unusual around here; for the most part, these are passive producers.

If we cannot attribute the successful introduction of Kashima's strategic reforms to the initiative of local farmers, how, then, can we explain it? The answer, very simply, is Kodama's leadership. It was Kodama who came up with the idea of reconfiguring the land to accommodate new crops and who mobilized area farmers behind the strategy, first as a thirty-three-year employee of the Kashima branch of JA Kamimashiki and then, from 1987, as an independent farm organizer.

The story of change in this corner of JA Kamimashiki is by no means a straightforward case of one man nudging farmers toward more profitable cultivation. Given their relatively traditional mindsets, Kashima farmers needed to be persuaded, cajoled, and incentivized into changing their attitudes and relationships with the co-op. That process took years. Nor was Kodama what one might call a market-oriented visionary. As he himself will admit, his actions were shaped more by a determination to help farmers make optimal use of their farmland and by simple sticks and carrots—including government subsidies—than by grandiose ideas about how to make local agriculture more broadly competitive. Change, in other words, was slow, incremental, adaptive, improvisational, often imperfect, and, compared to the sophisticated value-added marketing strategies some co-ops are introducing these days, relatively modest. The end results, however, repositioned the co-op and local farmers to more successfully navigate changing agricultural markets while reinforcing essential principles of agricultural cooperation.

The roots of Kodama's initiatives in Kashima extend to the 1980s, when Japan's growth economy was still driving rural youth into the cities in search of higher education and employment. An aging farm population was already a problem for Kashima, in other words—several years before the issue achieved national prominence. The co-op had been proactive in countering some of these challenges. In response to the introduction of gentan (see chapters 2 and 6) during the early 1970s, it encouraged area farmers to jump onto the rice-plus-alpha bandwagon by supplementing rice with wheat production on a rotational basis, and in 1983, it completed construction of a large country elevator in Kashima to store local raw product. A few years later, in response to the decline of grassroots farmer organizations, the co-op tasked Kodama, while still a branch employee, with the organization of farmer-members into hamletwide production associations (seisan kumiai) that could coordinate the application of collectively owned machinery. By 1990, associations were in place in all Kashima hamlets. The members of each association included the hamlet head as well as one representative each from JA Kamimashiki and the local agricultural committee (nōgyō iinkai).

Meanwhile, encouraged by the diversification of farm products elsewhere in the prefecture amid declining consumer demand for rice and rumors of an imminent end to government rice price supports, Kodama set out to expand the co-op's rice-plus-alpha strategy by adding soybeans to Kashima's two main products. The aim was to coordinate the cultivation of these crops under a block rotation arrangement. Farms were combined into large blocks (danchi) of plots that roughly approximated the boundaries of individual hamlets. During each two-year period, the blocks would produce harvests of each of the three crops on a rotating basis; while one block grew rice, others would grow soybeans or wheat. Farming blocks, or estates (einō danchi), devoted to specific crops had been around for years as a co-op—and prefectural government—strategy for improving productivity; as early as 1964, there were approximately 830 of them around the country.[9] But as Kodama explains, creating blocks for the purpose of crop rotation was a relatively new and challenging idea. Only five other co-ops in the country had introduced them by the time Kodama launched his project, and all were significantly larger than JA Kamimashiki's Kashima branch. And neither Kodama nor his co-op colleagues had any prior experience with block rotation.

At first, many of Kashima's aging, traditional, and mostly part-time farmers balked at the idea of producing soybeans, which were priced lower than rice during the mid-1980s. But Kodama was convinced that if incorporated into a block rotation scheme, soybeans could generate extra income for farm households over the long term. For Kodama and his co-op allies, in other words, the new production strategy seemed a promising antidote to declining consumer demand for rice in the context of gentan (see chapter 2). By propping up farm incomes, furthermore, it gave aging farmers a greater chance of securing successors—or least that was the hope.

Launching the scheme proved difficult. As a strategy, block rotation cannot work well unless all—or nearly all—contiguous farm households in the area participate and abide by the requisite operational rules. For example, farmers must communicate and cooperate closely as they reconfigure farmland and coordinate the irrigation and drainage requirements of each crop. They must also adhere to strict rotation schedules for the plan to work successfully, and that, in turn, requires close monitoring by co-op personnel.

Realizing that he could not do the time-consuming legwork for block rotation while simultaneously fulfilling his other duties as a co-op employee, Kodama resigned from JA in 1987. That same year, production by block rotation formally began in one of Kashima's hamlets. Other hamlets gradually followed suit. It was not until 2006, however, that twelve of Kashima's fourteen hamlets were fully on board and the farmland reconfiguration process largely completed. (The two Kashima hamlets that do not participate in the scheme are populated mostly by carrot-producing farm households.) By December 2015, 388 of Kashima's 562 farm households were participating in the arrangement. Time-specific area maps color coded by crop highlight the enormity of the accomplishment. Whereas maps from years past were splattered with small, irregularly shaped clusters of plots devoted to one crop or another, the map today is neatly divided into a few large, neat strips that evoke the lawns of Wimbledon in their precision.

Kodama's efforts were backed by key individuals, both in Kashima and beyond. While a co-op employee, he had the support of JA Kamimashiki's head and of many of his colleagues, although Kodama confesses that the co-op occasionally lost patience with the laborious processes involved in preparing for block rotation. Town and village officials were also supportive, as was the local agricultural committee. These groups were routinely represented in the fact-finding and town-hall meetings that Kodama organized over the years to facilitate the processes of farmland preparation and farmer organization. Kodama could also count on significant financial support. Funds for the reorganization of farmland came not from cash-strapped JA Kamimashiki but from Kashima's town coffers under the leadership of its long-serving, innovative mayor. Perhaps most importantly, Kodama made deft use of prefectural and national government subsidies. Well before three-crop block rotation was introduced, some local farmers were receiving subsidies under the national government's gentan policy to grow wheat on rested rice paddies. Kodama was well aware that those farmers would receive additional subsidies if they made further changes to their land and added that third crop, soybeans, to their production schedules. By Kodama's own admission, block rotation might have failed were it not for those subsidies.

Kodama worked closely with town and prefectural officials to distribute subsidies among farmers and in ways that closed the price differentials among rice, wheat, and soybeans. And herein lies one of the secrets to Kodama's effectiveness in persuading Kashima farmers to go along with the new production strategy. As we observed in earlier chapters, Japanese farmers have traditionally treated their farmland as cherished family assets rather than factors of production and are often suspicious of arrangements that might lessen their control over their land. Kodama overcame these cultural impediments to land reconfiguration by convincing potential participants that everyone would benefit financially from the block rotation strategy—and benefit equally. While this encouraged small-scale, part-time cultivators to remain on the land, thus curbing momentum toward formal farmland consolidation, it meshed well with local values and the principles of equality that characterize agricultural cooperation. And it helped build trust in Kodama among the community's traditional farm population.

Trust in Kodama was further reinforced by his commitment to transparency and democratic decision making. From the start, he logged hours each week conversing with individual farmers on their home turf, patiently explaining the objectives and requirements of block rotation to often reluctant cultivators and deliberately nurturing the support of individual hamlet leaders. Whenever he reached a new stage in the strategy's expansion, he carefully researched the requisite measures in collaboration with local stakeholders and encouraged communitywide discussions in public informational sessions. A few years ago, when it came time to discuss the venture's incorporation, local farmers were so used to Kodama that they needed no persuading. Indeed, Kodama recalls that particular series of consultations as the easiest to date: "We'd been at it for so long that there was virtually no need to debate incorporation. We had an approval rate of 103 percent!"[10]

The voices of local farmers imbue the organizational framework of the enterprise. That framework evolved slowly and somewhat haphazardly over the years before culminating, in 2015, in the incorporation of S. Mega-Farm, the largest corporation of its kind in Kyushu and a source of pride for the Kumamoto Prefectural government. Today, the enterprise is topped by a general assembly (sōkai) consisting of all 388 member-farm households. The general assembly then selects the corporation's twelve-member—one representative from each participating hamlet—board of directors, which Kodama heads. The general assembly and the board of directors are linked in two ways to twelve independent farm associations (einō kumiai) resembling the hamlet-based farm associations (shūraku einō) explored in chapter 3. First, representatives from the local farm associations sit on three organizations located at the base of the enterprise hierarchy; these three organizations work closely with Kodama and three vice directors in the implementation of the megafarm's affairs. Second, the corporation interacts on the ground with area farmers via more informal linkages with designated representatives of each of the twelve farm associations. In short, Kodama's enterprise is a *democratic cooperative* venture in every sense of the term; it is structured to support the sovereignty of area farmers over the enterprise's leadership and decisions, to facilitate regular and systematic communications among stakeholders as enterprise strategies are implemented, and to ultimately serve the farmer.

Why incorporate? It was no accident that Kodama chose to take this step in 2015, when the Abe government was in the throes of promoting the incorporation of farm enterprises. It was also at this point that the Kumamoto Prefecture's agricultural department under Hamada Yoshiyuki was promoting the establishment of incorporated megafarms as an antidote to the long-term deterioration of local farmer organizations—those foundational organizations that link farmers and JA's local cooperatives. By 2018, there were four of these megafarms in the prefecture.

Incorporation also has a number of perquisites. In Kodama's case, it entitles his enterprise to consumption-tax refunds and empowers him to hire employees who oversee a variety of tasks. It makes it much easier for him to formally cooperate with other firms and organizations; as of 2018, the megafarm has subcontracting relationships with thirty-five other organizations, including the local co-op. Finally, incorporation facilitates the bulk purchases of fertilizers, pesticides, and other inputs for distribution to member households. In sum, incorporation positions S. Mega-Farm to expand its capacity to enhance the productivity of its members.

Although much of the legwork involved in reorganizing Kashima farmers behind block rotation took place after Kodama left JA, he maintains a close relationship with the Kashima branch of JA Kamimashiki. The local co-op supported Kodama by assuming many of the administrative responsibilities involved in the reorganization of area farm households, helping with the incorporation process and participating in informational meetings at the local level.

The megafarm also leans heavily on JA Kamimashiki for basic agricultural services and is positioned to negotiate some of the terms of those services. The megafarm's access to a multipurpose combine is a typical case in point. Years ago, as part of a broader effort to maximize co-op receipts, the Kashima branch maneuvered to sell each of the predecessors of the megafarm's twelve independent farm associations their own combines. But Kodama balked at the expense. After several rounds of negotiations, he reached a compromise with JA: the co-op branch would own, house, and service one large multipurpose combine and lease it via the megafarm to farm households. The fees levied on households were low enough to satisfy users but high enough to ensure a satisfactory income stream for JA Kamimashiki.

The megafarm also purchases all fertilizers, pesticides, and other farm inputs for its farmer-members from JA Kamimashiki and has recently secured small but significant discounts (about 1.3 percent) for bulk purchases. And it delivers all the megafarm's raw product to market via JA Kumamoto's regional economic federation. Member product is pooled and entrusted to the co-op, and farmers receive a uniform price for the lot.[11] Kodama complains about those prices, arguing that JA Kamimashiki could be doing more to raise farmer incomes. He holds the co-op's feet to the fire by insisting on observing price negotiations between the co-op and the regional economic federation; Kodama recounts all this with an air of exasperation, but the fact that the co-op allows him through the door of these important—and usually closed—meetings attests to the mega-farm's clout.

JA Kamimashiki has fallen short on other measures, Kodama argues, most notably in the quality of its farm consulting (*einō shidō*) services to which all megafarm members—as regular co-op members—are entitled. The co-op sim-ply does not have enough trained consultants on hand to effectively do the job. Kodama and his employees help pick up the slack by offering megafarm mem-bers advice throughout the growing season.

Although Kodama complains that JA Kamimashiki is often slow to change and needs to do better by local farmers financially, he does not seriously enter-tain alternative routes to market. One reason for this is lack of time. Kodama's enterprise is simply too busy making sure that each farm household is well served to nurture branding and other sorts of marketing expertise. But for the most part, the status quo seems to work. Pooling raw product and working through JA meshes well with local tradition, and the area's mostly part-time cultivators can take pride in the fact that their rice will bear the prefecture's popular Mori no kumasan brand name. In 2018, Kodama seemed reasonably satisfied with the megafarm's partnership with JA: "Why do we purchase our inputs from JA? Because it gives us peace of mind! JA now gives us small discounts, which private-sector suppliers haven't always done. We feel similarly about JA's marketing and distribution services. JA has a huge economy of scale. It has power. We sell our stuff through JA because it's easy and fairly risk-free and because it works."[12]

Kodama knows full well that the relationship with JA works because of his megafarm's growing economic influence. As JA Kamimashiki's largest and most stable supplier of good-quality crops and largest purchaser of inputs, Kodama knows that if he threatens to defect by taking his business elsewhere, JA will lis-ten. And his negotiating power is likely to expand in coming years as the num-ber of big-box home centers and other independent input providers increases and as more farmers pursue contract farming independently of JA.

Kodama would not divulge concrete data about the financial fortunes of area farmers. Judging from his ongoing efforts to "give JA hell"[13] when it comes to negotiating good prices, however, things clearly could be better. But Kodama is confident that the introduction of block rotation and his strategic use of subsi-dies have improved agricultural productivity in Kashima, thus strengthening the capacity of area farmers to weather the pressures of Japan's increasingly com-petitive agricultural sector. In sum, farmers are better off than they would be otherwise, and the fact that no participating households have dropped out of the megafarm so far seems evidence enough of this. In the process, S. Mega-Farm has helped turn JA Kamimashiki into a "pretty good" co-op.

S. Mega-Farm not only incentivizes JA Kamimashiki to increase the economic returns of traditional co-op strategies to farmer-members; it also marks a departure from the typical postwar organizational linkages between co-ops and their farmer-members. As we have seen in chapters 2 and 4, local multipurpose cooperatives were normally tied to local farmers during the postwar era through a variety of traditional foundational organizations—independent agricultural groups at the grassroots level like production committees and their equivalent, hamlet consultative committees (*zadankai*) that dealt with both agriculture and nonagricultural issues, and the like. These eclectic organizations served as arenas for routine interaction between the farm community and co-op employees, both in the articulation of farmer preferences and input orders to the co-op and in the implementation of co-op strategies. S. Mega-Farm alters these organizational linkages between JA and local farmers in two important ways. First, Kodama's reorganization of farm households into first production associations and then larger, hamlet-based farm associations marks the *harmonization* of foundational organizations across hamlets. While multipurpose foundational organizations decline in size, focus, and influence as rural populations shrink and diversify, these hamlet-based farm associations may have a longer life expectancy precisely because they are focused exclusively on agricultural production and tethered to a single pole: S. Mega-Farm. The megafarm's grassroots associations have not, however, completely displaced foundational associations that fall directly under the co-op's purview; to the contrary, the co-op now has its own set of local, product-specific production committees. But there is enormous overlap between those co-op committees and megafarm associations in terms of both rank-and-file members and especially committee/association leaders—a product, Kodama explains, of the paucity of neighborhood farmers with the relative youth and wherewithal to both farm and play a grassroots leadership role. This level of overlap means that megafarm members are, in effect, heavily involved in co-op affairs, including the selection of JA Kamimashiki's general assembly, which chooses members of the co-op's board of directors.

Second, Kodama has positioned his corporation to function as the key intermediary between the hamlets, as organized through the megafarm's hamlet-based farm associations, and JA Kamimashiki—at least insofar as some of the day-to-day business of farming is concerned. Kodama is responsible for aggregating and articulating farmer input and other needs—tasks that would otherwise fall to the co-op's own local production committees—and then negotiates with the co-op for good prices. In sum, this is an example in which the presence of a large farm corporation in the area—JA's traditional nemesis—may improve communications between local foundational organizations and the multipurpose co-op and hence the implementation of productive farm strategies.

Kodama's story both within and outside of JA represents just one way in which the organizational linkages of co-ops to their member-farmers can be adapted to shifting demographic pressures and economic opportunities. And if the list of co-op representatives on Kodama's annual visitors log is any indication, we could very well see other co-ops in Kyushu and elsewhere duplicate this pattern of co-op-corporation interaction. But numerous challenges remain. Although his crop rotation scheme has worked to his farmers' advantage in the context of Japan's more open markets and, more recently, the termination of gentan (see chapter 6), Kodama now constantly grapples with the effects of fluctuating agricultural prices and declining consumer demand for rice, both of which complicate long-term planning and ongoing attempts to lower production costs and increase payments to farmers for their products. He also struggles to meet the growing demand for crops grown with fewer agricultural chemicals as new, more aggressive strains of weeds invade the area and the effects of climate change lower crop yields. What is more, the fertility of local farmland has been compromised as the production of three crops depletes the soil of nitrogen; this problem has become so pressing that area farmers opted in 2018 to drop wheat from their crop rotations. Finally, while block rotation has served as a lifeline for many traditional farmers, it has failed to attract younger cultivators into the community, where the average age of farmers nears seventy years old.

On top of these issues, S. Mega-Farm must constantly navigate Japan's complex subsidy regime. On the one hand, subsidies have substituted for price signals in terms of incentivizing the reform of co-op strategies, especially during the early years of Kodama's activism; in fact, it was the availability of gentan-related subsidies that convinced Kodama to pursue block rotation in the first place. On the other hand, different subsidies can conflict with one another in ways that complicate Kodama's efforts to implement new production strategies and grow his enterprise. Consider, for instance, subsidies connected to two of the government's pet projects: the promotion of certified farmers (nintei nōgyōsha—see chapter 3) and incorporated farm enterprises. Certified farmers are entitled to a number of special subsidies, but if those farmers join a larger, incorporated enterprise, like S. Mega-Farm, they are required to refund a significant portion of those funds to the government. The megafarm partially circumvented this problem by introducing three separate categories of household membership that vary in terms of the amount of farmland contracted to the enterprise, thus giving the megafarm's thirty-one certified farm households the option to contract only a portion of their land to the enterprise or none at all, in return for varying levels of access to megafarm services. S. Mega-Farm also avoids forcing difficult trade-offs on certified farmers by remaining—from a legal perspective—little more than an accounting entity rather than an incorporated enterprise with more hands-on involvement in the production process. The arrangement has the added benefit of preserving the eligibility of both S. Mega-Farm and its associated hamlet-based farm associations for certain types of governmental financial assistance. But while these measures help sidestep some of the contradictions inherent in the government's subsidy programs, it hamstrings the corporation's future development and the profitability of area farmers. Kodama would like to see S. Mega-Farm get directly involved in the cultivation and harvesting of local farmland and lease farmland directly—including that of retiring farmer-members who lack successors. For now, the best that S. Mega-Farm can do to ensure the future of agriculture in Kashima—at a time when only 70 to 100 of its 388 member households are expected to remain in farming over the short to medium term and half of its certified farmer-members lack successors—is to encourage its larger-scale members to purchase or lease the holdings of their retiring successorless neighbors.

As the Abe government exhorts stakeholders to think of Japanese agriculture as a profitable growth industry, it is important to remember that Kodama's venture is not a typical Japanese business, or *kigyō*. Yes, the enterprise is empowered to hire outside workers, just like any other Japanese business. And yes, it is interested in making more money. But the advantages of the megafarm's size and incorporated status are limited. Recall, for instance, the fact that Kodama does not concern himself with branding and marketing, preferring instead to let JA do the job: "I have no time for that sort of thing," he says. "I'm just too busy making sure that every megafarm member gets a fair shake."[14] And the vulnerability of his enterprise to climatic conditions often trumps the advantages of hiring outside labor. Hamada Yoshiyuki, the main architect behind the prefecture's promotion of incorporated megafarms, fully recognizes this: "What happens if a typhoon lands in your area in the middle of the night?" he asked during one of our interviews. "What use are your part-time employees then? Farming is not a 'factory.' You need to be on-site day and night!"[15]

Kumamoto farmers understood this only too well in April 2016, when the prefecture was struck by a massive earthquake. The tremblor damaged irrigation and drainage systems, leading to flooding of the surrounding fields and bringing planting to a standstill. But Kashima was among the first farming regions in the prefecture to recover—a point of great pride for Kodama. Within a matter of a few days, Kodama decided which systems could be quickly salvaged and used long-tested block rotation rubrics to determine who should plant what and when. Working through their hamlet-level farm associations and accustomed to following Kodama's lead and making speedy decisions, the farmers were quick to cooperate. As testament to Kodama's reputation for reliability and the effectiveness of his incorporated mega-farm, Kashima was among the first of the stricken farm regions to receive national emergency aid. In the end, an astonishing 96 percent of member farmland was recovered within the space of a few weeks, and the blow to household incomes was minimized. In the aftermath of the emergency, the accolades started flooding in—from the local and provincial governments and even from the Abe government. Today, a photograph of Prime Minister Abe, Kodama, and a former JA colleague standing in the fields of Kashima a few weeks after the disaster takes pride of place on one of the walls of S. Mega-Farm's tiny office. What began as a disaster is now remembered as an example of what cooperative relations among a multipurpose cooperative and an incorporated farm enterprise can achieve—not just for themselves but for an entire farming community.

Strong Farmers, Strong Co-ops: JA Saku Asama

The vegetable distribution center of the Goka branch of Nagano Prefecture's JA Saku Asama, headed by Tanaka Yukio, is remarkable for two reasons.[16] First, the vegetables it oversees are of Japan's highest quality. Consider, for instance, the cardboard boxes filled with heads of lettuce that line the concrete floors. The size of basketballs, the flawless, bright green produce captures the eye like gems in a jewelry store. In short order, the boxes will be run through special machines that quickly chill the lettuce to five degrees Celsius, vacuum sealed, and then loaded onto refrigerated trucks for shipment. Part of the well-regarded Shinshū brand of Nagano vegetables, the lettuce and other "tableland vegetables" produced in the area are a source of great pride for both local farmers and the co-op.[17]

Second, this distribution center—and others like it in JA Saku Asama—handles all but a tiny portion of produce grown in the area. What is more, the co-op channels all its produce into Zennō's distribution networks. This is puzzling. How can we explain the heavy reliance of the area's proud farmers on their multipurpose cooperative and in the very same prefecture where the likes of Shimazaki Hideki, the famous founder of Top River and advocate of "profitable farming," advises against an overdependence on JA?[18] And why does the co-op—indeed, why do all Nagano co-ops—depend so heavily on Zennō, that paragon of self-interested, rent-seeking behavior?

One possible explanation has to do with geography. In contrast to many farmers in, say, Ibaraki Prefecture, whose easy proximity to the massive Tokyo market enables many of them to bypass their local co-ops and sell directly to urban buyers, Nagano farmers are more isolated. Despite major improvements to its highway and train networks since the 1990s, the prefecture may still be too far removed from major urban centers to enable more than a few intrepid, larger-scale producers to forge independent channels to market. But make no mistake: Nagano farmers tend to be hardworking and resourceful, and many of the more competitive ones among them will abandon JA if they feel they can get a better price elsewhere. What, then, explains this dependence on the JA system?

Proactive leadership? Is there a "Kodama" in JA Saku Asama who has taken it upon himself to mobilize local farmers behind the co-op and its strategic initiatives? If our interviews with co-op employees are any indication, the answer is no; no one individual or group of individuals has stood out in this regard—perhaps because farmers are already behind the idea of strategic co-op reform.

The reason most farmers stick with JA Saku Asama, and the co-op with Zennō, is that JA organizations in Nagano give farmers what they want: a competitive, stable income stream and a cushion against market-related risks. And they have done so through the implementation of complex production and marketing strategies since 2001 that are rooted in strong organizational linkages between farmers and the co-op and that respond effectively to competitive price signals. The story of how the co-op and Zennō came by these strategies and their organizational foundations illustrates how agency can be exercised by farmers, as well as co-ops, and how market opportunities and the threat of farmer defections can in turn incentivize even Zennō to do better by local farmers.

JA Nagano's Production Adjustment Strategy

On one level, JA Nagano resembles the traditional JA system described in chapter 2.[19] Farmers hand virtually all their output to their local multipurpose co-op. After subjecting those products to light processing, the co-op then forwards them up the keitō. But there are important differences between the system of old and how JA Nagano operates today. First, while the traditional JA system reached its zenith largely because of rice, JA Nagano's successes rest on vegetables, a subsector in which JA did rather poorly in the past. Second, there are now far fewer local co-ops in the prefecture, at sixteen, than there once were, thanks to nearly fifty rounds of mergers since 1947, the year the Co-op Law was passed. Third, the Nagano keitō has been simplified through the 2001 elimination of the prefecture's economic federation, which had functioned for decades as an organizational layer between the local co-ops and Zennō; since 2001, Zennō has taken care of JA Nagano's marketing and distribution functions. But in contrast to some prefectures, the Nagano merger process has not significantly alienated farmers from JA. This is largely because of the commitment of Nagano co-ops and Zennō to boost the economic returns to farmers by implementing strategies that enhance the quality and hence prices of the prefecture's agricultural products.

For vegetables, the most important strategy is a market-conforming system of production adjustment (*jukyū chōsei*, lit., "demand-supply adjustment") that requires the cooperation of all prefectural co-ops and their farmer-members.[20] Zennō assigns product-specific production targets to the prefecture's multipurpose co-ops. Each co-op then subdivides its targets among its various branches, which contract with local farmer-members to fulfill them. Key to those targets are quality-specific grades that represent different price points: LL for the highest quality and most expensive grade, L for the next highest quality, then LA, LAA, LB, and so on down the list. Since the price for each grade at any point in time is determined in relation to that of the grade immediately above it, the aim is to manage the targets in ways that generate the highest possible price point for that top grade—for those basketball-sized gems, in the case of lettuce. In the event of a bumper crop, this means that some farmers will be asked to destroy a portion of their harvest, with the producers of the lowest grades being called on to cull the most and those of the top grade the least, if any at all. These strict, quality-related standards are among the most important operational rules among Nagano co-ops. What distinguishes them from operational rules in co-ops from most other parts of the country is the fact that they are shared by all participating Nagano co-ops and monitored by co-op employees in cooperation with Zennō.

One would think that farmers at or near the bottom rungs of this scheme would chafe at demands to trash the fruits of their labor, but in keeping with the equality principle of agricultural cooperation, JA ensures that everyone benefits. JA is clear that the point of the strategy is to keep prices relatively high for all producers. And without exception, in accordance with the buy-up sales (kaitori hanbai—see chapter 4), the co-ops pay farmers a final price within ten days of receiving their products at the Goka and other local distribution centers. Finally, JA generously subsidizes producers who bear a heavy financial burden for their sacrifices. As Tanaka and Shimura Tomoya, a long-term JA Saku Asama employee involved in vegetable production, see it, it is a system that delivers both high prices and peace of mind to area farmers. As in our Kumamoto case, Nagano co-ops strive to leave no farmer behind.

Nagano's production adjustment strategy occasionally fails. In June 2018, for instance, a glut in production prompted Zennō to orchestrate a major culling of the prefectural lettuce crop. At the time, no one could have predicted the record-busting heat wave that descended on Japan a few weeks later and its devastating effects on subsequent harvests. In retrospect, the lettuce that had been destroyed in June should have been chilled and stored to make up for those later shortfalls. Fortunately for producers, the effects of those shortfalls on household incomes were minimized by Zennō subsidies earmarked precisely for this purpose.

The production adjustment strategy for Nagano vegetables sounds a lot like gentan, the notorious production adjustment system for rice that was in effect between 1971 and 2018. Both systems are, after all, designed to prop up prices by regulating supply. But the two schemes differ in several respects. First, the Nagano system is not a national system, and although the national government provides Zennō with funds for farmer subsidies, it plays no role in the strategy's implementation. Second, farmers are not obligated to rest their farmland for predetermined periods, as rice farmers were under gentan. (Of course, this means that while precious farmland remains active in the Nagano system, the amount of food wastage can be considerable as farmers are instructed to regulate the size of their harvest by destroying parts of it.) Third, for many years gentan operated in a completely closed rice market, while the Nagano system functions in a market that is open to imports and where price fluctuations are the norm. Finally, whereas gentan was more about the quantity rather than the quality of the rice supply, Nagano's production adjustment system for vegetables also places a heavy premium on quality to secure good prices.

JA Nagano's strategy for vegetables also differs from JA's traditional rice collection strategies. When JA was at the height of its influence, it would offer its farmer-members relatively uniform prices within specific quality-related grades. To boost the overall quality of rice sold to consumers, moreover, it routinely mixed lower with higher grades; this was fairly easy to do for rice, the quality of which is not always discernible on the basis of its outward appearance. But JA cannot get away with these practices in the case of vegetables, particularly Nagano vegetables. Lettuce, cabbage, spinach, broccoli, and tomatoes are much larger than individual grains of rice and hence harder to pool. Moreover, vegetables must be carefully sorted even within specific strains according to discrepancies in appearance and quality, some of which result from production at different altitudes and/or in divergent soil conditions. Last but not least, discerning Japanese consumers have high expectations for the quality of the foods they eat, and for vegetables and fruits, they take choice for granted. JA Nagano knows that if it fails to meet consumer expectations, it could lose business to other prefectures and perhaps even to imports.

Nagano farmers pressure the cooperative system to act on that awareness. In fact, we view farmer pressure as a major reason why JA—and particularly Zennō—has done particularly well by vegetable farming in Nagano. Consider, for example, reactions to signals during the 1990s that Zennō was angling to dissolve JA's prefectural economic federation and assume its various functions. Worried that the move would trigger a race to the bottom in JA's regulation of product standards, angry farmers and many local co-ops forced long delays in the merger process. What ultimately paved the way for the federation's 2001 dissolution was intervention by then-governor Tanaka Yasuo, who spoke up on behalf of the prefecture's proud farmers and the integrity of Nagano brands and insisted that Zennō act on their demands. Farmer backlashes against even the possibility of lapses in product quality did not end there. Over the years, the area's best farmers—including Goka's lettuce producers—have on several occasions delayed the merger of individual local co-ops by being sticklers for standards. Shimura and Tanaka openly acknowledge the strengths of those farmer demands and the lengths the co-op will go to appease them. In response to the initial refusal of Goka farmers to approve a co-op merger a few years ago, for example, the co-op pledged to further minimize the scope of product pooling to protect local brands and their high prices.

In sum, strong farmer demands in the context of competitive markets have prompted both Nagano's multipurpose co-ops and Zennō to do well by local producers. It would be a mistake, however, to conclude that Zennō is now downplaying its self-interest, for when those production adjustment schemes work well, all boats rise; farmer incomes improve, and so long as farmer defections are limited, both the co-ops and Zennō can count on higher volumes of transactions and hence better revenue streams. Meanwhile, Zennō and Nagano co-ops have continued to benefit from the sale of large volumes of farm chemicals and other inputs to their farmer-members, thus underscoring our observation in chapter 4 that "working for the farmer" and "working for JA" can, in the end, be compatible goals. But none of this would happen in the absence of the coordinating functions of strong foundational organizations, as JA Saku Asama's production committees (seisan bukai) illustrate.

The product-specific committees of JA Saku Asama and other Nagano co-ops wear multiple hats. They are the main point of contact between farmers and the co-op and a forum through which farmers of like products develop and share expertise. They collect and channel member orders for fertilizers and other inputs into the JA system and select members to serve as representatives to the co-op's general assembly. In JA Saku Asama, co-op employees and committee members have cooperated on many an occasion to reorganize those committees, especially in the wake of mergers between the old economic federation and Zennō and among local co-ops. By all accounts, the primary purpose of those reorganizations has been to enhance the efficiency and effectiveness of farmer participation in JA Nagano's prefecturewide strategy for ensuring the quality and high prices of local vegetables.

The production committees, which, as the co-op's foundational organizations, are theoretically independent, also serve as arenas for enforcing the co-op's many operational rules and norms, a function that has grown increasingly important now that formal organizations within the JA system are legally prohibited from retaliating against nonconformity by their underlings. If farmers complain too much, they invite ostracism (*murahachibu*) by others in their committee. Those who leave the committee in search of a better deal might be refused reentry should their efforts fail. And farmers who do not abide by co-op standards for product size and chemical input use may be disciplined by the committee, since nonconformity can have a dampening effect on prices for all members. By pushing members to toe the strategic line, this sort of intracommittee peer pressure helps unify farmer voices vis-à-vis the co-op and Zennō. And it reflects and reinforces the sense of pride among area farmers, both in the quality of the foods they grow and in their participation in co-op management. Tanaka, from Goka's distribution center, laughingly points out that these sentiments are so strong that some farmers have trouble separating the production committee from the co-op itself, as evidenced by their proprietary attitudes toward the distribution center and other facilities that belong to the co-op. But he readily acknowledges that the effectiveness of JA Saku Asama is a function of those committees and their members: "The co-op is strong because the farmers are strong."[21]

This does not mean that the production committees function exclusively as a source of farmer control over the co-op and hence Zennō. They are a vehicle for top-down influence as well. JA Saku Asama insists that the farmers maintain these committees, and it requires farmers who sell through the JA network to belong to them. As Kaneshige Mikio, an entrepreneurial farmer and food retailer in neighboring Karuizawa further explains, it is through those committees that the co-op—indeed, co-ops throughout the prefecture—enforces compliance with various rules and standards. "The co-ops are really picky [*urusai*] about these rules," he explains. "If you don't obey them, the co-op expects the committee to ostracize you. The underlying fear, of course, is that if you don't follow these guidelines, your produce will earn lower prices!"[22]

Intrafarmer conflict does occur within JA Saku Asama. Production committees are susceptible to internal fissures, many of which reflect generational differences. This is certainly true within the co-op branches of Goka and Shirakaba, where farmers under forty compose roughly 30 percent of community totals. It is these younger farmers who are most likely to question JA practices, stand up in defense of the Nagano brand, and speak up on behalf of further change. Some of these farmers—and particularly those with incorporated enterprises—have been known to break away from their production committees and form alternative routes to market. Kaneshige, who belongs to a neighboring but similarly orga-nized co-op, offers one example of how this might work:

> I recently formed an association of organic farmers. It's hard to go or-ganic; it takes time and money to prepare the soil, and cultivating organic vegetables and other crops can be very labor intensive. But it's even harder to produce organically under JA, which insists that its farmer-members use certain minimum amounts of chemical fertil-izers, pesticides, and herbicides to maintain "product quality." If you want to go organic, you have to go "out" of JA and those production committees—at least that's the case around here.
>
> There are about twenty of us in the association, and we've just in-corporated it. I'm in my fifties, but the others are all young—thirty-something. We know there's a strong market for what we produce and we're confident that we will be successful. The fact that my organic shops are already doing well is proof of this.[23]

Entrepreneurial farmers like Kaneshige and his young colleagues represent the future of farming in Nagano. Since it is these types of farmers—the prefec-ture's most productive and profitable—who are most likely to defect from co-op services, JA Nagano has no choice but to pay attention to them.

Representatives of JA Saku Asama readily admit that the threat of farmer de-fection from co-op services is very real and that the co-op faces increasing compe-tition from incorporated farm enterprises established by the area's best producers. To help curb those defections, the co-op grants those all-important production committees a degree of authority to govern themselves. This is also necessitated, Tanaka explains, by the distinctive features of local agriculture. Area farmers pro-duce so many different kinds of vegetables (and fruits and flowers) and their input needs vary so markedly across both varietals and geographic conditions that only they can adequately determine their needs. Consequently, each committee has complete control over its input orders, but with the proviso that it meets those minimum requirements for chemical input usage. It is then up to the co-op to respond to those input orders, coordinate relations among the committees, and represent the committees to Zennō.

JA Saku Asama takes pride in the strength of its organizational connections to both local farmers and Zennō. "Our organization is strong," Tanaka boasts. "In fact, as a co-op, we may be organizationally the strongest in all of Japan!"[24] He credits co-op flexibility for this. The co-op is constantly responding to the requirements of individual farmers, he says, and it recognizes the need to do even more of that in the future. (To be sure, he makes no mention of the co-op's al-legedly rigid stance on the use of agricultural chemicals.) Tanaka is not just paying lip service to the JA system's commitment to self-reform (jiko kaikaku) in response to mounting criticisms of JA practices and pressures for change from the Abe government. Flexible responsiveness to the needs of local farmers seems embedded in the co-op's ethos. As if to remind visitors of this, Shimura brandishes a name tag with the words "CHANGE JA" written in English in large, capital letters along the bottom. And below that, the secret to how to fulfill that goal: "Hitori hitori ga kawarimasu," meaning, essentially, "change happens one person at a time."

Meanwhile, JA Saku Asama is responding to the relentless pressures of its younger farmers to keep upping the returns to cultivators by looking for ways to lower farmer production costs, although there is only so much cost cutting that a co-op can carry out before its own bottom line is compromised. In 2018, for instance, the co-op cooperated with Zennō to launch a new machinery rental service that targets farmers—often part-time cultivators—who lack the means to purchase their own machinery.[25]

More importantly, the co-op and Zennō are under constant pressure from their members to increase prices for farmer product. Today, Nagano vegetables wind their way to market via three JA channels. The first is a familiar one: produce travels through the local co-op and then Zennō, which sells it to private wholesalers. The second route eliminates the wholesaler as Zennō sells the produce directly to retailers and other buyers, thus lowering the commissions charged to local co-ops and hence farmers. The third, most radical route, links Zennō directly to buyers via preseason contract. Here, Zennō and buyers negotiate both the price and quantity of produce before crops are planted, and then Zennō works through individual co-ops to recruit interested farmers. JA members are under no obligation to participate in contract cultivation, but if they do take it on, they are informed of how much to grow and guaranteed a price on delivery. Although still in its infancy, the Zennō-led contract cultivation system is gaining traction among the farmer-members of JA Saku Asama, many of whom choose to join contracts in groups.

Of course, some younger farmers would like to see JA Saku Asama completely bypass Zennō—and hence unwanted commissions—and negotiate directly with distributors or end users like supermarkets or restaurant chains. But this is risky. The co-op has negotiated direct contracts in the past, but there have been instances in which buyers failed to pay for their orders. The advantage of working with Zennō, co-op representatives explain, is that the returns to both the co-op and the farmers are all but guaranteed. Moreover, the co-op has good reason to assume that demand for Zennō's services to support Nagano vegetables will likely expand in the future. Unlike in the past, when consumers purchased their fruits and vegetables at small, independent greengrocers (yaoyasan) located in neighborhood shopping districts (shōtengai), most now patronize large supermarket chains that offer prewashed, packaged fruits and vegetables or convenience stores that sell *obento* and other precooked meals. These retail behemoths depend heavily on processors to prepare their fresh produce, and those processors in turn require bulk purchases of raw product. It is Zennō, with its vast economy of scale, rather than the co-op that can most effectively meet these needs.

To be sure, the effectiveness of the co-op-Zennō partnership in Nagano depends heavily on the availability of government largesse. Subsidies influence the strategic choices made during the co-op reform process, grease the prefecture's production adjustment schemes, and compensate farmer-members for the effects of bad weather. And it is the MAFF that provides Zennō with the means to compensate farmers when buyers fail to deliver on their contractual obligations. Yes, co-ops like JA Saku Asama have learned how to adapt to price signals, but their ability to mitigate market-related risk—and in ways that serve all farmers—is still heavily dependent on those subsidies.

Despite this government safety net, numerous challenges remain. Thanks to robust demand and competitive prices for area products, farmers in JA Saku Asama appear to have an easier time attracting successors than in Kodama Kōyō's corner of Kumamoto Prefecture, but Nagano's small average farm size can impede such efforts. And while those favorable market conditions enable Nagano to attract new, younger farmers, the influx is not nearly enough to offset the aging of the overall farm population and a growing labor shortage. To compensate, JA Saku Asama has jumped on a national bandwagon to promote agricultural trainees. Although prohibited by law from training new farmers, the co-op recruits them from around the country and abroad, billets them with farm households, pays their housing allowances and wages, and provides them with educational resources. The program has drawbacks, though, including the MAFF-imposed prohibition on trainees working overtime—a problem in an agricultural prefecture like Nagano, observes a local tomato farmer, where the growing season is short but intense. (Never mind, he observes, that many trainees, including those from China, would welcome overtime and the extra wages it brings.) Furthermore, few Japanese trainees remain in farming after completing their terms—perhaps, the tomato cultivator muses, because the work is too tough.[26]

JA Saku Asama is also mindful of its many economic vulnerabilities. It is discovering, for example, the limits of large-scale contract cultivation. What is a co-op to do, Tanaka asks rhetorically, when crop failures prevent it from filling a direct order from a processor or retailer? The co-op may have no choice but to purchase the surplus of neighboring co-ops, but Nagano's competitive co-ops sometimes refuse such requests. The co-op also worries about the unpredictable actions of other agricultural prefectures. Even if all goes according to plan and the Nagano co-op network distributes just the right amount of high-quality produce to market, prices will plummet if co-ops in, say, neighboring Gunma Prefecture flood the market with too much of the same product. Finally, imports are a looming threat. Some fast-food chains like McDonald's are purchasing more of their lettuce and other produce from foreign suppliers via longer-term contracts and at favorable prices. Although the trend is not yet widespread, co-ops like JA Saku Asama are watching it with trepidation.

When all is said and done, has JA Saku Asama improved farmer fortunes? The lack of publicly available data on long-term farmer incomes prevents us from proving this definitively, but our answer is a qualified yes. High rates of farmer participation in those co-op production committees strongly suggest that farmers feel they have something to gain from the co-op—despite evidence of co-op strong-arming. And that something is risk mitigation and a stable long-term income. Farmer pressures on JA Saku Asama are evidence enough that the co-op could always do better in terms of increasing the financial returns to farmers, but the co-op's ability to lower risks and provide farmers with long-term financial security should not be underestimated. This does not mean, however, that the co-op's future is secure; it must constantly recalibrate that balance between income expansion and risk reduction as the prefecture's most competitive farmers establish more profitable routes to market.

While there is no shortage of criticisms of the performance of both the JA Kamimashiki–S. Mega-Farm partnership and of JA Saku Asama and other Nagano co-ops, our cases demonstrate how co-ops can implement market-driven strategies that better serve farmers when they are endowed with the right natural resources and market incentives, good leadership, and strategy-appropriate organizations that link farmers to their co-op. They also highlight the lengths that co-ops must go to adapt their strategies to Japan's more competitive and diversified agricultural market. Strategic adaptation is difficult, in part because there is no universally accepted script for how best to proceed; every co-op must chart its own course and in ways that reflect farmer voices as well as local opportunities and constraints—climatic, normative, legal, and financial.

Our case studies also underscore the prominent role of the JA keitō in the strategic reform and implementation processes. Again, most local co-ops reform within the organizational purview of the JA system. And contrary to prevailing opinion in some policy-making and academic circles today, sticking with that system—with Zennō—is not necessarily a bad thing. As chapter 7 elaborates, Zennō has been pursuing a degree of self-reform over the years, and not only because government demands it; the market increasingly requires it, and both farmers and co-ops, in many cases, have come to expect it. Of course, Zennō's definition of change remains deeply path dependent; it strongly favors changes that reinforce the basic organizational parameters of the traditional JA system. Nevertheless, the Nagano case suggests that it is possible for Zennō to ensure its longevity while simultaneously meeting farmer expectations vis-à-vis their revenue streams and risk mitigation.

But whether JA will continue to pull off this juggling act is an altogether different story. The challenge to JA from incorporated farm enterprise remains. While S. Mega-Farm is an example of an incorporated enterprise that enhances co-op performance to a degree, other farm-related corporations are more threatening to the JA system. As we saw in chapter 3, some traditional farm households are incorporating themselves and abandoning JA services. Nonfarm corporations are increasing their presence in agricultural production, both indirectly through their shares in agricultural production corporations and, more recently, directly through farmland leasing. And farmers—especially younger, organic farmers—are banding together to form incorporated associations that supply niche markets while simultaneously fulfilling some of the important objectives that used to fall solely under JA's remit: risk mitigation and income enhancement. As we explore in greater detail in our concluding chapter, the JA system must continue to find ways to adapt to Japan's diversifying farm enterprises and more competitive market forces, or local co-ops and Zennō will be reduced to serving Japan's smallest, most inefficient farmers.

JA'S SANCTUARY

The Challenge of Reform in Rice-Centric Co-ops

If any product symbolizes Japan, it is rice. Japan's short-grained, sticky rice is grown by 70 percent of commercial farm households and is viewed as central to the preservation of precious farmland.[1] Rice cultivation also lies at the heart of rural social networks and age-old Shinto rituals. And rice incites economic nationalism like no other product. Every time foreign trade negotiators demand freer access to the Japanese rice market, there is protest—and not only because imports might threaten domestic farmers or the country's already low rate of self-sufficiency in food production.[2] As a sacred symbol of Japanese identity,[3] rice, many believe, should be grown only on Japanese soil.

Rice is also JA's sanctuary. In fact, JA is what it is primarily because of rice. The co-op network's enormous economic power during the postwar era owed much to its near monopolization of the collection and marketing of rice. But rice is no longer the product it once was. Thanks to the partial liberalization of rice imports, the government's retreat from rice pricing, and steadily declining consumer demand, rice prices are much lower today than in 1994, when they reached their postwar peak. In contrast to, say, vegetables, there is now significantly less money to be earned from rice. Consequently, JA organizations now handle less of their members' rice output than they once did (see table 4.1).

Different JA organizations have responded to these market transformations in different ways. Predictably, Zennō fought to prevent the reforms that have shrunk its share of the rice market from 90 percent at its postwar peak to approximately 40 percent today,[4] and there is evidence that it colludes with independent rice wholesalers to curb price competition.[5] Nevertheless, there are signs that Zennō is adapting to the new reality. Meanwhile, some rice-centric co-ops—co-ops that produce far more rice by volume and sales receipts than any other agricultural product[6]—are devising strategies to boost, or at least stabilize, rice-farmer earnings. But this is hard to do in a market where a combination of declining consumer demand, increasing competition, and lower prices can wipe out the gains from, say, reducing input prices or negotiating with buyers for higher rice prices. Given these idiosyncratic market conditions, rice-centric co-ops must pursue alternative strategies to boost or stabilize farmer incomes. We identify three such strategies: (1) help farmers diversify away from rice to include vegetables, fruits, and/or livestock production; (2) diversify within rice by producing a wider range of varietals that can be used by food processing and retail firms or for livestock feed; and/or (3) transform the co-op's best rice into a branded product that can earn more competitive prices.[7]

Our purpose in this chapter is to explore how these three strategies play out in practice and to explain why some rice-centric co-ops do a better job than others. We make the case that the timing of reform is extremely important in rice-centric co-ops that pursue sophisticated value-added strategies; for example, early entrants to the branding game in the context of declining rice prices have an easier time securing name recognition and high prices than later entrants. But the three variables that shape success in all co-op reform processes are also at play in rice-centric co-ops: natural resource endowments and corresponding market opportunities, farmer organization, and co-op agency—highly skilled co-op agency, in this case. In chapter 5, we demonstrated that agency can emanate from among farmers as well as co-op staff, but for today's rice-centric co-ops that wish to improve farmer incomes, well-placed co-op personnel must become highly adept at not only producing rice but also selling it—a task, in today's challenging rice market, that requires mastery of logistics, branding, marketing, and other highly complex tasks. Rice may be Japan's most sacred food product, but only when rice-centric co-op leaders adopt the skills of effective business entrepreneurs can they reap significant returns. We illustrate these and related points through an analysis of two co-ops from Niigata Prefecture: JA Uonuma Minami and JA Echigo Jōetsu.

The chapter begins with an overview of JA's evolving role in Japan's changing rice market and of the context and content of the three rice-centric reform strategies outlined above. We then briefly explain our case selection. The bulk of the chapter explores and explains strategic reform in JA Uonuma Minami and JA Echigo Jōetsu. We conclude by assessing the importance of export markets to the future of the Japanese rice market.

Japan's Changing Rice Market

Postwar JA's power—both economic and political—owed much to the 1942 Staple Food Control Act, which was passed to alleviate wartime food shortages. Although the shortages were eradicated by the early 1950s, the act remained on the books for four more decades for no other reason than it served the interests of JA and the LDP. Together with a ban on rice imports, the Staple Food Control Act helped weaken private-sector competition in the rice market. It authorized the government to guarantee the high rice prices that enabled JA to deliver prosperity to its farmer-members, the vast majority of whom were part-time cultivators who looked to rice cultivation as an easy supplement to their off-farm employment. And by obligating farmers to sell nearly all their rice through the co-op system, the act empowered JA vis-à-vis the MAFF and facilitated the task of delivering the farm vote to sympathetic LDP politicians. JA's dominance in the rice market also gave it enormous influence over the highly politicized process of annual rice pricing—so much so that the LDP, in its quest to secure the farm vote, was known to succumb to JA pressures by increasing rice prices in the lead-up to elections.[8]

Of course, some farmers grew no rice at all. Others supplemented their rice production with vegetables, fruits, dairy, or livestock, all of which could be sold through the open market or via the special-purpose (marketing) co-ops (senmon nōkyō) that also fell under the JA Group's umbrella. Some local multipurpose co-ops went to great lengths to encourage product diversification—the plus-alpha movement (see chapter 2)—in the expectation that an overreliance on rice in the context of shrinking consumer demand would jeopardize the future of local agriculture. To be sure, multipurpose co-ops that encouraged diversification had a better chance of securing the loyalty of their members.

By the early to mid-1990s, a confluence of trends downgraded rice—and JA's influence—in the farm sector. At the forefront was the specter of rice imports. Anticipating the 1987 start of the Uruguay Round of GATT trade negotiations, the government of Nakasone Yasuhiro (1982–1987) voiced its support for agricultural trade liberalization and took steps to prepare the domestic market. By 1991, the Food Agency, which oversaw the Staple Food Control Act, promoted new entrants into the rice distribution system. And in the interests of cutting costs, the MAFF encouraged JA's prefectural economic federations (keizairen) to bypass Zennō and deal directly with rice wholesalers. In time, independent distributors were competing for the business of JA's farmer-members by offering higher prices. These developments slowly loosened JA's stranglehold on rice collection, distribution, and marketing.

In 1994, Japan affixed its signature to the Uruguay Round's Agreement on Agriculture, thereby opening the domestic rice market to imports for the first time in decades.[9] The move triggered waves of government deregulation that began with the 1995 replacement of the Staple Food Control Act by the more limited Staple Food Act and culminated in 2004 with an overhaul of the Staple Food Act that marked a significant liberalization of the rice market.[10] (Rice imports, however, remain subject to very high tariffs: 778 percent as of this writing.[11]) All the while, JA's edge in the rice market continued to shrink as more and more farmers exercised their post-1995 right to sell as much rice as they liked outside the co-op system. In 1985, the JA group handled 66 percent of all rice produced in Japan. By 2015, that total had dropped to about 50 percent (see table 4.1); roughly 40 percent was ultimately handled by Zennō or the eight independent prefectural economic federations.[12] These figures underscore that while JA remains the dominant purveyor of rice in Japan, many rice farmers are defecting from JA's distribution and marketing services and some co-ops are loosening their dependence on the keitō. Meanwhile, fruits and vegetables have surpassed rice as JA's biggest source of income, and by a significant margin; in 2015 vegetables alone generated 1.37 trillion yen for JA and rice just 791.3 billion yen.[13]

A long-term, precipitous drop in domestic consumption has further weakened rice as a source of prosperity for Japanese farmers. After peaking in 1962 at 357.2 grams—about five bowls—of rice per day, average per capita consumption shrunk to less than half that total—164.6 grams, or two and a half bowls—by 2015.[14] Several factors have driven these changes. First, rice consumption has declined as the Japanese diet diversifies. Today, Japanese eat more bread and dairy products than rice. And as the domestic markets for beer, wine, and other alcoholic beverages expand, Japanese are drinking less (rice-based) sake than they once did—two-thirds less than in 1970.[15] Second, declining demand reflects the rapid aging of the general population; while older people eat rice more frequently than young people, they tend to consume less of it at any one sitting.[16] Finally, lifestyle changes are dampening the demand for rice. Working mothers and one- and two-member households are often unwilling to devote the time it takes—up to two hours—to properly wash, soak, and steam rice. All but impossible to reverse, these price-dampening trends are the source of far more concern among farmers and JA organizations than the specter of rice imports, which, for now, remain very low.

The rice market confronted further changes in late 2013, when the Abe government announced gradual but sweeping changes to gentan (see chapter 2), the scheme for propping up rice prices by limiting production that was implemented in 1971. Determined to encourage rice farmers and local co-ops to respond more directly to changes in demand and to ultimately lower prices for consumers, the government, by 2018, eliminated its annual production targets and the direct subsidies for farmers who fulfilled them. Fears that these changes would trigger overproduction have yet to materialize; the 2018 planting, for instance, grew by a mere 1 percent over the previous year.[17] Nor have rice prices declined much because of these recent changes; as we elaborate later, they have increased for some rice strains. Given overall consumer trends, however, it is very possible that rice prices will soon resume their downward trajectory. To prepare for that contingency, some prefectural governments are partnering with local co-ops to introduce their own voluntary, prefecturewide rice production targets.

Two features of the rice market that have not changed much over the years are high consumer standards and a complementary distribution system. These points were drummed into us during a conversation with Yoshida Yūji, the owner of a small rice shop in Tokyo's Minato Ward. Lodged at the front of his home and consumed by a rice polishing machine and piles of neatly stacked bags of rice, the shop has changed little since Yoshida's grandfather built it decades ago. One might have expected vendors like Yoshida to disappear following the mid-1990s repeal of the 1942 Staple Food Control Act and the subsequent diversification of rice retailing. But these tiny businesses continue to dot the city landscape. Yoshida explains why:

> I get all my rice from Shinmei, the rice wholesaler. I sell about 40 percent of it to households and the rest to local restaurants. These consumers have different needs. Housewives like to purchase their high-end rice from me rather than their local supermarket because they know it'll be fresh. They also prefer me to the internet because sometimes you get a bad bag, and no one wants the hassle of returning that heavy thing through the mail.
>
> Matching restaurants with the right kind of rice can be tricky. Chinese restaurants want drier rice that can be easily fried, and sushi shops need sticky rice. *Donburi* restaurants want rice that won't get mushy.[18] Farmers aren't always good at meeting these requirements, but I've got it down to a science. And I do all the polishing. It makes no sense for farmers to polish their own rice before sending it off. The equipment is expensive, and besides, rice loses freshness with each day it takes to travel from the farm to a restaurant's doorstep. And no restaurant in its right mind is going to invest in its own polisher. "Farm-to-table" may work for vegetables—restaurants, after all, can peel their own carrots—but it doesn't work for rice.

Businesses like mine may not be very profitable, but they survive because consumers are picky [urusai] about their rice. In fact, I'd say that nowhere else in the world is such a premium placed on a perfect product.[19]

Yoshida's business represents just one stage in a complex distribution system that simply adds to the consumer price of rice. But consumer standards are such that he will likely remain in business for years to come. Yoshida's place in the distribution system also symbolizes the limits of agricultural entrepreneurship. It is hard for the typical, small-scale, part-time rice farmer to reduce costs by selling directly to restaurants and other retailers; for the most part, that farmer must rely on well-established distribution systems.

Strategic Change in Rice-Centric Co-ops

The rice-market trends chronicled above are changing the relationship between JA's local multipurpose co-ops and their farmer-members. As lower rice prices complicate producer efforts to prop up their incomes and secure those all-important successors, some large-scale, entrepreneurial farmers are loosening their dependence on their local co-ops and contracting directly with rice wholesalers, processors, and restaurant chains. The co-ops know that to curb these defections, they must increase returns to farmers by lowering input prices and raising payments to farmers for their raw product. Unfortunately, the declining demand and price of rice can erase the gains of both strategies.

Rice-centric co-ops have three additional strategic options, each of which comes with a raft of challenges and trade-offs. First, they can help their members diversify away from rice by producing more fruits, vegetables, dairy, and/or livestock. The merits of this plus-alpha strategy include stronger consumer demand and more competitive prices for nonrice products and access to varying levels of government subsidies. Unfortunately, some regions simply do not have the soil or climactic conditions to do this successfully. The strategy also comes with a substantial learning curve and start-up costs, including those associated with preparing paddy fields for nonrice crops. And then there are the social risks. Switching to nonrice crops entails breaking away from communal irrigation systems and other infrastructural supports for rice production, as well as from the cooperative social networks that arise to maintain those systems—networks that often take years to develop and that in some communities are populated mostly by blood relations. Neighboring farmers, meanwhile, may end up bearing some of the costs of rerouting water flows. Many farmers—particularly older ones—would prefer to stick with rice than invite the opprobrium of their neighbors, not to mention the ostracism they might face should they seek reentry into those communal systems at some later date.

The second—and easier—strategy is to diversify within rice. Today, Japanese rice normally falls into one of three categories, the first two of which are known collectively as table rice: rice for household use (*kateiyōmai*), which is used by both households and high-end restaurants, and business rice (*gyōmuyōmai*) purchased by restaurant chains and other food preparation services, sake breweries, and the manufacturers of rice crackers (*sembei*) and other processed foods. The third category is feed rice (*shiryōyōmai*), which is fed to livestock.

Diversifying within rice has several advantages. The start-up costs and social risks are relatively low, since neither the soil nor the irrigation systems and other supporting infrastructure need to be significantly changed. Business rice and especially feed rice have higher yields than table rice, and both are easier to grow. Feed rice, moreover, is exempt from many of the standards governing agricultural chemicals (fertilizers, pesticides, and herbicides) that apply to table rice—hence its appeal to part-time farmers seeking to minimize their time in the paddies. And since both business rice and feed rice have shorter growing seasons than highly popular *koshihikari* and other types of household rice, entrepreneurial farmers have an easier time supplementing their rice with soybeans and other crops that can be grown in the same soil. Finally, feed rice—but not, before 2019, business rice—receives generous government subsidies.

The Abe government introduced feed rice subsidies to boost national food self-sufficiency levels—increasing feed rice production lessens dependence on corn imports from the United States[20]—following its abolition of the former Democratic Party of Japan (DPJ) government's (2009–2012) direct household income subsidies.[21] The subsidies are generous. Farmers who grow feed rice are eligible for direct subsidies (*chokusetsu shiharai kōfukin*) of up to 105,000 yen per 1,000 square meters and an additional 12,000 yen per 1,000 square meters if they grow high-yield varietals. In 2017, when the wholesale price of feed rice was just one-tenth that of business rice, these subsidies effectively closed the price gap.[22] In sum, today's farmers can make a decent living from feed rice.

The problem is that feed rice subsidies have triggered a major shortage of business rice since 2015 that is occurring even though business rice consumption has been steadily increasing over the last four decades as a proportion of total table rice consumed. These trends highlight not only the market-distorting effects of some types of government subsidies but also the fallacy that gentan's formal "abolition" marks the government's retreat from the rice market.[23] The shortage has also triggered spikes in business-rice prices and a concomitant sense of crisis within the restaurant, food processing, and retail industries.

What for buyers is a crisis is for farmers an opportunity to diversify into business-rice production. To secure optimal prices for business rice, farmers should ideally manage their output by setting production targets and prices through direct negotiations with corporate buyers. But most farmers lack bargaining power vis-à-vis processors, restaurants, and retail chains. And as the rice vendor Yoshida Yūji reminds us, it can be hard for farmers to meet the exacting standards of their buyers. The co-ops, however, can help bridge that gap by representing their farmer-members in the contract negotiation process.

The third strategy for rice-centric co-ops is the development of a high-priced, branded table rice—the ideal strategy for many co-ops. Nothing boosts the reputation of a co-op more than a good rice brand. Effective branding can also increase co-op incomes, although the long-term decline in rice prices has certainly offset some of those gains in many cases. And the reason for this strategy's appeal has to do with those high consumer standards: despite the overall decline in consumer demand, households appreciate high-quality table rice, and many are willing to pay for it.[24]

Rice branding is also the most challenging of the three rice-centric co-op strategies. Since the 2013 announcement of gentan's abolition, farmers and co-ops have scrambled to brand their top rice. There are 795 registered brands as of November 2018, an increase of 50 percent over the previous decade,[25] and vendors purchase manuals the size of telephone books to help keep track of them all. Only the tastiest koshihikari earns top prices in Japan, however, and few co-ops are able to produce it. Soil and climactic conditions must be optimal. And the co-ops must be sufficiently in control of the production process to ensure that all participating farmers generate raw product that is of consistently uniform quality. Even then, there is no guarantee that an entrepreneurial co-op can earn high prices in today's already saturated rice market. As we elaborate in our case studies, only co-ops with leaders who are skilled in the fine art of marketing have a chance to succeed. When it comes to strategies like branding and marketing, moreover, timing is key. Consider, for example, Mori no kumasan, an increasingly popular brand from Kumamoto Prefecture launched in 2000 that is known for its quality and lovable mascot—a black bear named Kumamon, a prefectural symbol. A 60 kg bag of unpolished Mori no kumasan earned on average just 14,514 yen in the wholesale market in 2018; this trailed the national average of 15,595 yen and was far less than the 20,782 yen earned by Uonumasan koshihikari, the industry leader that has been around for decades.[26]

As earlier chapters demonstrated, there is a growing consensus among Japanese agricultural stakeholders that good co-ops strive to increase, or at least stabilize, farmer incomes. This can be hard to do, given the pressures of aging farm populations, increasing market competition, and, in some cases, geographical handicaps. Thanks to those rice-market idiosyncrasies, the task is even harder for rice-centric co-ops. With only a few exceptions, the most these co-ops can hope for is to minimize the negative effects of these structural challenges.

Case Selection

To illustrate how rice-centric co-op strategies play out in practice and explain variations in their success, we turn to Niigata Prefecture—Japan's rice country. Niigata is the twelfth largest of the country's top fifteen agricultural prefectures in terms of production.[27] As of March 2018, all of Niigata's twenty-four local multipurpose co-ops focused predominantly on rice, but like local multipurpose co-ops more generally, some have been more successful than others in terms of earning top prices for farmers. We illustrate this in our analysis of two co-ops: JA Echigo Jōetsu and JA Uonuma Minami.

With 4,536 regular and 4,533 associate members, JA Uonuma Minami is much smaller than JA Echigo Jōetsu, which has 17,571 regular and 21,683 associate members. But in keeping with our observation in chapter 4 that large size does not necessarily translate into high agricultural performance, JA Uonomu Minami is considered Niigata's top co-op, and hence one of the nation's best, while JA Echigo Jōetsu struggles to do well by its members. This reputational discrepancy is underscored by differences in the amount marketed and handled (AMH—see chapter 4) per regular member in 2018: 1.099 million yen for JA Minami Uonuma and 664,000 yen for JA Echigo Jōetsu. There was also a significant gap between the two co-ops in terms of AMH profits per regular member: 44,530 yen for JA Minami Uonuma and 22,020 yen for JA Echigo Jōetsu. This performance does not, however, fully conform with our observation in chapter 4 that co-ops that put more money in the pockets of their members tend to have higher ratios of regular to associate members; while JA Echigo Jōetsu had both the lowest ratio (0.81) and the lowest financial returns to members of our four co-ops, JA Uonuma Minami had the second-lowest ratio (approximately 1.0) but the highest returns.

In addition to the differences in the financial performance indicators of these two co-ops, the similarities and differences in their strategies render them prime cases for comparative analysis. Both produce high-quality rice while simultaneously pursuing a mix of strategies to lower farmer risk and increase incomes— strategies that are necessitated by shrinking demand, increasing competition, and lower prices in the saturated rice market. Most notably, the two co-ops have branded their highest-quality rice—the most challenging of the three strategies. But while JA Echigo Jōetsu's top rice falls in the highest category of taste-test scores from the influential Japan Grain Inspection Association, it has yet to earn top prices.[28] JA Uonuma Minami's branded rice, by contrast, is by far Japan's most popular and expensive rice, and it has been so for many years.

We seek to explain these discrepancies between the two rice-centric co-ops by exploring the interplay of those three sets of variables that play a crucial role in shaping the outcomes of strategic reform in co-ops more generally: favorable growing conditions and corresponding market opportunities, farmer organization, and entrepreneurial agents of change. To these three universal variables, we add a fourth: the timing of reform. Timing matters in all co-ops that seek to corner markets through branding and sophisticated marketing strategies. But in the idiosyncratic Japanese rice market, as we shall see, it is especially important. Finally, we underscore the magnified importance of entrepreneurial agents of change in the form of highly skilled co-op leadership in rice-centric co-ops.

Our choice of cases is also influenced by differences in the co-ops' relationships with Zennō. Niigata co-ops have long depended on Zennō, but that dependence is waning. In 2005, 89.9 percent of all agricultural product was sold through the keitō; that figure declined to 76.7 percent in 2015 and to 71.9 percent in 2017.[29] JA Echigo Jōetsu is an example of a rice-centric co-op that continues to lean heavily on the keitō. JA Uonuma Minami, by contrast, depends on Zennō less than any other Niigata co-op. The story of how it achieved this degree of independence illuminates the challenges facing Zennō as it struggles to prevent further declines in its share of the rice market.

JA Uonuma Minami

Located along Niigata Prefecture's border with Gunma Prefecture, JA Uonuma Minami is a multipurpose local co-op with a small landmass and a big reputation.[30] Sandwiched between rolling hills to the west and the Echigo mountain range to the east, this co-op in the heart of Japan's snow country encompasses some 3,600 hectares of farmland, all but 600 hectares of which are paddy fields. From the fertility of the soil to the quality of the water supply and the temperatures during peak growing season, growing conditions here are ideal. This is where Minami Uonumasan koshihikari is grown, Japan's most famous—and expensive—brand of table rice.

The product of a merger between two co-ops in 2000, JA Uonuma Minami is the biggest rice producer among Niigata Prefecture's twenty-four co-ops. In 2018, the co-op's koshihikari yield for commercial purposes totaled 29,600 tons, or 15 percent of the 195,200 tons produced in the prefecture.[31] Over the past gen-

eration, the co-op has pursued several strategies to maximize the financial returns to its farmer-members. Like many conscientious co-ops, it strives to lower
farmer costs in part by purchasing many of its farm inputs directly from manufacturers, both domestic and foreign, rather than through Zennō. And as we
shall see, it has become highly adept at maximizing product sales at prices favorable to producers. Finally, the co-op has pursued two of the three rice-centric
co-op strategies introduced above. While as of this writing it sees no need to diversify within rice, it has achieved a degree of diversification away from rice.
Most significantly, its success in rice branding is unsurpassed.

Grown in every prefecture except Hokkaido and Okinawa, koshihikari is by
far Japan's top-selling table rice. It is planted in 35 percent of the country's rice
paddies, while the second most popular strain—*hitomebore*—is grown on just
9.2 percent of national paddy land.[32] In what may be the co-op's most significant set of operational rules, JA Uonuma Minami divides its koshihikari into
four quality-specific categories. In 2014, 75 percent of member rice qualified as
conventionally grown, or regular rice (*kankō saibai mai*), which is of high—but
not the best—quality. Twenty-four percent fell under two categories of special
rice (*tokubetsu saibai mai*), each of which relies on the reduced use of agricultural chemicals—one more than the other. Special rice earns the highest prices in
the country and is at the heart of the co-op's reputation. The final category—only
1 percent of the total—is organic rice,[33] which is completely free of agricultural
chemicals.[34]

JA Uonuma Minami has organized sections (*ka*) within the co-op that oversee these koshihikari grades and other co-op products and that serve as the main
point of contact with farmer-members. Of particular note is the Special Rice
Sales Section (Tokusan hanbai ka) devoted to that all-important special rice.
Membership in this section, which functions as a de facto foundational organization (kiso soshiki), is mandatory for farmers who wish to sell their best koshihikari through the co-op. And the membership is small, totaling just 240
households in 2014—less than 15 percent of the co-op's 3,400 member households.
(Those 240 households represented roughly 90 percent of farmer-members who
produced the rice; the remaining 10 percent marketed their product through
non-co-op channels.)

It is through the Special Rice Sales Section that JA Uonuma Minami plans
and executes its production strategies to ensure strict quality control. Co-op staff
are in close contact with their members in much the same way that agricultural
consultation (einō shidō) officers are with their local farmers (see next section),
but with one notable difference; whereas the business of agricultural consultation is often an improvisational affair designed to help farmers with the basics,
the staff of the co-op's Special Rice Sales Section work with highly skilled farmers

and according to a carefully prepared script. Farmers have access to detailed manuals on co-op-wide standards for everything from cultivating seedlings to weeding and the harvest. And technology is prioritized—high-tech tractors and other sophisticated devices that help optimize and standardize production across different plot sizes and other variant conditions in this cold, snowy corner of the country.

In a revealing illustration of the fallacy of equating good farming only with full-time, large-scale farms, most farmers who belong to the Special Rice Sales Section are part-time cultivators with average-sized plots. Few farmers, moreover, have incorporated their farms. Although incorporation makes it easier for farms to share ownership of sophisticated machinery, many traditional family farms balk at the legal requirement that family members who work the paddies only part-time be put on the "company" payroll—an impractical and costly requirement in a region where the growing season is just a few weeks long. A few farms belong to hamlet-based farm associations (shūraku einō), but they do so voluntarily; in contrast to JA Echigo Jōetsu, neither local and prefectural governments nor the co-op have pushed for its approximately three hundred constituent hamlets to participate in these arrangements. For JA Uonuma Minami's best farmers, the primary point of organized contact with the co-op is the Special Rice Sales Section. And the proof of the section's ability to ensure farmer conformity with the co-op's operational rules is in the quality of the farmers themselves. "The abilities of our farmers have really increased over the last ten to twenty years," noted Kaneko Kunio, one of the section's high-ranking officers, in 2014. "And we attribute that to our section's promotion of sophisticated technologies, those manuals, and other ongoing efforts to help educate the producer."[35]

JA Uonuma Minami's top growers defy our intuitive assumptions about what goes into an entrepreneurial farmer mindset. In a sense, growers resemble the passive producers of old in terms of their small size, part-time orientation, focus on rice, and preference for traditional forms of family management (kazoku keiei—see chapter 2). But these farmers are anything but passive producers. As evidenced by their willingness to adhere to high cultivation standards and to defect to non-co-op rice wholesalers, they prioritize their incomes and take pride in their work as much as larger-scale, full-time entrepreneurial farmers. The fact that area farmers learned to be this way, as Kaneko's comments suggest, is testament to the co-op's top-down leadership and organizational skills.

In sum, JA Uonuma Minami's farmer-members are positioned to produce high-quality rice—rice that looks good, smells good, and tastes good. But other co-ops are learning to do this as well. Even Kaneko will admit that the differences in quality among Japan's top rice brands are miniscule; what distinguishes one from another, he admits, are consumer taste preferences and cooking methods. Clearly, the secrets to Minami Uonumasan's market dominance extend beyond the area's optimal growing conditions and the co-op's high standards and effective organization of participating farmers.

The success of Minami Uonumasan also rests in the timing of the co-op's branding efforts. Among the first co-ops to brand its high-end koshihikari rice—it launched production during the mid-1950s—JA Uonuma Minami earned something of a first mover advantage. Since then, the co-op has worked hard to preserve the brand's quality and reputation in the face of mounting competition, thus earning it the nation's highest possible prices—year after year. Six municipalities in Niigata Prefecture produce the Uonumasan brand of koshihikari table rice, and two of them are located in JA Uonuma Minami. Since it introduced its ranking system in 1989, the Japan Grain Inspection Association has awarded that brand the highest taste scores in all but one year (2017). The brand also earns the highest wholesale prices; it pulled in 19,597 yen per 60 kg bag in 2015, 2,721 yen more than its closest competitor, and 20,782 yen per bag in 2018—fully 5,187 yen more than the national average.[36] But if Uonumasan is considered Japan's top rice, the co-op's contribution—Minami Uonumasan—to that brand is considered the best of the best. And when JA Uonuma Minami sells its best rice under a separate label, it earns even more than Uonumasan.

Translating that first-mover advantage into consistently high prices over the years owes much to the marketing skills of co-op staff members like Kaneko. Long before the 2015 amendments to the 1947 Co-op Law required co-ops to include individuals with professional skills on their boards of directors, JA Uonuma Minami was pulling precisely these sorts of individuals into its ranks. Kaneko, for instance, worked for a luxury department store before joining the co-op as an employee. His arrival was not without controversy. How, skeptics asked, could someone with no farming experience help run an agricultural co-op? The answer, Kaneko explains, is that he knows how to sell rice.

Selling rice in ways that maximize farmer incomes is a tricky business. As we noted in chapter 4, the dominant custom has long been for Japanese farmers to hand whatever rice they produce to their local co-op, which then pools it and sends it up the keitō. Farmers receive an advance payment (*kariwatashikin*) from JA, and then the co-op adjusts those payments once prices are finalized.[37] The problem with unconditional consignment sales (mujōken itaku hanbai), however, is that it can shoulder a co-op with a short-term oversupply of rice. When this happens, the co-op stockpiles what it cannot send up the keitō or sell directly to market and tries to sell it the following year as old rice (*komai*)—or the year after that as very old rice (*kokomai*)—to food processors. Since the older the rice, the lower the price, one would think that the co-op would get rid of as much of the old rice as possible to make room for the sale of coveted new rice (*shinmai*). But not so. Selling off too much old rice can eat into overall demand for new rice.

A co-op that bypasses Zennō must also weigh the interests of rice wholesalers in its marketing strategies by taking care not to overload them with too much old or new rice. For if the wholesalers find themselves with more rice than they can sell downstream in any given year, they may very well purchase less rice from the co-op the following year, thereby increasing co-op stockpiles (assuming, of course, a good harvest). Kaneko notes that if wholesalers were transparent about their anticipated sales and stockpiles, the co-op could plan accordingly. But few wholesalers divulge this kind of information. The best a co-op like JA Uonuma Minami can do is estimate what its wholesalers have on their hands at any given time and work closely with its farmer-members through the relevant co-op sections to adjust production accordingly. Needless to say, this requires a high degree of skill.

JA Uonuma Minami opted long ago to alleviate these marketing challenges by handling much of its rice via the buy-up sales (kaitori hanbai) method, which involves direct contracting with private-sector buyers. The trick is to negotiate both the supply and price of rice with wholesalers or corporate customers before seedlings are planted. To fulfill those contracts without adding to rice stockpiles, the co-ops work closely with its farmer-members through the requisite organizations to produce only the targeted amounts. The fact that JA Minami Uonuma reduced its dependence on Zennō's rice collection, marketing, and sales services to less than 10 percent by 2018 is evidence of its skills in the contracting game.[38]

The co-op works with a variety of different corporate customers. Around 2007, for instance, it began partnering with the Aeon Group, the conglomerate of retail and financial services based in Chiba Prefecture that is best known for its nationwide chain of supermarkets. It later forged a series of contracts with Ito-Yokado, a rival supermarket chain; luckily for the co-op, the ensuing competition between the two chains for its top rice helped keep prices high. But while the co-op welcomed the efficiency and predictability that these contracts brought to the production process, Kaneko and his colleagues worried that its corporate buyers would collude with one another to force a decrease in prices. Since JA Uonuma Minami lacked the size and hence bargaining power to counter such a move, it hired private wholesalers to act as middlemen between itself and its corporate customers—wholesalers that have the market presence to help keep prices high.

The diversification of JA Uonuma Minami's corporate customers goes beyond supermarket chains. To cite just one example, the co-op now supplies the rice that Japan Airlines (JAL) serves to its first- and business-class passengers on international flights. JAL had been purchasing Niigata koshihikari from trading companies and department stores since 2005 but in 2012 started dealing exclusively—and directly—with JA Uonuma Minami.[39] The relationship helps stabilize demand for the co-op's top brand and has enormous advertising benefits; first- and business-class airline passengers are, after all, precisely the demographic with the means to purchase Japan's most expensive rice. Meanwhile, the co-op has been moving aggressively to market its rice overseas, most notably to high-end retailers in cities in Taiwan, Hong Kong, Singapore, and other wealthy East Asian countries.

Kaneko is not averse to sending a small portion of JA Uonuma Minami's rice through the keitō. Zennō can be trusted to deliver on its obligations. And it will purchase the co-op's rice even if there is a decline in quality, a development that would constitute a breach of contract for the co-op's high-end corporate customers. Most significantly, the co-op now has leverage over Zennō. "Since we know how to sell our best rice through private channels," Kaneko explains, "we are in a position to get top prices from Zennō. Zennō needs our rice for its more discriminating buyers; if it cannot promise to pay up, we can always go elsewhere."[40]

But even though Zennō has been taking steps to entice Niigata co-ops to remain within the keitō fold, JA Uonuma Minami clearly prefers those alternative routes to market. Consider, for instance, the drawbacks of selling rice to Zennō using the unconditional consignment sale method. "Zennō has been doing a lot more recently to increase the prices it pays to co-ops through this method," Kaneko explains, "but it is not doing enough to manage its inventories. This means that even if we get a high price one year, Zennō may buy less from us the following year."[41] Taking its cue from the growth in independent contract sales by JA Uonuma Minami and a few other prefectural co-ops, Zennō, in 2012, started purchasing some of its rice via advance contracts with Niigata co-ops. While this is a step in the right direction, Kaneko observes, the co-op still expects to earn higher prices through the private market.

When we focus just on its rice-branding strategy, JA Uonuma Minami is a very good co-op.[42] In terms of putting money into the pockets of its farmers, it compares exceptionally well to other co-ops. Nevertheless, the co-op faces difficult challenges—the same sorts of challenges that confront rice producers around the country. First, while the co-op secures higher prices for its top rice brands than any other co-op, it, too, is feeling the effects of declining rice prices over time. That 20,000-plus yen per 60 kg bag of unpolished koshihikari rice that it earned for its farmers in 2015? This was roughly half what it earned in 1995.

The co-op has taken steps to hedge against the long-term decline in the demand for and price of rice. First, it constantly introduces measures to ensure the consistent production of high-quality rice. As we have seen, it remains in close contact with participating farmer-members and encourages the use of high-tech devices during the production process. It has equipped its two country elevators with sophisticated cooling and monitoring equipment. It pours resources into the inspection and classification of raw product.[43] And it participates in collaborative efforts to improve production. For example, it cooperated with the MAFF and other co-ops that market Uonumasan rice to produce the March 2007 Uonuma Rice Charter (Uonumamai kenshō), a set of production guidelines for achieving the highest possible product standards and prices.[44]

Second, the co-op participates in campaigns to help boost the demand for rice. As early as 1992, the co-op partnered with the Minami Uonuma City government to encourage local schools to purchase—with the help of government subsidies—higher-quality koshihikari rice for their school lunch programs. The co-op figured that if the 4,900 school-age children in the municipality were to be served its rice four times a week, it would have a secure outlet for sixty-five tons of rice per year. The co-op partnered with the municipality once again in 2013 to introduce a "koshihikari ordinance." Based on the recognition that even consumers living in the heart of rice country are drifting away from rice (kome banare), the ordinance promotes rice for breakfast, as well as in school lunches.[45]

Third, the co-op seeks to add value and accessibility to its top brands. It developed new technologies to ensure bacteria-free packaging. It built a facility in Los Angeles that steams, flash freezes, and then transports high-end rice to area school lunch programs. And the co-op is adjusting its marketing techniques to address the specific needs of the growing demographic of older consumers; these include the expansion of farmers' markets in areas that serve the elderly, express delivery options for distant customers, and the like.

The above examples all speak to JA Uonuma Minami's efforts to support its branded table rice. But there are two other broad strategies open to it as it hedges against future market pressures: diversifying within and away from rice. The co-op has taken a pass on the first strategy, and for understandable reasons; given the excellent performance of its koshihikari table rice, there is simply no pressing need to produce lesser strains.[46] But it is still an open question whether the co-op can continue to convince its farmer-members to remain loyal to koshihikari. As we have seen, the demand for lesser strains for use by chain restaurants and food processors is now on the rise. And there are strong incentives in place for farmers to move into feed-rice production. In 2014, once gentan's days were numbered, Kaneko predicted that the national government's introduction of generous subsidies for feed-rice production would tempt many area farmers away from koshihikari. He dreads the thought: "I would rather see farmers make our high-quality table rice at a lower price than get a comparable subsidy for feed rice, even though that lower-quality rice is much easier to grow. But I know that many farmers will disagree!"[47]

JA Uonuma Minami has, however, been diversifying away from rice. It is now Niigata Prefecture's second-largest grower of watermelons, distributing 450,000 of them in 2014 alone; the melons are known for their unusual sweetness—a result, the co-op boasts, of the region's daily temperature swings during the summer.[48] And the co-op has made a success of shiitake mushrooms. Area farmers have been producing shiitake since 1984, when a co-op employee partnered with eight part-time rice farmers in search of an off-season (i.e., winter) project that would avert the need for off-farm employment beyond the prefecture. Despite some setbacks, including competition from cheaper Chinese imports, the venture gained traction with the co-op's strong support;[49] a JA Uonuma Minami subsidiary operates the hothouses in which the mushrooms are grown, as well as a center established in 2013 for the cultivation of mushroom spores. As of 2017, shiitake composed 26 percent (or 1.38 billion yen) of the total products marketed and handled by the co-op (5.40 billion yen). But at 58 percent (or 3.11 billion yen), rice remains by far the co-op's dominant product.[50]

In 2016, JA Uonuma Minami concluded a preliminary agreement with its neighbor to the south, JA Shiozawa, to merge on March 1, 2019. The expanded co-op, now known as JA Minami Uonuma, remains headquartered in the city of the same name and is the eleventh largest of Niigata's now twenty-three multipurpose co-ops in terms of membership.[51] JA Shiozawa had considered merging with JA Uonuma Minami in 2000, only to retreat for fear of tarnishing the reputation of its successful mushroom industry. The farmers and co-op staff who produced and marketed Minami Uonumasan harbored similar concerns. Would the postmerger co-op lose its control over product quality? And would unqualified farmers try to lay claim to the label?[52] Other co-op leaders saw things differently; in the context of a relentlessly shrinking farm population, concomitant successor shortage, and declining consumer demand, merging would help shore up co-op resources, improve the efficiency of services, and encourage product diversification.[53] In a professed signal of its commitment to farmer welfare that no doubt did more to placate its nervous staff, the newly-merged co-op opted to retain all of its combined employees.[54] Meanwhile, JA Uonomua Minami's growing success with mushroom production likely reassured JA Shiozawa of its commitment to quality.

The postmerger co-op is now in the throes of a Niigatawide discussion on the merits of more mergers. In November 2018, Niigata's agricultural cooperative union (chūōkai) formally resolved to reduce the number of local co-ops in the prefecture to just five—one per region[55]—by 2024 and has established a special committee to that effect. The goal may prove elusive. Co-op mergers require the approval of at least two-thirds of each participating co-op's general assembly (sōkai), which represents farmer-members. But Niigata farmers are proud and competitive. They have a keen sense of what distinguishes the quality of their products from those of farmers next door, and they are loath to see their co-ops cede control over their production and management strategies to a larger, more distant entity.[56]

The events of 2017—JA Uonuma Minami's annus horribilis—are likely to fuel both sides of the debate. That year, Uonumasan koshihikari lost its top rating from the Japan Grain Inspection Association for the first time since 1989. The ostensible culprit: bad weather.[57] But it was also revealed that JA Uonuma Minami and other contributing co-ops were mixing their top rice with inferior strains.[58] These actions are not illegal, but they violate consumer expectations at a time when the number of—and competition between—regional brands increases. The resulting scandal prompted a co-op-wide reassessment of its production strategies and a commitment to greater transparency;[59] despite record-high temperatures in the summer of 2018, Uonumasan quickly regained its top rating. For local farmers, events like these are proof that good co-ops must remain in close contact with their members if they are to ensure product quality and serve farmers; increasing the size of co-ops through further mergers would defeat this goal. But from the vantage point of many co-op leaders, 2017 underscores the importance of creating economies of scale and further professionalizing the co-op. It remains to be seen how this debate will ultimately be resolved.

JA Echigo Jōetsu

Located in Niigata Prefecture's Jōetsu City not too far from the Japan Sea coastline,[60] Sanwa is a city ward that in May 2018 had 5,622 residents, forty-six hamlets (shūraku),[61] and forty-four full-time and many more part-time rice-farming households. From the looks of it, the area is thriving; the roads are wide and freshly paved, and the lush, flat paddies are neat and evenly apportioned. But the future of farming in Sanwa is uncertain. More than two decades of falling rice prices have made it harder for farmers to earn a good living. Farms in Sanwa and surrounding farm communities tend to be fairly small, and many farmers struggle to find successors. And there has long been a high risk in the area that farmers who retire will abandon their land.[62]

To address these challenges, the local co-op, JA Echigo Jōetsu, and the municipal government have encouraged land consolidation through leasing. Once uniformly tiny, many Sanwa farms are now fairly large by Japanese and especially Niigata standards; at least five households have holdings of thirty hectares or more, while the number of farms with ten hectares or more is increasing. In compliance with national government policy, moreover, there has been a push to concentrate more land in the hands of certified farmers (nintei nōgyōsha), who, as we saw in chapter 3, are eligible for special government subsidies. In 2018, all of Sanwa's full-time and twenty-two of its part-time farm households were certified, and roughly half of them had expanded their holdings through leasing. Certified farmers now control about 60 percent of the ward's total farmland.

Since the 1970s, and particularly between 1994 and 2012, Sanwa has been a major beneficiary of Niigata Prefecture's penchant for land improvement projects—hence the area's excellent infrastructure, evenly shaped rice paddies and good drainage systems, and improved soil fertility.[63] To ensure that users remained good stewards of these structural changes, the prefecture made the receipt of certain subsidies contingent on farmer participation in hamlet-based farm associations (shūraku einō, or HBFAs). Farm households and their HBFAs were also encouraged to incorporate, again in the understanding that their eligibility for subsidies would increase.

Despite these efforts to improve the productivity of local agricultural lands, the successor shortage in Sanwa and neighboring communities persists.

Kikuchi Sadao's experiences as one of Sanwa's full-time, certified farmers illustrate both the opportunities and challenges of farming in the area. Kikuchi hails from a farm household, but like many others of his generation, he turned his back on the family business after graduating from college and went to work for a firm in Nagoya. After the 1973 oil shock halved his salary, he returned to the family farm, eventually inheriting a combine and 2.2 hectares of paddy land. Since the combine was more than he needed for such a small plot, he launched a small business to rent it out to rice farmers in the northern part of neighboring Nagano Prefecture. He did all the extra work himself but soon tired of it. Nagano during the 1970s and early 1980s had yet to undergo significant land improvements, and the uneven, eel-shaped paddies—many of them carved precariously out of the sides of hills and mountains—made for taxing, even dangerous work. Kikuchi gave up his combine-renting service, only to indulge his entrepreneurial spirit by purchasing a small sake brewery.

Kikuchi's passion is his farm. Over the years, he gradually increased his holdings to fourteen hectares of farmland, two of which he leases from neighboring farmers. He is the largest farmer in his hamlet, controlling 80 percent of its total farmland. Unlike most farmers in Sanwa, however, Kikuchi does not belong to an HBFA, but this is not for lack of trying. The law requires a minimum of five farmers with a combined total of twenty hectares or more to form this type of cooperative arrangement, but there are only two other farmers in the hamlet besides himself, both owning tiny plots and one getting on in years. Nor has Kikuchi incorporated his farm. Incorporation would have allowed him to hire outside labor, but he dreads the required paperwork. Kikuchi admits that it is tough tending to fourteen hectares on his own, but he makes a decent living from his one-man show. He is careful to update his machinery; some years ago, he sold his combine and replaced it with four smaller, task-specific tractors that are easier to operate and cheaper to repair. And he strives to maximize his profits. By any measure, he lives up to his personal motto of "Farm as if you are in America," save for one thing; he struggles to increase his holdings—and hence his farm's efficiency—to twenty hectares.[64] The problem, he explains, is that none of his neighbors are ready to give up their land.

As the price of rice dropped after the mid-1990s and demand continued to decline, many farmers in Kikuchi's area gradually faced the difficult truth that rice was no longer the ticket to a prosperous lifestyle. But despite incentives to diversify, including those provided under gentan, many Sanwa hamlets were slow to jump on the rice-plus-alpha bandwagon. Sanwa had always been about rice, and the community's land-improvement projects were largely predicated on that fact. By the early 2000s, however, local farmers were shifting gears. With the support of the prefectural and city governments, some began to diversify away from rice by cultivating soybeans, buckwheat, cucumbers, and other vegetables that can be grown in hothouses; winter vegetables like daikon radishes, carrots, cabbage, and leeks; and edamame—young soybeans contained in their pods that are a popular mainstay of Japanese bars and restaurants.

Kikuchi was eager to start cultivating edamame, but preparing Sanwa paddy land proved a major undertaking. The problem was too much clay in the soil. Clay, which retains water, may be acceptable—if not optimal—for wet-rice cultivation, but it is bad for most other crops; too much of it, and the plants will drown. To solve the problem, during the 2010s the prefectural and city governments embarked on another round of land improvement, or in this case, plot preparation (*hojō seibi*), trucking in massive amounts of topsoil to cover a select number of paddies that had been cleared of clay. Only farmers like Kikuchi, with ten hectares or more of farmland, were eligible to receive the replacement soil and its accompanying subsidies.

Kikuchi has to carefully rotate his crops, since the edamame can quickly deplete the soil of essential nutrients. Only two of his fourteen hectares have been devoted to edamame, which he grows between May and August. In September, he plants buckwheat and, the following year, business rice for his sake brewery. He devotes his remaining twelve hectares to koshihikari. Planting buckwheat on the heels of the edamame crop makes good sense, he explains, since buckwheat is easy to cultivate and can be harvested in just a few weeks. And it is important to follow the buckwheat with rice, since flooding the fields in preparation for rice seedlings will eliminate any stray pieces of buckwheat that have fallen from his tractor during harvesting and lodged in the soil. All in all, Kikuchi is pleased with this arrangement and is doing well financially. His diversification venture also marks a major departure from custom in the area, where the long winters and the fixation on rice mean just one crop per year for most farmers.

Kikuchi illustrates how rice farmers can successfully diversify both within and away from rice. Nevertheless, his farm faces a precarious future. His farmland is now worth just a quarter of its value during the early 2000s. And Kikuchi has no successor lined up: "I have no children. And I have no idea who, if anyone, is going to buy my farm from me. I'm in no rush, though. I'm only sixty-eight, and I plan to keep working for at least another ten years. There's no need to start looking for a successor until I'm closer to retirement. Until then, why bother incorporating my farm? Look at all the farms around here that have incorporated; hardly any of them have successors! Why go to all that trouble—for nothing?"[65]

Sanwa rice farmers have options to market their products independently of JA. Kubota Nōki, one of Japan's leading farm equipment manufacturers, has a wholesaling subsidiary in the area that collects unpolished rice (*genmai*) and ships it to Southeast Asia; before the rice reaches the market, the firm's wholly owned, rice-polishing facilities in the region strip it of its outer layers. Niigata farmers who contract with Kubota Nōki can expect a price for their raw product that is roughly 20 percent higher than what the local co-op offers. But few farmers take this route. Even larger-scale, diversified farmers like Kikuchi, who has the economy of scale and profitability to shoulder more risk, are deterred by the independent distributor's strict quality standards and refusal to offer long-term contracts. Kikuchi admits that his advancing age also fuels his hesitation.

Kikuchi, like so many of his neighbors, is a JA man.[66] He purchases all of his farm machinery and other inputs through the Sanwa branch of JA Echigo Jōetsu and sells all of his rice, buckwheat, and edamame to the co-op, where it is pooled with the raw product of other farmer-members. Kikuchi values the security that comes with the co-op's implicit guarantee to buy his output for as long as he remains a regular co-op member. And he has no complaints about how the co-op has treated him. JA Echigo Jōetsu has undergone numerous mergers over the years, he explains, but as far as he can tell, those mergers have yet to adversely affect the quality of service at his branch.

Bordering the coastline in the southwest corner of the prefecture, JA Echigo Jōetsu is Niigata's largest multipurpose cooperative. Formed in 2001 through the merger of seven co-ops, it covers two cities: Jōetsu, where co-op headquarters are located, and Myōkō. As of March 2018, the co-op has 17,571 regular (farmer) members, nearly three times the prefectural average, and it encompasses 1,418 square kilometers of agricultural and nonagricultural land. It is not as farmer-centric as JA Uonuma Minami; like most co-ops today, its associate member-ship (21,683) surpasses that of its regular members by a significant margin. JA Echigo Jōetsu has a large staff: 706 full-time and 481 part-time employees, many of whom work in the co-op's nonagricultural services. And it encompasses twenty-four branch offices, many of which were once the headquarters of pre-merger co-ops, and one small outpost (*shutchōjo*) staffed by a few part-time staff and seventy local agricultural consulting (einō shidō) officers.

As befits a Niigata co-op, rice is at the co-op's core. As of March 2018, 9.98 billion yen of the 11.67 billion yen of agricultural product (86 percent) collected and marketed by the co-op came from rice. Livestock totaled 0.48 billion, and fruits and vegetables, 0.36 billion.

Like JA Uonuma Minami, JA Echigo Jōetsu has been caught up in prefecture-wide talks to create a single co-op for Niigata. Co-op employees and farmers are lukewarm to the idea. The co-op is already large, they complain, and this complicates the close farmer-co-op communications needed to successfully adapt to changing market conditions. As the size of the co-op increases, would it continue to staff local branches with skilled, full-time employees who can ef-fectively meet the specific needs of local farmers? Since one of the purposes of mergers is to cut costs, would those employees get paid enough?

These questions weigh heavily on the minds of employees who work in the co-op's agricultural consultation services. Offered gratis to farmers, the services are a money loser for most co-ops. But no good co-op can afford to neglect them, argues Inoue Yoshifumi, a retired JA Echigo Jōetsu staff member and agricultural consul-tant who now works part-time for the co-op. Consultants, he explains, work on-site to help farmers—particularly those without farmhands—with everything from planting to the harvest. As the consultants work alongside farmers, they chat—about insects, weeds, quality control, good management practices, farm profitability. Cynics may claim that this intense co-op-farmer interaction is a sub-terfuge for persuading farmer-members to buy JA inputs and sell their raw product through co-op networks, but Inoue sees things differently. Agricultural consultation helps farmers learn about best practices at a time when farm manage-ment is becoming increasing technical and complex. And it builds farmer trust in the co-op, which is essential if the co-op is to meet individual farmer needs. As co-ops merge, many are cutting back on consultation or staffing the services with part-time and/or inexperienced employees. Others are centralizing consultation in one or a handful of consultation centers in their jurisdictions. But as Inoue ex-plains, these centers are only effective if farmers take the trouble to visit them. Most visitors, however, are farmers like Kikuchi who already know what they are doing. Others are unaware of the challenges they face or of strategies for widening their profit margins; these are the farmers, argues Inoue, who justify the continuation of routine farm visits by local co-op consultants.

As it embarks on strategic reform, JA Echigo Jōetsu is determined to strengthen these close, individualized ties with farmers. It has also made organizational changes at the co-op-wide level. Some fifteen years ago, the co-op established a management committee (keiei kanri iinkai) that operates alongside—and selects the members of—the co-op's board of directors (rijikai), which runs the day-to-day operations of the co-op. Some co-ops tried and failed to make this two-tiered governance structure work, but as the co-op veteran and committee head Aoki Katsuaki explains, the system works well in JA Echigo Jōetsu's case: "We view the relationship among the various members of the co-op in a very holistic way. Our farmer-members are the co-op's hands. The board of directors and the staff are its feet. And the management committee, which includes a few farmer-members, is the brains of the operation. It is primarily in the management committee that we formulate and implement strategies designed to maximize co-op and farmer returns in response to the changing domestic market."[67]

In sum, JA Echigo Jōetsu has worked within the guidelines established by the Co-op Law to devise a governance system that helps maximize the in-house production and management expertise that is required for the design and implementation of the many operational rules that shape co-op strategies. And in the context of declining consumer demand for rice, the co-op has pursued all three of the hedging strategies open to rice-centric co-ops. First, it is encouraging farmers to diversify away from rice. Like the farmers it serves, JA Echigo Jōetsu was slow to initiate this strategy, but by the early 2000s, it was an enthusiastic promoter of edamame and other vegetable production. It helped implement prefectural and local government plans for the replacement of paddy soil, and its agricultural consultants and other branch employees worked closely with farmers to help them grow high-quality products. To facilitate more organized interaction with its farmer-members, the co-op recently established a special sales section just for horticulture and livestock that connects to corresponding foundational organizations—producers' associations—at the grassroots level.[68] It also cooperates with local government to open up new sales routes and promotes the establishment of farm-to-table restaurants as part of the nationwide trend toward local production for local consumption (chisan chishō). These services are essential to many farmers in today's economy, for as Aoki observes, "Farmers are pros at growing things, but they are amateurs at marketing!"[69] So far, vegetable and livestock sales have been on the uptick, but there is still room for improvement; in FY 2017, the co-op's 70 million yen in edamame earnings fell 30 percent short of its goal.

Second, JA Echigo Jōetsu has been striving to promote its high-end brand of koshihikari rice, Echigojōetsumai. Since 2013, the brand has consistently earned the highest possible marks for quality and taste from the Japan Grain Inspection Association.[70] But Echigojōetsumai has failed to secure prices on par with those of other comparable leading brands, a problem it attributes to weak name recognition. To rectify this, the co-op recently launched a new advertising campaign led by a mascot named Ekomorin, an anthropomorphized, snowy-white grain of rice with rosy cheeks and a bow in her hair. Ekomorin appears on the co-op's website and promotional literature, and life-sized versions of her show up at department stores and events around Niigata and beyond. As of this writing, however, Ekomorin has yet to generate the kind of brand loyalty that translates into higher prices. Aoki explains why:

> The media expects us to have a mascot these days. But it's not doing much for us. Part of the problem is that most of JA Echigo Jōetsu's koshihikari is sold to Zennō and then wholesalers, and wholesalers couldn't care less about mascots; they're interested in buying rice that's of consistently good quality and that will sell well. Another challenge we face is generational. Younger people don't eat much rice nowadays, and fewer and fewer cook it themselves. But if you don't cook your own rice, you're not going to pay much attention to brands. Finally, we face strong competition from JA Uonuma Minami, which has been branding its rice for years. Once a brand gets stuck in consumers' heads, it's hard to drive it out of them.
>
> Because of all this, we pour most of our effort into getting higher ratings on taste tests and clinching better prices in the market. One advantage we have in this co-op is that we grow a very high volume of rice, which gives us more negotiating power.[71]

The high name recognition of—and respect for—both JA Echigo Jōetsu and Aoki Katsuaki in the Japanese co-op world is evidence enough that this is a co-op led by highly skilled leaders who work hard for farmer-members. Nevertheless, one gets the sense that things could be better in terms of generating higher returns to farmers. Arriving late to the diversification and branding games is one possible reason for this. This timing issue, in turn, may be symptomatic of the need for soil improvements in parts of the co-op's jurisdiction a generation ago. The high clay content in Sanwa Ward's soils was a major impediment to the cultivation of the best vegetables and rice—the kinds of products that could command top prices from Japan's demanding consumers. The fact that the co-op and local and prefectural governments took it upon themselves to rectify the problem in Sanwa and other affected communities in the co-op speaks to their foresight and commitment to farmers. But as Kikuchi observes, the time to diversify into nonrice products was the 1970s, after gentan was launched; perhaps then, he argues, the co-op could have established a stronger competitive edge in these products. As for rice, the co-op should have debuted Ekomorin and its other branding efforts a generation ago rather than during the 2010s.

Our interviews also suggest that despite the presence of skilled leadership at the co-op-wide level, there may be a disconnect between JA Echigo Jōetsu headquarters and at least some local branches in the introduction of new strategies, as Inoue's musings illustrate:

> Right now, our branch is about to participate in yet another co-op-wide survey of certified farmers in the area. Look at the pile of surveys on that desk over there. So much work for our busy staff, and particularly the secretaries! But nothing much ever comes of these things. Once the co-op tallies the results, there's never much discussion about how to increase profits, plan for the future, or that sort of thing. These surveys are a colossal waste of time.
>
> There's not enough leadership in this co-op. Take my work in agricultural consultation. There is no manual for what we do. We have to learn the ropes as we go along. Some of this is to be expected, since every farmer's needs are different. But it would be nice to have more guidance in this job.
>
> This business of self-reform that Prime Minister Abe and his government are promoting? It's all just talk down here. Sure, sometimes guys from co-op headquarters or the prefectural level [of JA] will come down to talk to us about new ideas, and they'll give us a bunch of numbers, but our branch doesn't know what to do with all that. Nobody here knows much about marketing. None of us has been to business school! Abe wants us all to become management consultants for our farmers. But how are we supposed to do that without the proper tools?[72]

This organizational disconnect between co-op headquarters and at least some of its branches may very well be the product of too many mergers over the years; the co-op, in other words, appears too big to manage. There is also evidence that farmers are not always organized to optimize co-op strategies. Yes, farmers who now grow vegetables have been grouped into producers' associations that are linked to a special section in co-op headquarters. But for many rice producers, one of the main points of organizational contact with the co-op is those hamlet-based farm associations that were formed with government and co-op assistance as a byproduct of land-improvement efforts in decades past. These are not the ideal settings for nurturing active, entrepreneurial farmers, since many of the management decisions of farm households—usually small-scale, part-time, and aging households—are subcontracted to HBFA managers. As our interviewees confided, moreover, many HBFA managers have little to no training in business management. As such, the HBFAs seem to be reinforcing more traditional farmer mindsets—passive producers who pour their energies into the straightforward task of cultivation and neglect the management skills that are essential to profitable businesses.

Nevertheless, there are clear signs that this co-op continues to change. Most notably, the co-op has recently embraced the third strategy of rice-centric co-ops: diversification within rice. Recognizing the limitations of koshihikari in today's domestic market, the co-op, since 2015, has been helping interested farmer-members produce less rice for household and high-end restaurant consumption and more rice for feed and business use. By 2018, the co-op was supplying about 25 percent of all the feed rice produced in Niigata.[73] The real challenge, though, lies in the production of business rice.

JA Echigo Jōetsu farmers were initially skittish about growing business rice. As noted earlier, business rice prices are volatile, and farmers are well aware that they can earn a good, more stable income growing heavily subsidized feed rice. Buyers, for their own part, are not always keen to purchase business rice from Niigata Prefecture, which has long been associated with koshihikari. Undeterred, JA Echigo Jōetsu began venturing into business-rice production following the announcement of gentan's abolition and shifted into high gear by 2016 once it was clear that business rice was in short supply. The co-op developed new strains of high-yield business rice (*koshiibuki*, *tsukiakari*, and *mizuho no kagayaki*) that can be produced relatively cheaply. It also launched a sophisticated contracting system. Following the 2017 harvest, the co-op collected information about future demand from Zennō and several dozen private buyers, drew up its own demand estimates, and then submitted individualized shipment volume requests (*shukka irai sūryō sho*) to participating farmers. Based on farmer feedback, the co-op concluded preliminary sales contracts with buyers and finalized them at planting. The scheme effectively calibrated business-rice production to market demand and generated virtually no rice stockpiles. Meanwhile, koshihikari's share of the total volume of rice collected and sold by the co-op has been decreasing, dropping by several points to 45 percent by 2018.[74] Farmland devoted to the contracted production of business rice grew during that same period from 57 hectares to 671 hectares and is expected to increase further.[75]

While the timing of JA Echigo Jōetsu's foray into product diversification and rice branding may have been off, the fact that the co-op is setting prefectural standards for business-rice production suggests that it has grown more adept at recognizing and responding to new, price-making market opportunities; in the words of one co-op representative, JA Echigo Jōetsu is shifting from "selling what is produced" to "producing what will sell."[76] This positive development is unlikely to make much of a dent in the severe successor shortage that plagues farm communities like Sanwa. But for now, the co-op's price-making strategy promises to put a little more money in the pockets of aging farmers.

To the extent that a good co-op is measured in financial terms, JA Echigo Jōetsu lags behind its famous neighbor, JA Uonuma Minami. The reasons for this, we have argued, have to do with its particular mix of resource endowments, organization, co-op leadership, and the timing of reform. JA Uonuma Minami, as we have seen, has been blessed with ideal growing conditions, highly skilled co-op leaders, tightly knit organizations that wed the co-op and its farmer-members to common strategic goals, and a good sense of timing. But while JA Echigo Jōetsu appears to have no shortage of skilled leaders within its headquarters, it has been handicapped by soil deficits and weaknesses in the organizational linkages between both headquarters and local branches and local branches and farmer-members; these shortcomings, in turn, no doubt exacerbate the co-op's relatively weak capacity for effective strategic timing. Nevertheless, JA Echigo Jōetsu is clearly learning how to adapt its strategies to new market-related opportunities and in ways that stand to strengthen its organizational linkages with its farmer-members.

Exports and the Future of Rice

In 2013, when Japan formally joined the negotiations for the Trans-Pacific Partnership (TPP), a twelve-nation, comprehensive free-trade agreement, JA was up in arms. To the leaders of JA's national organizations and many local co-ops, an increase in cheaper agricultural—and particularly rice—imports from abroad would spell the demise of Japan's inefficient part-time farmers, the backbone of JA membership. Despite Prime Minister Abe's pledge to shield what were commonly referred to as "five sacred items" (rice, wheat, pork and beef, dairy, and sugar) from detariffication, many farmers and JA organizations continued to view TPP as an existential threat.

Others saw things differently. Shimada Toshio, the prosperous, full-time farmer in Kumamoto Prefecture whom we met in chapter 3, summed it up well: "I support TPP. Japanese agriculture is in decline, and it's going to keep declining because of our aging population and the farm sector's successor shortage. TPP will help us get rid of deadwood and trigger an agricultural rebirth, so the sooner it starts, the better. I think those demonstrations against TPP in Kasumi-gaseki are ridiculous—a waste of an opportunity. We need to say yes to TPP for the future of agriculture!"[77]

To Shimada, TPP promised greater access to foreign markets as participating countries tear down their barriers to agricultural imports. Of course, TPP negotiations collapsed following the United States' withdrawal under President Donald Trump in January 2017. The eleven-nation alternative that went into effect in late 2018, together with a recently concluded trade agreement between Japan and the European Union, will invite an increase—but only a modest one—in rice and other agricultural imports.

Exports, meanwhile, have become integral to the future of Japanese rice production because they represent new sources of consumer demand at a time when domestic demand is sharply waning. Several factors drive international demand, the first of which is the growing affluence of Asian consumers and their concomitant interest in safe, high-quality foods. Second, the international popularity of Japanese cuisine (*washoku*) received a huge boost after UNESCO added it to its Intangible Cultural Heritage List in late 2013. Third, the price of Japanese rice in recent years has occasionally dropped to levels comparable to—or even cheaper than—those of its closest international competitor, California rice,[78] a development that, ceteris paribus, works to Japan's advantage. Finally, the demand for made-in-Japan rice is on the rise among Japanese chain restaurants as they expand abroad.

In keeping with these trends, rice exports nearly doubled between 2016 and 2019—from 9,986 metric tons to 17,381 tons.[79] Hong Kong has consistently been the top destination, followed by Singapore, the United States, Taiwan, China, and Australia, in that order. Most economists agree, however, that rice exports have yet to reach their full potential. Kawai Naotada, the former chairman of Ōtoya, agrees.[80]

Ōtoya, a chain of low-priced restaurants that targets middle-class families, is a ubiquitous presence in Japan. But by the early 2000s, Japan's shrinking middle class and sluggish growth rates convinced the chain to set its sights abroad. First, it looked to markets that were part of the "chopstick culture" (*ohashi no bunka*)—Thailand, Taiwan, Hong Kong, Singapore, Indonesia, and even China. It then expanded to New York City, where by 2018 it operated three restaurants. As of 2014, Ōtoya had eighty-five restaurants overseas.

Rice is central to Ōtoya's success as an outlet for "authentic Japanese food," explains Kawai. But procuring rice for those foreign restaurants has been a challenge. Ōtoya refuses to purchase rice directly from non-Japanese suppliers, since it is unlikely to meet the company's standards. That leaves two other options. The first is to have the rice grown in the countries where the restaurants are located. But this, too, can be tricky. While there is no shortage of farmers willing to contract with Ōtoya, particularly in Southeast Asia,[81] Ōtoya must expend resources to help them meet the firm's standards for quality. Moreover, good rice depends on fresh, clean water, but this is often in short supply in Asian agricultural communities; Ōtoya must therefore install special water filter systems to guard against contamination. But these systems are expensive to purchase and maintain, and most local farmers lack the skills to keep them in good repair.

Because of these headaches, Ōtoya would prefer the second option: importing rice directly from Japan. But this is easier said than done. As Kawai sees it, Japan does not export enough rice for Ōtoya to secure a stable supply. The Abe government announced an agricultural export push in 2013, but it did not do enough to help farmers and co-ops meet that goal. Logistical bottlenecks make it hard to get product to market—particularly overseas markets. And variations in product safety standards across countries have slowed things down. Kawai thinks the MAFF could help farmers and co-ops adapt to these standards by conducting tests on rice exports before they leave the country or by negotiating with foreign governments to loosen their restrictions.

For years, Ōtoya has purchased rice for its domestic restaurants from co-ops in Ibaraki and Tochigi Prefectures, where farmers and co-ops are flexible enough to produce rice according to the chain's specifications for high volume, low price, taste consistency, freshness, and the like. ("Farmers in these prefectures," observed Kawai in 2014, "are much more flexible than many of Niigata's proud farmers, who are used to growing rice 'their way.'")[82] Kawai would like to see changes that make it easier for these co-ops to export their rice directly to Ōtoya's foreign restaurants. But many such changes are still in the future.

Critics share Kawai's frustration with the government's agricultural exports policy. The Abe government, argues Yamashita Kazuhito, an economist, paid insufficient attention to the fact that Japanese rice is still too expensive for many foreign buyers. But instead of introducing more measures to bring down those prices, he observes, the government flaunted World Trade Organization rules by providing hefty subsidies to rice farmers—subsidies that do nothing to incentivize farmers and co-ops to lower production costs.[83] Yamashita is deeply skeptical that the abolition of gentan will lower prices and stimulate exports; to the contrary, he argues, the introduction of subsidies for feed-rice production has had the opposite effect.[84]

Rice-centric co-ops recognize the importance of exports for the welfare of both themselves and their farmer-members. Some, like JA Minami Uonuma and JA Echizen Takefu, have already established successful footholds in niche markets abroad; these achievements suggest that co-ops with popular brands enjoy something of an advantage. Zennō, for its part, is banking on the allure of Japanese rice abroad as it forges partnerships with companies like Kubota, which operates rice-polishing facilities in East Asia. But Zennō is also struggling; in 2015, it set an export target for 2016 of 10,000 tons, but failed to meet it.[85] Rice-centric co-ops, meanwhile, are mindful of a fundamental dilemma inherent in exports: to do well, rice prices must decline, but declining prices means less money in the pockets of farmers.

In sum, there is a strong and growing consensus that the future of rice and co-ops depends heavily on exports. But for rice exports to expand, Japanese agriculture needs far more than entrepreneurial farmers and reformist co-ops; it needs more structural reform. We address this topic in the next chapter.

ABENOMICS, JA SELF-REFORM, AND THE FUTURE OF AGRICULTURAL COOPERATIVES IN JAPAN

This chapter revisits the big picture of Japanese agriculture and agricultural cooperatives by exploring the second Abe Shinzō government's (2012–2020) efforts to transform Japanese farming into a growth industry (*seichō sangyō*). What did the Abe government accomplish—or not—in its quest to change the laws, regulations, and other formal rules of the game that define many of the constraints and opportunities facing farmers and JA organizations? What remains to be done to empower stakeholders as they grapple with Japan's ongoing farm crisis? And what can we say about the future of JA?

To answer these questions, we begin by chronicling both the Abe government's co-op reforms and a growing movement toward self-reform (jiko kaikaku) at the national level of JA, a movement that reflects precedents for change set by innovative local co-ops and other incentives internal to the JA system. In so doing, we examine how the rhetoric and goals of contemporary reform are shaped by changes to both the national policy process and competition between two competing visions of Japanese agriculture—one neoliberal, the other more holistic. We then draw from Niigata Prefecture's JA Echigo Jōetsu to make the case that the future of agriculture and JA depends on the further empowerment of local actors—farmers, co-ops, local governments—to respond as flexibly as possible to the distinctive geographic, demographic, and economic challenges that confront their farm communities.

Reforming JA from the Top Down

At a November 6, 2014, press conference at JA's Tokyo headquarters, then-president Banzai Akira of Zenchū released details of a sweeping plan for self-reform at all levels of JA. A former rice farmer from Niigata Prefecture, Banzai had deep roots in JA; his father had served as a vice president of Zennō, and Banzai himself had once headed Niigata's Zenchū chapter. A "JA thoroughbred,"[1] Banzai was repelled by the Abe government's proposals for radical JA reform and determined to control the terms of the reform debate.

Banzai had good cause for worry. Shortly after assuming power in December 2012, Prime Minister Abe turned his attention to agricultural reform as a fundamental component of the third arrow, or structural reform prong, of Abenomics. Amid great fanfare, in December 2013 the Abe government released the Plan for the Creation of Agricultural Regional Vitality (Nōrinsuisangyō・chiiki no katsuryoku sōzō puran), its basic blueprint for agricultural and rural reform in the context of economic and demographic decline in the countryside. The plan and accompanying policies launched a string of reforms that indirectly influenced JA by further diversifying and empowering competitive farmers and loosening government controls over the agricultural sector. The government resolved, for example, to double agricultural incomes within ten years. It pledged to concentrate 80 percent of farmland in the hands of core farmers by 2023 and, to that end, establish prefectural farmland consolidation banks (nōchi chūkan kanri kikō, FLCB) to coordinate the demand and supply of farmland leasing.[2] It promoted the sixth industrialization (rokuji sangyōka) of agriculture through an assemblage of programs to fund and facilitate the integration of agricultural production with food processing and retailing. It pushed for the incorporation of more farm households and, controversially, greater participation of nonfarm household corporations in agricultural production. Building on precedents set under Prime Minister Koizumi Jun'ichirō (2001–2006),[3] the government established two national strategic special zones (kokka senryaku tokku) for agriculture. It sought to compensate for shrinking domestic demand for rice and other foods by incentivizing farmers and co-ops to export. And it abolished the production targets and accompanying subsidies of gentan, the government-led production adjustment program implemented in 1971 to prop up rice prices by reducing production. These are just a few examples of items on the government's long list of actions for creating aggressive agriculture (seme no nōgyō)—a profitable growth industry with global reach. Although critics were quick to highlight the many flaws in these and other initiatives, most agreed that they were long overdue responses to rural decline and flagging agricultural incomes.[4]

JA viewed these reforms with ambivalence. On the one hand, efforts to increase agricultural productivity and exports promised new opportunities for JA organizations. On the other hand, JA feared that the further empowerment of larger-scale, full-time farmers relative to small-scale, part-time farmers, as well as the promotion of enterprises other than the family farm, would lower demand for JA services over the long term. They feared, in other words, that the reforms would indirectly diminish JA's already shrinking edge in the agricultural economy.

Be that as it may, Banzai and other JA leaders pulled their punches on this dimension of the government's agricultural agenda. For like all agricultural stakeholders by this point, they recognized that Japanese agriculture was sorely in need of reform. They were far more vocal, by contrast, in their opposition to the Trans-Pacific Partnership (TPP), the Abe government's main portal for integrating the Japanese economy into global markets. Despite the government's pledge to cushion five sacred items (rice, wheat, pork and beef, dairy, and sugar) from imports, Banzai and his colleagues openly condemned the proposed twelve-nation pact as a major threat to struggling agricultural areas and part-time farmers. Privately, they fretted that market openings under TPP would significantly weaken JA power.[5]

In reaction to JA's relentless opposition to TPP, the Abe government took a politically unprecedented step: it revised the Vitality Creation Plan in 2014 to put JA itself on the official reform agenda.[6] In May 2014, the Council on Regulatory Reform (Kisei kaikaku iinkai, CRR) delivered on this pledge by proposing an audacious set of reforms to the 1947 Agricultural Cooperative Law. It called for an end to the prohibition on profit making among co-ops as part of its overall effort to expand agricultural production and increase farmer incomes. It pushed for the outright abolition of Zenchū and its prefectural equivalents (chūōkai) and a concomitant end to their control over local co-ops via mandatory audits (kansa) on the grounds that they curbed the co-ops' capacity to develop their own management expertise.[7] It recommended the conversion of Zennō and its independent counterparts in eight prefectures from cooperative organizations into joint-stock companies, thus stripping them of their sweeping antimonopoly and tax exemptions. To help co-ops expand their expertise to adapt more effectively to changing agricultural market forces, it called for a majority of members of co-op boards of directors to be either certified farmers (nintei nōgyōsha) or private-sector management experts (puro, or "professionals"), and for the reduction of co-ops' credit and insurance responsibilities, which would enable co-ops to transfer their best staff into agricultural services. It recommended a reduction in the usage of nonagricultural co-op services by associate cooperative members (jun kumiaiin) to less than half that of regular (farmer) members (sei kumiain). And the CRR proposed changes to the wording of the Co-op Law to emphasize farmers' voluntary participation in co-ops. In no uncertain terms, the CRR sought to free local co-ops from the stifling embrace of prefectural and national organizations in the JA hierarchy; reduce their multifunctionality, one of the hallmarks of postwar Japanese agricultural cooperation; and expand their capacity to innovate as agricultural enterprises—thereby positioning them to boost flagging farm incomes and alleviate the deepening farm successor shortage.[8]

Banzai's November 2014 announcement of a blueprint for self-reform signaled JA's official response to the CRR's bombshell proposals. Given Zenchū's long history of resisting change, it is tempting to dismiss the announcement as empty posturing. But the rhetoric of JA's November 2014 reform blueprint suggested otherwise. Here, JA acknowledged the severity of agriculture's demographic and economic crisis and pledged to do more to increase agricultural productivity and farmer incomes by promoting strategies that better served the individual needs of core farmers.[9] The Abe government itself could not have said it better.

That JA's national leadership was already reconciling itself to reform was further corroborated by years of pro-reform proclamations. At its triennial national conventions (*taikai*) between 2003 and 2012, JA trumpeted the need to improve support for individual farmers and expand product sales channels, build value-added chains in cooperation with local processors and restaurants, promote the structural reform of farm households via their participation in hamlet-based farm associations and contract farming, and lower farm input costs.[10] In its noteworthy 2012 meeting, which took place weeks before Abe's electoral victory, JA brought a heightened sense of urgency to the proceedings and introduced a five-year reform blueprint to help restore agriculture for the next generation of cultivators by transforming it into a growth industry and revitalizing rural areas.[11] Those two goals reappeared in a more comprehensive JA plan to promote change that was released in April 2014; among other things, the April plan called for more co-op support for core farmers, improving farm-related—as opposed to financial—services at the local co-op level, and reforming co-op management and governance practices.

Was this mere lip service to reform? Zenchū's and Zennō's slowness to act on these pledges suggest precisely that. Viewed in this light, JA's release of its April 2014 reform plan just weeks before the CRR dropped its much-anticipated bombshell can be interpreted not as evidence of its commitment to change but as an effort to deflect criticism and stall future reforms. But the fact remains that JA now had a compelling reason of its own to take co-op reform seriously. And that reason was a growing sense of crisis within JA as Japan's increasingly diverse and competitive agricultural market incentivized more farmers—and even co-ops—to defect from the JA system.

JA's national organizations could have reacted to this crisis by doing what they always did: jack up input prices and service commissions and coerce farmers to remain within the co-ops and co-ops within the JA system. But declining rent-seeking opportunities and changing economic and political conditions have rendered those tactics nearly obsolete. As we observed in chapter 6, the liberalization of the rice market during the mid-1990s and long-term declines in the domestic demand for rice have weakened Zennō's dominant position in that subsector and triggered drops in rice prices, thus decreasing JA revenue. The gradual dismantling of gentan's key pillars diminished what remained of JA's influence as an agent of the state and narrowed Zennō's capacity to force farmer compliance with its dictates. Meanwhile, the media's expanded coverage since the 1990s of JA-related scandals, many of which have involved antimonopoly violations, and the Japan Fair Trade Commission's increasing willingness to take JA to task for those violations have tarnished JA's reputation. And the long list of small-scale agricultural reforms that have gradually empowered both core farmers and JA's competitors over the years have made it harder for JA to keep Japan's most productive farmers under its wing. As JA is well aware, those farmers may still form a significantly smaller percentage of Japan's farming population than part-time farmers, but they collectively produce far more output in terms of both volume and value than their part-time counterparts. Declining revenue from JA's credit, insurance, and other nonfarm services makes it imperative for JA in general and Zennō in particular to step up its efforts to serve the interests of Japan's more competitive farmers.

Co-op defections from JA services are also incentivizing JA's national organizations to embrace reform. In chapter 6, we explored efforts by Niigata Prefecture's JA Uonuma Minami to forge new marketing channels outside of Zennō; as of this writing, the co-op markets approximately 90 percent of its member product outside of the keitō (Zennō's distribution channels). Fukui Prefecture's JA Echizen Takefu is another example of a co-op that has almost completely bypassed Zennō for its input and marketing needs. These are just two of the more dramatic examples of hardworking co-ops that have strived to diversify their input sources and marketing channels. Of course, suboptimal growing conditions, leadership deficits, organizational weaknesses, and other disadvantages make it next to impossible for many co-ops to take these steps; these are the co-ops that will continue to depend most heavily on Zennō. But Zennō knows that if it is to attract and retain the business of top-performing co-ops, it must learn how to better serve them and the competitive farmers they represent by paying more attention to price signals and other market incentives.

Our evidence suggests that Zennō has learned many of these lessons independently of government pressures—and not only because of the increasing threat of local farmer and co-op defections from the keitō. Zennō also sees opportunities in tailoring its strategies to local conditions and appears to be responding to reform precedents among local co-ops. Consider, for instance, the story recounted in chapter 5 of Zennō's relatively successful partnership with Nagano co-ops on behalf of production adjustment schemes for vegetables. This partnership was shaped in part by the bottom-up demands of entrepreneurial farmers and co-ops for higher returns on their raw product. But the timing of the introduction of this prefecturewide strategy following the JA Group's organizational reforms during the 1990s and early 2000s suggests that Zennō itself was thinking proactively. It is also worth noting that Zennō embraced this scheme nearly two decades before the Abe government had embarked on its structural reform crusade. Finally, there is evidence that JA's top leadership is learning important lessons from the initiatives of innovative local co-ops, such as their growing willingness over the last few years to help disseminate best practices and introduction of new programs to assist local co-ops that seek to improve local farmer productivity.

Put simply, JA's national leadership had plenty of reasons of its own to concur with the Abe government that JA/co-op reform was imperative. The two sides differed, however, over the scope of reform. While the leadership remained intent on introducing reforms from within the extant JA system, the CRR was proposing nothing less than the wholesale transformation of that system itself, including co-op multifunctionality and JA's top-heavy hierarchical structure. As JA saw it, the CRR had declared war on the very essence of JA identity.

Contending Visions of Reform and the Battle for JA

Conflicts over JA reflected two competing visions of the future of agriculture and how best to turn it into a growth industry. Officially, the government favored a neoliberal approach to reform. While it never lost sight of agriculture's important place in rural communities, it prioritized sweeping structural reforms to enhance farm and co-op competitiveness and profitability, encourage losers to leave the scene, and enable local co-ops to respond more profitably to market-based incentives and the winners among their farmer-members. In theory, at least, the government also favored a reduction of subsidies and other forms of government interference in the agricultural sector.[12] By contrast, JA, its supporters, and policy makers at the prefectural and local levels subsumed the language of reform under a broader rubric of local policy (*chiiki seisaku*). This approach assessed not only the economic but also the demographic, societal, and even environmental implications of agricultural and co-op reform and was far more accepting of subsidies and other redistributive policy measures (see chapter 2) to soften the blows of structural reform on the farm sector's weakest players.

The language of neoliberalism permeated the government's unofficial rhetoric and official statements on agricultural and co-op reform. For example, Suga Yoshihide, the prime minister's long-serving chief cabinet secretary and one of the major facilitators of Abenomics, was a vocal proponent of market-conforming agricultural reform. The son of an Akita Prefecture farmer who had abandoned rice in favor of strawberry production, Suga saw significant potential in the farm sector and frequently pushed for its transformation into a growth industry. The aforementioned Vitality Creation Plan, for its part, was steeped in the language of freer market principles and a determination to transform agriculture into a globally competitive growth industry. The plan pledged to double farmer incomes by heeding consumer preferences, lowering production costs, and raising farm revenues and to promote larger-scale farm enterprises and their participation in value-added production. Similarly, the CRR's 2014 co-op reform plan sought to level the playing field between JA organizations and other market players in the agricultural sector by reducing the co-op network's multifunctionality, stripping key players of antimonopoly exemptions, and the like.

This neoliberal ethos was especially pronounced in the Kantei's CRR and Industrial Competitiveness Council (Sangyō kyōsōryoku kaigi, ICC). JA took umbrage at the predominance of businessmen in these advisory commissions who allegedly knew little about agriculture or the complex demographic challenges confronting the countryside.[13] One partial exception was Niinami Takeshi, former president and CEO of Lawson and then Suntory Holdings, who headed the agricultural committee of the ICC; Niinami had received positive press for Lawson's employment-generating ventures into farming following the 2009 liberalization of farmland leasing. But like other members of the committees, Niinami seemed fixated on running farms like businesses.

The advocates of neoliberal reform were by no means in lockstep with one another. On the subject of co-op reform, while some would have liked to see JA disbanded altogether, more moderate advocates like the MAFF's Okuhara Masaaki, administrative vice minister (*jimu jikan*) from 2016 to 2018, envisioned a strong and continuing role for co-ops in rural Japan. Okuhara wanted the co-ops freed from the controls of Zenchū and their prefectural counterparts and from government interference.[14] Every local co-op, he argued, should function as an independent entity that could respond creatively to the particular strengths of the surrounding environment and profitably represent farmers in the marketplace. Co-ops, he concluded, should undergo a rebirth (*saisei*) and return to the core principles of agricultural cooperation.[15] Here, Okuhara sounded no different from the reformist co-op leaders we have described in this book. Where Okuhara distanced himself from many JA voices was in his emphasis on the economic or business side of co-ops. The co-ops, he suggested, should do more to structure themselves, think, and act like for-profit businesses and to cooperate more with other private enterprises.

JA and its allies bristled at this kind of rhetoric. They opposed the conflation of agriculture with other industries and the government's alleged obsession with "market fundamentalism"—an overemphasis on neoliberal market principles and the pursuit of profit at the expense of some of the noneconomic principles of agricultural cooperation and the livelihoods of less competitive farmers.[16] They were mindful of agriculture's inherent disadvantages—of the fact that some regions were handicapped by uncontrollable climactic and other conditions, that agricultural prices can be unpredictable, and that farms, unlike shoe or car factories, cannot be closed at night and on weekends. As JA and others saw it, free markets do not alleviate the many challenges facing agricultural production—they exacerbate them. If it was to be transformed into a growth industry, JA concluded, agriculture would need special treatment. So, too, would the co-ops.

JA's national spokespersons deftly evoked these convictions in their efforts to ensure that co-op reform would remain narrowly path dependent—that it would preserve, in other words, the very organizational hierarchy and multifunctionality that the CRR seemed so intent to destroy. It linked, for example, its self-preservation efforts to the important goal of rural revitalization (*chihō saisei*). Although the Abe government was elevating rural revitalization on its agenda, it glossed over JA's multifaceted contributions to rural communities in its fixation on growing rural economies.[17] JA was only too willing to connect the dots. In its two 2014 self-reform reports, it upheld rural revitalization as one of its three main objectives, alongside expanded agricultural production and increased farm incomes, the two overriding goals of the CRR report. And it trumpeted the centrality of the JA hierarchy and co-op multifunctionality to the health of rural communities by emphasizing, for example, its role as a one-stop, cradle-to-grave service provider in depopulating rural communities, especially those experiencing shrinking local-government programs following waves of municipal mergers. Although JA conveniently overlooked the fact that it, too, was abandoning some of Japan's most disadvantaged farm communities (see the epilogue), its message was clear: rural Japan depended on co-op multifunctionality, which in turn depended on the co-ops' close organizational linkages to national service providers and their regional affiliates.

JA used similar rhetoric to defend its auditing and supervisory functions. The CRR report had called for the outright elimination of these functions as a step toward the emancipation of local co-ops from the controlling influences of Zenchū and its prefectural counterparts. In response, Zenchū pledged to increase the autonomy of those prefectural organizations, in part by replacing mandatory, one-size-fits-all audits and supervision with a system that would enable more flexible prefectural responses to the needs of specific local co-ops.[18] At the same time, it defended its auditing authority as integral to the financial health and organizational viability of the co-ops, arguing that spinning it off to independent public accountants would leave some struggling co-ops—and hence rural communities—underserved.[19]

In a similar vein, JA linked its perceived indispensability to the fate of JA's associate members. Given how essential JA's multifunctional organizational structure was to the future of rural communities, JA argued, it stood to reason that the co-ops' nonfarmer associate members should continue to have full access to the system's financial services and panoply of consumer and social-welfare offerings. Many of them, after all, were aging residents who were unlikely to leave their villages or retired farmers, some of whom had leased their farmland to neighboring core farmers. To deprive these residents of these essential services was to deny beleaguered rural communities one of their last remaining safety nets.[20]

Banzai and his colleagues knew that the Abe government was acquiring the political wherewithal to make significant headway in its neoliberal vision of co-op reform. Building on the effects of the electoral and administrative reforms of the 1990s (see chapter 3), Prime Minister Koizumi Jun'ichirō's efforts to empower the Kantei, and deepening fissures within the political alliance of the LDP, the MAFF, and JA, the Abe government further strengthened the Kantei's hand in the agricultural reform process. It ceded policy formulation processes that had traditionally fallen under the MAFF's umbrella to neoliberal Kantei organizations like the CRR and the ICC. It encouraged the rise of reformist officials like Okuhara Masaaki inside the MAFF and appointed reformist politicians like Hayashi Yoshimasa as minister (2012–2014, 2015). Meanwhile, the notoriously anti-reformist farm *zoku* (policy tribe) was undergoing something of a sea change. While some zoku members were determined to soften the effects of neoliberal change on their farm constituents, several now advocated for reform, including Inada Tomomi, head of the LDP's influential Policy Affairs Research Council (PARC); JA favorite Moriyama Hiroshi; and Nishikawa Koya, the one-time don of the farm zoku and minister of agriculture between late 2014 and early 2015. Finally, key LDP positions that had once been monopolized by zoku traditionalists were falling to their enemies. This trend came to a head in October 2015, when Abe defied the wishes of more conservative zoku members by filling the chairmanship of PARC's all-important Agricultural Committee with Koizumi Shinjirō, a young, antizoku politician and neoliberal advocate whose passion for agricultural reform resembled that of his father for postal privatization.

At the end of the day, the 2015 amendments to the 1947 Co-op Law represented a compromise between these two competing visions of reform—one that highlighted the lingering influence of JA and its allies in the MAFF and the LDP.[21] Most notably, JA multifunctionality and the broad organizational parameters of the JA system emerged from the reform process relatively unscathed. JA Bank and the cooperatives' associate members were spared the reformers' ax. The transformation of Zennō into a joint-stock corporation was stipulated as an option rather than a requirement, and the question of reducing associate-member access to co-op services was postponed for five years. And Zenchū and its prefectural chapters were preserved. The changes that were introduced were modest but significant.[22] The law was amended to eliminate the prohibition of co-ops' pursuit of profit and to underscore the co-ops' primary mission to improve farmer incomes,[23] and both the co-ops and JA federations were expressly prohibited from forcing members to use their services. The CRR's recommendations for the reform of co-op boards of directors were adopted. Zenchū was converted from a cooperative organization into a general incorporated association (*ippan shadan hōjin*), comparable to any other Japanese trade association. Zenchū was also stripped of its authority to impose mandatory audits on local cooperatives, which it had used to shape their management and financial decisions, and to collect levies (fukakin) from the co-ops, which funded not only those audits but also Zenchū's political lobbying campaigns. (Zenchū's prefectural counterparts, however, remain free to collect those levies.)[24] JA's power had been reduced, albeit not as much as the CRR had hoped.[25]

The Past, Present, and Future of Co-op Policy Reform

Looking back on recent history, it is clear that Japanese agriculture is once again changing. As farm populations shrink and agricultural markets open up, farmers and co-ops continue to diversify. And JA at the national level is resigned to at least some degree of market-conforming reform that puts the financial needs of farmers first.[26]

The manner in which the various organizational components of JA interact is also changing. Once pressured to meet virtually all their input and marketing needs through JA channels, local co-ops now have more opportunities to pick and choose their providers; this, in turn, is incentivizing organizations at all levels of the JA hierarchy to work harder. At the same time, JA's national and prefectural leaders are becoming more attentive to local co-op and farmer voices by conducting more site visits, developing new two-way channels of communication, soliciting more co-op opinions into JA policy processes via hearings and symposia, and the like. Similar changes are underway at the government level. Not too long ago, prefectural- and municipal-government officials would complain bitterly about the imposition of one-size-fits-all policies (think gentan) on local agriculture. Now, there is more back and forth between levels of government during the policy formulation process to adjust national policy to local contingencies. As representatives from local co-ops and prefectural governments are wont to complain, Zenchū and Zennō and the national government can still get it wrong.[27] But gone are the days when agricultural decision making in JA and government was mostly a top-down affair.

The Abe government's agricultural reforms, including the 2015 amendments to the Agricultural Cooperative Law, marked a high point in these trends. Indeed, the Abe reforms were pathbreaking insofar as JA's organizational structure was targeted for major changes for the first time since 1954, when the government passed legislation to establish Zenchū and its prefectural counterparts. But the Abe reforms nevertheless failed to transform agriculture into a growth industry. This is hardly surprising. In marked contrast to the critical juncture of the occupation era, when US and Japanese authorities had the political space to transform the rules of agricultural and cooperative engagement (see chapter 2), the Abe government was shouldered with the remnants of the occupation's handiwork, including a mature cooperative system backed by a panoply of vested—albeit more weakly vested—interests.

The government scored a few additional victories in the wake of the 2015 Co-op Law amendments, most notably with the spring 2017 passage of the Law to Support the Strengthening of Agricultural Competitiveness (Nōgyō kyōsōryoku kyōka shien hō). The law promises to lower farmer production costs by encouraging more competition in the farm input sector and by requiring all providers, including co-ops, to publicize their input prices. But no sooner was the ink dry on the new law than key reformers began to leave the scene. In late 2017, lower house member Nishikawa Koya lost his bid for reelection, and Koizumi Shinjirō was replaced as head of PARC's agricultural committee by Nomura Tetsuro, a former JA official. In 2018, the MAFF's Okuhara Masaaki retired, and old-guard members of the farm zoku, like the upper house's Yamada Toshio, found themselves with more influence in agricultural policy-making circles.[28]

Meanwhile, local co-ops are facing new challenges. Over the short term, COVID-19 is creating hardships for many farmers and co-ops as sudden drops in the demand for rice from school lunch programs, chain restaurants, and other retail buyers eat into co-op sales and hence farmer-member incomes. The producers of high-end vegetables are also experiencing drops in demand as consumers avoid restaurants and cook more at home. Meanwhile, shrinking demand has been especially hard on JA defectors who have been forging their own routes to market, among them larger-scale, full-time farmers who produce expensive rice for restaurants. Some of these defectors, it appears, are returning to the co-op in an effort to lower their risks and stabilize their incomes. If co-ops wish to prevent those entrepreneurial farmers from defecting again in the future, they would do well to increase the returns to farmers by reforming their purchasing and sales strategies.

Over the long term, JA faces technological pressures. For years now, Fujitsu, NEC, and other major Japanese firms have been marketing new technologies to streamline and lower the costs of agricultural production, from high-tech fruit and vegetable sorters to sophisticated GPS programs for fine-tuning the application of water, fertilizers, and other farm chemicals to each square meter of farmland. More recently, firms have been introducing smartphone applications to help farmers compare input prices and find independent buyers for their products. Since many of these technologies are best suited to Japan's largest and most competitive farmers, they represent yet another incentive for those farmers to defect from their local co-op. But high-tech innovation can also be an opportunity for JA. If JA can find ways to partner with the providers of high-tech applications that are adapted to the needs of smaller-scale farmers, it stands to benefit. (So will the providers, which gain access to Japan's largest network of farmers and, as a result, to sources of valuable data.) JA's August 2020 announcement of a joint venture with a smartphone app developer suggests that it is learning how to adapt.[29] Ventures like these may not do much to transform Japanese agriculture into a growth industry, but they can help make life easier for struggling farmers.

Farmer and co-op diversification and the high-tech revolution illustrate that even if the government does nothing on the agricultural reform front for the next few years, slowly but surely, both farmers and JA will continue to change. For when all is said and done, decades of small-scale changes to the formal-legal foundations of Japanese farming and agricultural cooperation have unleashed reformist momentum in the farm sector that that will transcend any one government. It is unlikely, however, that this momentum will be enough to enable beleaguered local farm communities to overcome their many challenges. As the next section illustrates, even some of Japan's most fertile farm regions and hardworking co-ops are fighting to stay afloat.

Local Problems, Local Solutions: Insights from JA Echigo Jōetsu

Aoki Katsuaki, career co-op employee and now head of the management committee (keiei kanri iinkai) of JA Echigo Jōetsu in Niigata Prefecture, fears for his co-op's future.[30] As we saw in chapter 6, JA Echigo Jōetsu is a prominent rice-centric co-op that has introduced some noteworthy strategic reforms over the years. But as Aoki reminds us, local conditions, including the distinctive challenges inherent in rice production, are limiting the scope for further change.

Geography is one of JA Echigo Jōetsu's biggest headaches. The co-op covers territory that is extremely hilly and mountainous (chūsankan chiiki), and this fact alone explains much of the area's population decline. As Aoki explains,

> Today, Jōetsu City has about 200,000 people. But it has been losing between 1,000 and 1,400 people per year. People aren't exactly moving away; the problem is that no one is moving in to replace those who have passed away. This is true for farmers as well as the general population. What prospective farmer would want to move into a mountainous area when there are plenty of employment opportunities these days on flat land? It's hard to live and work in a place like this!
>
> To address all this, we are taking steps to make rice farming more productive, help elderly farmers keep up their farms, and encourage young people to move into farming. But none of these initiatives is enough to reverse the ravages of population decline and their effects on regional agriculture. The best we can do is slow the pace of decline.[31]

The most obvious strategy for boosting farm productivity in areas with shrinking populations, Aoki notes, is the application of more high-tech machinery to local rice paddies and other farms. This can be difficult in areas that are mountainous and populated by elderly farmers: "In flat farming regions, all farms can use the same machinery. But in mountainous areas, the machinery must be customized to the specific requirements of individual plots. This can get expensive. And many older farmers are not physically up to the task of operating heavy machinery on uneven terrain; it's very tiring—even dangerous—work."

Since technological approaches to boosting agricultural productivity in this geographically and demographically challenged part of the country are limited, JA Echigo Jōetsu looks to farmer reorganization as its best hope. The co-op has partnered with local governments to promote the expansion of hamlet-based farm associations (HBFAs—see chapters 3 and 6), which have long had a foothold in the area. The co-op invests in many of these HBFAs and cooperates with their managers to assist farmers. Unfortunately, several hamlets are losing population so rapidly that the HBFAs themselves are struggling. To counter this, JA Echigo Jōetsu and Jōetsu City have created networks of as many as twelve individual HBFAs to promote cross-hamlet resource and service sharing. Given their sheer size, these networks qualify for national subsidies that exceed what is normally paid out to farm hamlets in mountainous regions. The initiative has scored some successes, earning the co-op and city government a special prize from the MAFF.

One major objective of these HBFA networks is to help aging farmers contract with younger farmers to perform much-needed services, from operating that dangerous machinery to harvesting fields, preparing raw product for transport, and delivering it to JA collection centers. Everyone gains from the arrangement. Aging producers shore up their incomes by keeping their farms in production, while younger farmers, who are paid in part from those national subsidies, earn extra cash. JA Echigo Jōetsu, which manages the contracts, has more raw product delivered to its collection centers, and that, in turn, can translate into higher revenue and profits.

JA Echigo Jōetsu also promotes the incorporation of farm enterprises, including those alliances of HBFAs. But the results of this initiative have been mixed. As we saw in chapter 3, incorporation positions a farm enterprise to hire outside labor and engage more effectively in various kinds of business transactions; this, in theory, should make it easier for the enterprise to secure successors. In this corner of Niigata, however, incorporation has made nary a dent in the successor crisis. Aoki estimates that between 50 and 70 percent of incorporated enterprises in the area are led by individuals age sixty-five or older; many will be active for only five more years or so, and most of them lack successors.

"Then what?" he asks rhetorically.

For stakeholders like Aoki, letting farms die is not an option. Topographical handicaps notwithstanding, this is prime rice-growing country with a long history and deep cultural significance. But if those HBFA networks should find themselves rudderless once their CEOs retire, Aoki explains, JA Echigo Jōetsu could assume control of them. This would likely involve reorganizing the networks as specific kinds of JA-invested agricultural corporations (JA shusshigata nōgyō hōjin—see chapter 4). These JA-invested corporations, which have been increasing in recent years, are actively promoted by Zenchū and its prefectural counterparts. A few, moreover, have functioned as agricultural production cooperatives (see chapter 2) in that they engage directly in cultivation.

But Aoki dreads the thought of harnessing those HBFA networks to his co-op as JA-invested agricultural-corporations-cum-production-cooperatives. It would mean another marked departure from owner-cultivatorism—that widely espoused postwar principle that farmland be tilled by those who own it, and vice versa.[32] It would push the traditional multipurpose cooperative well beyond its mission, which stops short of direct cultivation. And it would increase co-op risks to potentially intolerable levels. The co-op would be in charge of vast amounts of farmland, Aoki explains, not all of it of good quality. And it would have to hire and train scores of farm workers—a costly and challenging undertaking in the context of Japan's rapidly declining farm population.

JA Echigo Jōetsu strives to avoid this scenario by offering more support to existing farmers and recruiting new farmers. To accomplish these goals, it works closely with a variety of local stakeholders and participates in initiatives launched by JA's central authorities. In April 2016, for example, JA's national leadership set out to establish prefectural core-farmer support centers (ken'iki ninaite sapōto sentā) in all forty-seven prefectures to assist competitive farmers. Rather than wait for farmers to visit the centers, representatives from the prefectural JA offices and local co-ops make joint visits to targeted farms to determine their specific needs, and the center then works with the JA Group's banking, insurance, and farm services to devise specific policies for both the local co-op and its core farmer-members.[33] The initiative seems to strike the right chord in that it strives to serve the specific needs of individual farms, but it is too soon to tell how effective it will be. What is more, it does not do much for the legions of older, smaller-scale farmers who compose the bulk of rural communities.

JA Echigo Jōetsu has also set up an incorporated subsidiary to train recent high school graduates in cultivation, farm management, marketing, and other essential skills. When a local enterprise hires one of the trainees, it pays a fee to the subsidiary. The municipal government is also pitching in, providing internships to trainees and monitoring local incorporated farm enterprises to ensure they provide their interns with attractive benefits.

The co-op has also made good use of its Team for Agricultural Coordination (TAC). Part of a nationwide initiative launched in 2008 by Zennō to help curb the defection of farmers from its services, the TAC program places teams of experts at the local co-op level to help individual farmers improve their farm management and marketing practices. As originally envisioned, TAC addresses the needs of local co-ops and farms that are attempting to become more competitive and profitable.[34] But the team that operates under Echigo Jōetsu emphasizes the provision of educational opportunities for all farmers.

It is in training and education that Aoki pins most of his hopes. He is proud of the fact that JA Echigo Jōetsu has helped roughly three hundred people become farmers over the past ten years and that as many as two hundred of these new farmers are first-generation cultivators. And he is grateful for the support of local government and private businesses. But when all is said and done, Aoki fully recognizes that these initiatives cannot fully correct the area's farm successor shortage. Aging and economic competition are problems in any agricultural community, he observes, but they are almost insurmountable in hilly and mountainous areas.

How, then, does Aoki view the Abe government's 2015 amendments to the Co-op Law? Will the reforms help position his co-op to more effectively address the tangled skein of economic, demographic, and geographic challenges that plague his region? Aoki gives the question some careful thought. "I think the changes will definitely help some co-ops," he replies, seemingly in agreement with the goal of empowering local co-ops.[35] But there are limitations to what the reforms can achieve. Some co-ops, he notes, for example, will have trouble finding certified farmers and professionals to recruit onto their boards of directors. And some of the reforms still smack of a one-size-fits-all approach—the assumption that if all co-ops conform to the new guidelines, things will fall into place:

> The reforms will not be enough to help co-ops like JA Echigo Jōetsu resolve our distinctive problems. Why can't there be more flexibility in how these problems are defined and addressed? Take, for example, the government's resolve to eventually reduce co-op services for associate members. This overlooks the fact that not all associate co-op members are alike. Many of them in our area are former farmers who have leased their land to HBFAs and who deserve our help—particularly in depopulated areas lacking alternative service providers. Why can't the government recognize that what works for one co-op may not work for another?[36]

Aoki Katsuaki, like many other entrepreneurial co-op leaders, knows that the future of Japanese agriculture and multipurpose cooperatives will be decided at the local level, village by village, co-op by co-op. He is pessimistic that his co-op and locality will be able to cure what ails them. But he is hopeful that the worst effects of Japan's agricultural crisis can be mitigated—at least for now.

What more, then, can government and JA do to help co-op leaders like Aoki Katsuaki and other local stakeholders stave off the inevitable?

For starters, government can fix Japan's mind-numbingly complex farm subsidy regime. As chapters 5 and 6 illustrated, there is a subsidy for just about everything, and one would be hard-pressed to find a bureaucrat at any level of government who can list—let alone make sense of—them all. Many subsidies, moreover, conflict with one another, thus working at cross-purposes to farmer and co-op innovation. These problems must be resolved.

The government can do more to compensate for declining domestic demand for rice and other foods by facilitating exports. To be sure, the Abe government took some noteworthy steps to help farmers and co-ops export. What was missing, however, was a concerted government effort to negotiate with foreign governments that have erected barriers to agricultural imports from Japan.

Both the government and JA can further empower local co-ops to respond to the challenges of their environments while remaining mindful of the fact that every local co-op is different. Since not every co-op has an Aoki Katsuaki at the helm, both can take steps to improve training for prospective co-op leaders, particularly in disadvantaged rural areas, and provide more resources to enable co-op partnerships with local governments and businesses on behalf of common goals. Several years ago, the Abe government took steps in this direction when it established those national strategic economic zones for agriculture we noted earlier. Located in Niigata City and Hyogo Prefecture's Yabu City, the zones seek to accelerate the deregulation of farmland, diversify farm enterprises, and encourage partnerships among local stakeholders. In Yabu City, at least, the partial liberalization of farmland acquisition has led to some noteworthy reforms.[37] But the conditions that enable these private-public partnerships in the agricultural sphere are confined to the zones, and JA has been sidelined in local decision making. Government can and should do more to promote deregulation in other farming areas, incentivize more active co-op participation in reform projects, and disseminate best practices.

Meanwhile, the government must recognize that independence from Zennō need not be a prerequisite for co-op reform. Yes, there are pockets of resistance inside Zennō—and Zenchū—that slow the pace of change. And yes, the large JA system has a stubborn penchant for path-dependent reform that renders change slow and cumbersome. But as our analysis of JA Nagano's production adjustment scheme in chapter 5 reveals, Zennō-co-op partnerships can serve the interests of multiple stakeholders, from the farm household to the legions of food processors and large food retail chains that buy rice and other commodities in bulk. In future, the government should take care to avoid reforms that preclude Zennō from taking a mutually beneficial leadership role in the coordination of local co-op strategies.

For the foreseeable future, JA and the small-scale family farm are here to stay. Neither will be supplanted by large-scale, North American–style agribusinesses; at the very least, the lingering distrust of neoliberal economic values in local agricultural communities and the topographical constraints on farmland consolidation will see to that. For as long as JA and the family farm remain the dominant players in Japan's agricultural landscape, the reforms that stick will be those that work with rather than against the JA network and in ways that leave no farmer behind.

EPILOGUE
It Takes a Village

On a cool, rainy day in early June 2014, we drove the steep, twisting roads to Yamato, a 545 sq km town nestled in a remote and mountainous corner of Kumamoto Prefecture served by JA Kamimashiki. Accompanied by two officials from the prefecture's agricultural department, our aim was to explore the state of agricultural reform and rural revitalization in Japan's mountainous areas, or chūsankan chiiki. The fact that there is an oft-used Japanese term for rural communities like Yamato is telling, for it is here that the ravages of demographic and economic decline are most keenly felt.

The result of a 2005 merger of two independent towns and one village, Yamato's roots extend back to feudal times. The Tsūjun Bridge, a massive stone aqueduct from the late Tokugawa era (1600–1868), still irrigates some of the surrounding terraced rice paddies. Typical of postmerger municipalities in rural Japan, Yamato encompasses many farm communities that were once independent villages, and they all struggle to retain population and stay afloat economically. Suge, a village of 212 aging inhabitants known for the deep gorge that cleaves it in two, joined the national terraced rice paddy owner (tanada ōnā) movement (see chapter 3) some years ago to invite outsiders to help plant and harvest its local paddies. No one expected the program to make much of a dent in the village's labor shortage, but it was enough to attract some extra funds and attention; the village later joined a similar program in support of its beleaguered tea fields. In a bid to draw more tourists to the area, Suge also secured government funding to construct a suspension bridge over the gorge.[1] In 2013, Suge's community building (machizukuri) earned it an award from the agricultural ministry. But neither the villagers' hard work nor the government accolades have expanded tourism beyond a modest trickle. And the population continues to shrink. When we returned to the area three years later, tiny Suge had lost some 30 more people.

Neighboring Yamato communities have similar stories to tell. In Shimaki village, relentless population decline has led to the shuttering of many homes, schools, and small businesses. Entrepreneurial residents have tried to shore up the local economy by building a solar panel park and converting an abandoned nursery school into a plant for grinding bamboo—never in short supply in rural Kyushu—into a powder that can be sold as both a fertilizer and a high-fiber dietary supplement. But the village remains mired in an economic slump. Even JA Kamimashiki, Shimaki's agricultural lifeline and one of its last organized sources of community cohesion, is in retreat. In keeping with the overall downward trend in the JA Group's sales of household goods and other daily necessities in Japan (see table 4.1), the co-op abandoned at least one of its gasoline stands as well as the village's sole grocery store (A-Co-op); like many other tiny rural communities around the country, Shimaki now relies on volunteers to keep the store stocked with a few basic supplies.

Should communities like Suge and Shimaki be allowed to shrink—even die? From a hard-nosed economic perspective, the answer is yes. This is not prime habitat for rice cultivation. In fact, were it not for postwar Japan's artificially high rice prices, there would be even fewer farmers in the area. Put simply, Yamato's predicament is to be expected as Japan's agricultural market liberalizes and globalizes. The laws of economic competition should be allowed to take their course and public investments limited to efficient stakeholders who can help transform the remnants of regional agricultural into a growth industry.

The locals see things much differently. For them, the loss or decline of a mountainous farm community disrupts ecosystems and regional transportation routes and affects the management of prefectural waterways that originate at high elevations. It destroys regional employment opportunities and social networks, severs rural-urban linkages, and diminishes the living standards of the elderly residents who are left behind. And since there is not always an efficient farmer waiting in the wings to purchase an inefficient farmer's assets, the decline of rural communities wastes precious farmland. These economic, social, political, environmental, and even cultural concerns—the stuff of local policy—help motivate local residents, politicians, and officials to put up the good fight against demographic and economic decline, even at the expense of economic efficiency. They also deepen many of the challenges currently confronting JA as it contemplates its future.

That Yamato is typical of small rural communities battling demographic and economic decline was drummed into us during our June 2014 meeting with

Yamamoto Naoki, a career bureaucrat from the Ministry of Internal Affairs and Communications who had been dispatched to the town to serve as vice mayor for two to three years. Since the municipal offices were under reconstruction, we sat down with Yamamoto and his colleagues in the government's temporary offices on the outskirts of the main part of town. The vice mayor quickly ran through a litany of statistics with the air of an official long used to explaining the town's grim circumstances to outside visitors. In 2005, the year of the merger, Yamato had 20,154 people. By the time of our visit, that number had shrunk to 16,704.[2] Yamato is also an elderly community, with more than 40 percent of residents aged sixty-five or more. Between 2000 and 2015 the number of commercial farm households shrunk from 2,446 to 1,876, while the overall farm population was cut roughly in half, from 12,678 to 6,545. Approximately 10 percent of area farmland has been abandoned, and many of those who remain on the land cannot find successors.[3]

Yamato's economy reflects national trends in other ways as well. Farming is no longer the rural municipality's main employer; just 37.9 percent of employed residents were engaged in agriculture or forestry in 2018, while 15.5 percent worked in manufacturing and 46.6 percent in services. And farming itself has been diversifying. Some farmers follow tradition by cultivating rice or tea, but others are now producing fruits, flowers, livestock, and especially vegetables that do well at cool, higher elevations. Meanwhile, the traditional farm household is starting to lose ground to incorporated farm households, a small but growing number of enterprises are operating outside of JA, and farmland leasing is taking root among some larger-scale cultivators. But most farms in Yamato remain small— too small, Yamamoto remarked, to qualify for government subsidies—and land consolidation via leasing is devilishly hard to pull off, thanks to the rugged terrain.[4] When all is said and done, Yamato remains a community dominated by small-scale, part-time farmers and hence high production costs—hardly the sort of community that can transform its farms into a growth industry.

Yamato's future is bleak, but this does not deter town officials and intrepid residents from throwing their energies into rural revitalization. From the transformation of the Tsūjun aqueduct into a tourist attraction to Suge's impressive new bridge and Shimaki's microbusinesses, Yamato is scrambling to build new economic lifelines. Revitalization efforts also extend to the agricultural realm. As Yamamoto explained, Yamato recognizes that the key to agriculture's revival is to create larger, more profitable farms that attract younger cultivators into the area. To that end, the town promotes hamlet-based farm associations (shūraku einō)— one of the few viable strategies for achieving economies of scale among small-scale farmers confronting formidable impediments to land consolidation. By consolidating farmland management, the associations earn the label core farmers, and that, in turn, qualifies them for special national- and prefectural-government subsidies. Yamato also does what it can to facilitate farmland leasing by larger-scale cultivators, although the area's small plots are not always attractive to potential leasers. Finally, Yamato has jumped onto the sixth-industrialization bandwagon by promoting the acquisition and servicing of produce sorters (*senkaki*) and other machinery, strengthening policies to expand and support the distribution of branded organic and processed foods, and helping local entrepreneurs set up farm-to-table restaurants that showcase local foods.[5] Yamamoto readily acknowledged that JA Kamimashiki has played a central role in some of these initiatives. Although it has scaled back its presence in tiny communities like Shimaki, the co-op has lent its support to hamlet-based farm associations and provides helpful farm management advice (*einō shidō*) to small-scale farmers as well as social welfare services to Yamato's aging residents.[6]

JA Kamimashiki's contributions to local farming and community revitalization took an interesting turn in spring 2017 with the election of its former leader as mayor of Yamato. Born in 1947 in Yabe, one of the towns that had been folded into Yamato in 2005, Umeda Yutaka served as head of Yabe's co-op prior to its merger with JA Kamimashiki during the 1990s; by 2005 he was at the helm of JA Kamimashiki. Umeda went on to play leading roles in JA's prefectural-level welfare and banking organs and in 2014 assumed the leadership of Zenchū's prefectural counterpart. In 2017, he left JA to run for mayor.

On our return visit to Yamato in June 2017, we met with Mayor Umeda and several town officials at his spacious offices inside the town's bright, newly completed municipal headquarters. Speaking in the folksy dialect of the area, the gregarious seventy-year-old mayor grew pensive when we pointed out that the municipality had lost more than 1,600 residents since our 2014 visit. There was no denying that the town was still aging and shrinking at alarming rates, he observed, and that this would likely continue for some time. JA, he believed, was integral to those left behind: "JA Kamimashiki has some shortcomings. It is still too heavily centered on its banking and insurance services and the income derived from those services. Nevertheless, JA does do a lot to help local farmers—many different types of farmers, though not so much the top performers. And it provides many other essential services to the community. JA is, in other words, part of Yamato's very foundation [*kiban*]."[7]

Mayor Umeda's observations highlight a pattern that is being duplicated in rural communities throughout Japan. As farmers diversify and many of the top performers venture outside the JA network, most small, part-time farm households remain heavily reliant on JA for their financial, input, and marketing needs. Mayor Umeda sees no need to state the obvious: if JA turns its back on these cultivators, the town will die.

Serving those left behind in Yamato has been hard for the co-op, because it, too, has suffered the effects of depopulation. The co-op's local organizational presence has been loosened via a string of mergers that reduced the number of local branches from about thirty in the 1990s to just six today. For financial reasons, the co-op has also had to pare down its staff—changes that happened more or less naturally, Mayor Umeda explained, as staff members retired or moved to larger towns. Today, the co-op struggles to attract and retain good staff—so much so that it occasionally defies tradition by hiring people from outside its jurisdiction. As JA Kamimashiki's organizational and human presence shrinks, so, too, does contact between co-op employees and local farmers.

Nevertheless, the co-op continues to perform vital functions for Yamato farmers and residents. Mayor Umeda is especially proud of its welfare (*fukushi*) services for local elderly residents, including home visits, a seniors' daycare center, and a retirement home. While co-op leader, the mayor reacted to declining government offerings in the wake of municipal mergers by joining forces with the remaining local governments in JA Kamimashiki's jurisdiction to train the co-op's female members as licensed caregivers. It was a rational response to the needs of the community that also expanded employment opportunities for local women. "Most of the women JA recruits for eldercare are the wives of local farmers who are looking after aging family members anyway," the mayor explained. "Why not train and license them to provide comparable services to the broader community?"[8] Because of these initiatives, the co-op has an unusually active women's committee (*joseibu*). And in Yamato, at least, the services make money for JA, which is unusual among multipurpose co-ops. The reasons for this success: the quality of services rendered; the strong, unanimous support of top officials in JA Kamimashiki; and Umeda Yutaka's proactive leadership.

Despite JA's traditional opposition to reforms that might weaken demand for its services, JA Kamimashiki has learned to coexist with incorporated farm households and nonfarm household corporations. 7-Eleven runs a few hothouses in the area, and some local farmers have partnered with Kagome, MOS Burger, and other food processors and retailers to grow foods by contract. One of the mayor's colleagues explained that these ventures have been around for so long that no one really questions them anymore. Mayor Umeda went on to note that the town government has long supported the incorporation of family farms. "It used to be hard for farms to incorporate," he noted, "but the application process has been simplified over the years. And the town government wants to do what it can to help. All kinds of farms are welcome here. And we all must step up to help the community."[9] These words are all the more significant coming from a man who spent the bulk of his career inside JA.

Although it is unclear just how much impact Umeda Yutaka's initiatives have had on Yamato agriculture, the data current to 2015 are encouraging. The total number of farm households is still declining and the spread of abandoned land increasing, but the number of more efficient, full-time farm households is on the rise—from 554 households in 2000 to 668 in 2015. Finally, between 2014 and 2015, the combined income from agricultural production and food processing in Yamato rose from 9.7 billion yen to 10.4 billion yen, a small but impressive increase given the shrinking farm population.[10]

But when all is said and done, Mayor Umeda argued, "the key to Yamato's farming future is bringing young people back into the community. And that's not an impossibility! Yamato has lots of charm and potential, and with the right incentives, we can and will attract more youth into the area."[11]

As proof of his convictions, Mayor Umeda introduced us to Nagasaki Sachi, the leader of a municipal program for community development launched in 2014 that includes a training program for young farmers, and two of the training program's first graduates, Yatsuda Shogo and Nakahata Yoshihirō. Both in their twenties and transplants from other parts of Japan, the two men now run their own incorporated farms. They have applied what they learned as trainees to good effect; Yatsuda is contracted to produce vegetables for Itoyokado, the nationwide supermarket chain, while Nakahata has tapped into several non-JA channels—including the internet—to sell his strawberries. But the farming acumen of these two friends was not the only reason we were introduced to them. In February 2017, Yatsuda and Nakahata launched Yamato Deshika,[12] an agricultural corporation (nōgyō hōjin) that helps young farmers and restauranteurs maximize access to local resources—agricultural, human, and financial. The two entrepreneurs were inspired by similar experiments in the town of Kamiyama in Tokushima Prefecture, long viewed as a pioneer in the juxtaposition of farming and community building, and Nagasaki Sachi saw to it that they had the necessary funding to spend time within their Tokushima mentors. Yatsuda and Nakahata strive unabashedly to maximize their farm profits, and they encourage their Yamato Deshika coworkers and clients to do the same. They also contribute to the local culture by promoting farmers' festivals and rock concerts—all in the hopes of attracting twenty-somethings from the cities looking for a radical lifestyle change.[13]

Yatsuda and Nakahata have struggled in Yamato. The shrinking town has no shortage of vacant houses, but the absence of a rental culture made it hard for them to find suitable accommodation. And the two have had trouble finding investors for Yamato Deshika. The Japan Travel Bureau is on board, and the Yamato government does what it can to help, but the town is legally prohibited from using public funds to invest in for-profit firms. As for JA, it had not yet thrown its support behind the firm at the time of our 2017 visit. Did the co-op perhaps see Yamato Deshika as a competitor? "Maybe," answered one of the two farmers while within earshot of one of the prefecture's top former JA leaders: "But we aren't out to compete with the co-op. JA has been so integral to the development of farming infrastructure in this region. In fact, without JA and its long history here, we wouldn't exist. However, JA's not doing a whole lot to train new farmers here—and that's where we come in. But we hope to someday attract JA investment. After all, we're all in the same boat. We all want to secure successors for Yamato's farms and prevent the decline of our town."[14]

Yamato Deshika's young leaders are among the top performers Mayor Umeda referred to earlier in our conversation: full-time producers with viable, incorporated farms and a knack for branding, marketing, and turning a profit. They are the kinds of farmers most likely to thrive and secure successors in Japan's increasingly competitive agricultural economy. But they are more than just economic actors; they are also committed to preserving rural communities in ways that resonate with more traditional producers and other rural residents. For them, agriculture is a potential growth industry and then some. It is the ultimate expression of the economic, social, ecological, and cultural dimensions of rural Japan—a crucible for the blending of tradition and modernity, emotion and rationality, and something to be carefully preserved.

Where does this leave JA? As we have illustrated throughout this volume, JA must continue to adapt to and complement the changing agricultural market if it hopes to contribute to the survival of agriculture in this era of economic and demographic upheaval; for only if agriculture survives—nay, thrives—will JA do so as well. This requires putting the interests of farmers first, and not just small-scale, part-time farmers who cannot help themselves; these farmers are in irrevocable decline. To remain relevant, JA must also do more to serve those top performers like Yatsuda Shogo and Nakahata Yoshihirō. What is more, Mayor Umeda reminds us, JA must address not only the economic requirements of those top performers but also the collective needs—social as well as economic—of the localities in which they reside. JA, in sum, must strike a sustainable balance between conforming to market forces while upholding the basics of traditional agricultural cooperation.

Notes

1. ADAPTING TO THE MARKET

1. The English title Japan Agricultural Cooperatives, or JA, was voluntarily adopted by the co-op system during the early 1990s. Before that, the postwar system was known as Nōkyō (*nōgyō kyōdō kumiai*, lit., agricultural cooperative associations). Today, co-ops have formal names that begin with JA (e.g., JA Eichizen Takefu) but are also referred to by the generic term *nōkyō*.

2. This figure is current as of January 1, 2018. The number of co-ops has been steadily shrinking over the years as a result of inter–co-op mergers. JA Zenchū, *JA fakuto bukku*, 10.

3. "Tomita Takashi: 'Hoka no nōkyō ni sakigakete kaikaku dankō, gentan haishi wa mushiro chansu da'" [Tomita Takashi: "As we leap ahead of other co-ops on reform, the abolition of gentan is instead an opportunity"], *Daiyamondo*, February 18, 2017, 68.

4. "Itan nōkyō no chōsen: kindan chokubai, nōka no tame, zenkoku no JA kara onmitsu shisatsu" [The challenge of heretical co-ops: direct sales forbidden for the sake of farmers, participants in covert inspections come from co-ops nationwide], *Asahi shimbun*, March 26, 2014.

5. "Itan nōkyō no chōsen."

6. See, for example, Milly, *New Policies*; Suzuki, *Globalization*; Vogel, *Freer Markets, More Rules*; Vogel, *Japan Remodeled*; Vogel, *Marketcraft*; and Watanabe, *Labor Market Deregulation*.

7. See, for instance, the writings of the noted Japanese agricultural economist Yamashita Kazuhito: Canon Institute for Global Studies (website), "Kazuhito Yamashita," https://cigs.canon/fellows/kazuhito_yamashita.html.

8. For related analyses of how government policies shape corporate and/or market behaviors, see Schaede, *Choose and Focus*; and Vogel, *Marketcraft*.

9. See, for example, Mulgan, "Loosening the Ties that Bind."

10. For compelling, locally oriented perspectives on institutional change in Japanese agriculture more generally, see the work of Hanno Jentzsch, especially *Harvesting State Support*, which was published as this book was going to press.

11. In a similar vein, Jentzsch explores how the national farmland consolidation policies are "sourced" from "local farmland governance models." See Jentzsch, "Tracing the Local Origins."

12. Of particular note is Ang, *How China Escaped*. At the risk of overstatement, there are some parallels between Ang's analysis of institutional and economic development in reform-era China and our story of institutional change inside JA. Like the Chinese government, JA is a hierarchical system of organizations that, during its postwar heyday, had significant authoritarian tendencies. And like China's local government officials, reformist co-op leaders are often masters of improvisation as they adjust their strategies in reaction to shifting conditions. But given the maturity of the JA system, Japanese co-op leaders today may very well have *less* room to innovate than local Chinese officials.

13. Ostrom, *Governing the Commons*, 25.

14. World Bank, "Agriculture, Forestry, and Fishing, Value Added (% of GDP)—Japan," accessed September 9, 2020, https://data.worldbank.org/indicator/NV.AGR.TOTL.ZS?locations=JP.

15. See Davis, *Food Fights*; and Naoi, *Building Legislative Coalitions*.

16. See Hall and Soskice, "Introduction," esp. 8–12.

17. North, *Institutions, Institutional Change*, 3.

18. North, 4.

19. Moe, "Power and Political Institutions," 32; and North, *Institutions, Institutional Change*, 3–6.

20. Moe, "Power and Political Institutions"; and Pierson, "Power in Historical Institutionalism."

21. Hall, "Historical Institutionalism"; Mahoney and Thelen, "Theory of Gradual Institutional Change," 4; North, *Institutions, Institutional Change*, 6; Pierson, *Politics in Time*, 142–53.

22. North, *Institutions, Institutional Change*, 37.

23. For more on the differences between formal and informal institutions, see Helmke and Levitsky, "Informal Institutions"; and Brinks, "Informal Institutions."

24. Helmke and Levitsky, "Informal Institutions," 728–30. See also Kellee S. Tsai, "Adaptive Informal Institutions"; and Lily M. Tsai, "Solidarity Groups."

25. For more on markets as institutions, see Hall and Soskice, "Introduction," 9–11.

26. Heclo, *On Thinking Institutionally*, 38.

27. North, *Institutions, Institutional Change*, 5, 7; and North, *Understanding the Process*, 59.

28. Ostrom, *Governing the Commons*, 51–52.

29. Our definition of *strategy* is based on Hall and Soskice, "Introduction," 14–17. For more on the relationship between organizations and strategies in organization theory, see Scott, *Institutions and Organizations*, 210–16.

30. North, *Institutions, Institutional Change*, 7.

31. For more, see Mulgan, *Politics of Agriculture*, 64–68.

32. Mulgan, 55–64. In addition, JA's national organizations include a travel agency, an organ that provides social welfare services, and two organs that oversee JA's in-house newspaper, publication, and cultural activities.

33. MAFF, "Nōkyō ni tsuite," November 2017, 2. It is important to note that the number of local co-ops is constantly shrinking as a result of mergers. In April 2020, there were just 567 special-purpose co-ops and 584 multipurpose co-ops. MAFF, "Nōkyō ni tsuite," April 2020.

34. Dunn, "Basic Cooperative Principles," 85.

35. As chapter 2 elaborates, these observations reflect a range of insights from both institutional economics and the work of agricultural economists.

36. The politics of Japanese agriculture is a major focus of academic inquiry and, in many ways, beyond the objectives of this book. We therefore limit our references to this topic to aspects of farm-related electoral and bureaucratic politics that shape the contours of institutional and economic reform within JA. For more on those complex political themes, see the various works of Aurelia George Mulgan, including Mulgan, *Politics of Agriculture*; Mulgan, "Where Tradition Meets Change"; and Mulgan, "Loosening the Ties." See also Maclachlan, "Electoral Power"; Maclachlan and Shimizu, "The Kantei vs. the LDP"; Maclachlan and Shimizu, "Japanese Farmers in Flux"; and Maclachlan and Shimizu, "Japanese Agricultural Reform."

37. The term *keitō* is used by JA insiders to denote the agricultural distribution network that connects Zennō to its prefectural affiliates and the co-ops. It is to be distinguished from the JA Group.

38. Bates, *Markets and States*, xii.

39. The term "mindset" corresponds roughly to the Japanese word *ishiki*, which can also be translated as "consciousness" or "awareness." Some younger Japanese farmers use the anglicized version of the word: *maindo setto*.

40. See, for example, Brinks, "Informal Institutions"; and L. Tsai, "Solidarity Groups."

41. See Boettke and Coyne, "Context Matters," 8–9.

42. See, for instance, Hayami, *Japanese Agriculture under Siege*.

43. MAFF, "Nōgyō rōdōryoku ni kansuru tōkei."

44. Yamashita Kazuhito estimates that the number of farm households selling their products exclusively through JA decreased by 20 percent between 2005 and 2010 alone. Yamashita, *Nōkyō kaitai*, 180.

45. In our readings and interviews, we frequently encountered criticisms of the lack of managerial or entrepreneurial mindsets and expertise among traditional Japanese farmers. For example, Yoshida Makoto, agricultural adviser to Mitsubishi Shōji, interview, Tokyo, May 10, 2016; Shimazaki, *Mōkaru nōgyō*.

46. Boas, "Conceptualizing Continuity," 45; and March and Olsen, "Elaborating the 'New Institutionalism,'" 8.

47. See, for example, Moore, *Social Origins of Dictatorship*.

48. See, for example, Steinmo, *Evolution of Modern States*; and Thelen, *How Institutions Evolve*.

49. North, *Institutions, Institutional Change*.

50. Boas, "Conceptualizing Continuity," 45.

51. Rhodes, Binder, and Rockman, *Oxford Handbook of Political Institutions*, xv.

52. Capoccia and Keleman, "Study of Critical Junctures."

53. Pierson and Skocpol, "Historical Institutionalism," 699–700.

54. North, *Institutions, Institutional Change*, 6.

55. Pierson, *Politics in Time*, 10–11. See also Rixen and Viola, "Putting Path Dependence."

56. Pearson, *Politics in Time*, 37.

57. Pierson, 38.

58. Mahoney and Thelen, "Theory of Gradual Institutional Change," 3; and North, *Institutions, Institutional Change*, 7.

59. Mahoney and Thelen, *Explaining Institutional Change*. For other analyses of the potentially transformative effects of gradual, path-dependent institutional change, see Boas, "Conceptualizing Continuity"; Steinmo, *Evolution of Modern States*; and Thelen, *How Institutions Evolve*.

60. Ostrom, *Governing the Commons*, 51–52.

61. While Peter Hall rejects the notion that "shirkers are the motors of history," he reminds us that member defections from institutions can be "important elements" in institutional change. Hall, "Historical Institutionalism," 218. In the case of Japanese local co-ops, the specter of member defection looms over all co-ops and certainly constitutes an incentive to change, but it does not fully explain actual incidents of change.

62. Of JA's 10.37 million members in 2015, 4.43 million were regular members, and 5.94 million were associate members. JA Zenchū, *JA fakuto bukku*, 11.

63. The role of agency has been a major preoccupation for institutionalism scholars in a variety of traditions. For historical institutionalism, see Mahoney and Thelen, *Explaining*

Institutional Change; and Mahoney and Thelen, "Theory of Gradual Institutional Change." For organization theories, see relevant chapters in Adler et al., *Oxford Handbook of Sociology*; and Scott, *Institutions and Organizations*, esp. 114–26. See also Ang, *How China Escaped*. Finally, it can be said that the bulk of Douglass North's relevant writings in institutional economics are fundamentally concerned with explaining the rule-based and organizational contexts in which agents make choices.

64. Ostrom, *Governing the Commons*. See also Ang, *How China Escaped*.

65. The importance of deliberative forums in any cooperative setting cannot be overstated. As Peter Hall and David Soskice observe, "Deliberation provides the actors with an opportunity to establish the risks and gains attendant on cooperation and to resolve the distributive issues associated with them." Hall and Soskice, "Introduction," 11.

66. Hamada Yoshiyuki, former director general, Department of Agriculture, Forestry and Fisheries, Kumamoto Prefectural Government. Interviewed on several occasions between 2016 and 2018.

67. Certified farmers (*nintei nōgyōsha*) are officially designated by local governments as farmers with economically viable farms. (Most are full-time farmers.) As such, they are entitled to special government subsidies.

68. "Itan nōkyō no chōsen."

69. Please contact the authors for access to the data set.

2. THE POSTWAR JA MODEL

1. Torgerson, "Farmer Cooperatives," 92.

2. Yamashita, *Nōkyō kaitai*, 150.

3. Ostrom, *Governing the Commons*, 25.

4. Dunn, "Basic Cooperative Principles," 85. Dunn's definition may be the most widely cited definition of the traditionally organized agricultural co-op.

5. Buccola, "Agricultural Cooperatives."

6. Torgerson, "Farmer Cooperatives," 92.

7. Seipel and Heffernan, "Cooperatives," 1.

8. Buccola, "Agricultural Cooperatives."

9. Cross and Buccola, "Adapting Cooperative Structure," 1254.

10. Chaddad and Cook, "Understanding New Cooperative Models," 350.

11. In some co-ops, voting rights are distributed in proportion to a member's patronage of co-op services. Buccola, "Agricultural Cooperatives."

12. Chaddad and Cook, "Understanding New Cooperative Models," 350.

13. Coltrain, Barton, and Boland, "Differences between New Generation Cooperatives," 3.

14. Nilsson, "Co-operative Organizational Models," 455.

15. Buccola, "Agricultural Cooperatives."

16. Zeuli and Cropp, *Cooperatives*, 27–32.

17. Chaddad and Cook, "Understanding New Cooperative Models," 357.

18. See Alho, "Farmers' Self-Reported Value."

19. Zeuli and Cropp, *Cooperatives*, 20.

20. Nilsson, "Co-operative Organizational Models," 456.

21. Farmers tend to view these investments as essential to the maintenance of co-op management; they do not expect to profit from them. Masaaki Ishida, "Development of Agricultural Cooperatives," 31.

22. See Ōtahara, "JA no 'sōgōsei,'" 5.

23. Kajiura, *Datsu nōkyō*, 22.

24. Yamashita, *Nōkyō kaitai*, 40, 47.

25. France has had by far the highest rate of farmer co-op membership among European and North American countries. Today, the rate stands at approximately 75 percent. Note, however, that this figure reflects farmer participation in *one or more* co-ops, while the Japanese rate of nearly 100 percent reflects membership in the multipurpose co-ops only. Filippi, *Support for Farmers' Cooperatives*, 23.

26. Capoccia and Kelemen, "Study of Critical Junctures," 341.

27. Yamashita, *Nōkyō kaitai*, 38.

28. Fujitani, "Nōkyō at a Crossroads," 376.

29. Ogura, *Agricultural Development*, 86.

30. See Embree, *Suye Mura*, 139–53; Najita, *Ordinary Economies in Japan*, 64–87. See also Morris-Suzuki, "Cooperatives and Grassroots Developments."

31. Najita, *Ordinary Economies in Japan*, 64–66, 73.

32. See Ishida Masaaki, *JA no rekishi*, 10–15.

33. Ishida Masaaki, 12, 22.

34. Yamashita, *Nōkyō kaitai*, 39.

35. Yamashita, 36.

36. Ishida Masaaki, *JA no rekishi*, 9.

37. Ishida Masaaki, 32–33.

38. The co-ops were mobilized primarily to implement national food policy.

39. Ōtahara, "JA no 'sōgōsei,'" 6.

40. Kitade, *Nōkyō wa kyōdō kumiai*, 49–51.

41. In 1946, agricultural productivity was estimated to be less than 20 percent of 1943 levels. Kitade, *Nōkyō wa kyōdō kumiai*, 55.

42. Ishida Masaaki, *JA no rekishi*, 52; Ōtahara, *Nōkyō no taigi*, 44.

43. Mulgan, *Politics of Agriculture*, 49–50.

44. Yamashita Kazuhito, Canon Institute for Global Studies, interview, Tokyo, May 27, 2014.

45. Yamashita, *Nōkyō kaitai*, 39–40.

46. Kajiura, *Datsu nōkyō*, 39.

47. Yamashita, *Nōkyō kaitai*, 52.

48. Kitade, *Nōkyō wa kyōdō kumiai*, 79.

49. Yamashita, *Nōkyō kaitai*, 49.

50. As Mary G. McDonald has observed, these provisions ensured that access to farmland was "much more directly state-regulated in the second half of (the) century than in the first." McDonald, "Agricultural Landholding," 58.

51. McDonald, 59.

52. Jentzsch, "Abandoned Land," 39.

53. Ostrom, *Governing the Commons*, 51–52.

54. The system also facilitated vote mobilization. Mulgan, *Politics of Agriculture*, 383.

55. By 1951, 48 percent of local co-ops were operating in the red; they were resuscitated by a massive government bailout. Ishida Masaaki, *JA no rekishi*, 61–62.

56. Ishida Masaaki, 61–62.

57. For a comprehensive analysis of these and related issues, see Mulgan, "'Japan, Inc.' in the Agricultural Sector."

58. "JA Zenchū shihai hōkai zen'ya" [On the eve of the collapse of JA Zenchū dominance], *Daiyamondo*, November 29, 2014, 37.

59. Primary responsibility for the implementation of JA's electoral tasks is assumed by ostensibly independent "farmers' political leagues" (*nōmin seiji renmei*, or *nōseiren*). See Mulgan, *Politics of Agriculture*, esp. 82–92, 186–92.

60. Ishida Masaaki, *JA no rekishi*, 67; Mulgan, *Politics of Agriculture*, 61–63; and Ogura, *Agricultural Development*, 260.

61. Yamashita, interview, May 27, 2014.

62. The reasoning here was that co-ops and local governments would be better positioned to cooperate on behalf of common goals, as they did during the 1940s and 1950s in the implementation of food rationing programs. Godo, "Japanese Agricultural Cooperative System."

63. Kitade Toshiaki argues that the postwar co-ops were established too quickly; their leadership was weak and they had few assets beyond what they had inherited from their predecessors. Kitade, *Nōkyō wa kyōdō kumiai*, 64.

64. Kitade, 93–102.

65. Kitade, 67.

66. The figures in this paragraph are drawn from MAFF, "Nōkyō ni tsuite," April 2020, 3, 11.

67. Matsuoka, "'Jidai e tsunagu,'" 28.

68. The farm population was already in decline by 1960, however. Just ten years earlier, 16.4 million Japanese, fully 45 percent of the total workforce, were working on farms. Nōgyō to keizai henshū iinkai, *Kīwādo de yomitoku*, 68.

69. Honma and Hayami, "Distortions to Agricultural Incentives," 12.

70. Ogura, *Agricultural Development*, 203.

71. Mulgan, *Politics of Agriculture*, 33.

72. Kelly, "Japanese Farmers," 35–36; Dore, *Land Reform in Japan*, 284; and Iwata Jun, transport company owner, interview, Kumamoto City, June 5, 2014.

73. Price supports for other commodities were dismantled during the 1950s.

74. There were other, less prominent routes to market: the black market and a government approved route for voluntary distributed rice (*jishuryūtsūmai*). The latter was officially introduced in 1969 for higher-quality rice that could not be effectively priced by the government; prices were instead set by government-designated collection organizations and wholesalers. Ironically, the co-ops were officially recognized as collection organizations under this scheme, which simply increased farmer dependence on the co-ops. Since voluntary distributed rice was costly and sometimes difficult to sell, moreover, the Food Agency ended up subsidizing it to a degree—even though the scheme's ultimate purpose was to reduce government debt caused by the subsidization of government rice. Kitade, *Nōkyō wa kyōdō kumiai*, 135–36; Godo, "History."

75. Mulgan, *Politics of Agriculture*, 3–4.

76. Babb, "Making Farmers Conservative."

77. Maclachlan, "Electoral Power."

78. Nōgyō to keizai henshū iinkai, *Kīwādo de yomitoku*, 80–81.

79. In 2017, approximately 940,000, or 72.3 percent, of the 1.3 million commercial farm households in Japan cultivated rice. MAFF, "Inasaku no genjō," 2.

80. See Honma, *Nōgyō mondai*, 64–66.

81. Yamashita Kazuhito, Canon Institute for Global Studies, interview, Tokyo, May 20, 2015.

82. For a comprehensive analysis of gentan, see Arahata, *Gentan haishi*.

83. "Seme no nōsei, dare no tame nōgyō" [Aggressive agricultural policies, agriculture for whom?], *Asahi shimbun*, December 6, 2014.

84. Yamashita Kazuhito, Canon Institute for Global Studies, interview, Tokyo, July 18, 2018.

85. North, *Institutions, Institutional Change*, 5.

86. Kitade, *Nōkyō wa kyōdō kumiai*, 75; Bullock, "Nokyo," 1.

87. Yamashita, *Nōkyō kaitai*, 171.

88. Yamashita, 100–101.

89. Yamashita Kazuhito, Canon Institute for Global Studies, interview, Yabu City, June 8, 2017.

90. Yamashita, interview, June 8, 2017.

91. Kajiura, *Datsu nōkyō*, 64–65.

92. Yamashita, *Nōkyō kaitai*, 100.

93. Masaaki Ishida, "Development of Agricultural Cooperatives," 25.

94. Masuda Yoshiaki, "JA gabanansu no kōzō," 18, 26.

95. Kobayashi, "JA no kiso soshiki," 121–24.

96. See Saitō Yuriko, "Shūraku soshiki."

97. Dore, *Land Reform in Japan*, 290–92.

98. Kobayashi, "JA no kiso soshiki."

99. Masuda Yoshiaki, "JA gabanansu no kōzō," 18.

100. Boland, Hogeland, and McKee, "Current Issues."

101. Masaaki Ishida, "Development of Agricultural Cooperatives," 22.

102. Masaaki Ishida, 28. Some employees fill their quotas by using their own funds to purchase JA products, a practice known as "self-destruction" (*jibaku*). Yamashita, *Nōkyō kaitai*, 117.

103. One prominent JA insider complained that many local co-ops served merely as "yes men" to their prefectural federations. Kajiura, *Datsu nōkyō*, 58.

104. Yamashita Kazuhito, interview, June 8, 2017.

105. For more, see Iiguni, "Kazoku keiei," 34.

106. North, *Institutions, Institutional Change*, 25; Yoshida Makoto, Mitsubishi Shōji, interview, Tokyo, July 18, 2016.

107. Dore, *Land Reform in Japan*, 56–58, 61, 92–93.

108. Matsuoka, "'Jidai e tsunagu,'" 28.

109. Bates, *Markets and States*.

110. Ōtahara, *Nōkyō no taigi*, 16.

111. Unless otherwise specified, the material in this paragraph and the two that follow is drawn from Ōtahara, 45–46.

112. Mulgan, *Politics of Agriculture*, 54.

113. Ōtahara, *Nōkyō no taigi*, 46.

114. The material in this paragraph and the one that follows is drawn from Kajiura, *Datsu nōkyō*.

115. See, for example, Hayami, *Japanese Agriculture under Siege*.

116. Hayami, xii.

117. Ogura, *Agricultural Development*, 86; and JA keiei senryaku kenkyūkai, *Hieiri soshiki no keiei senryaku*, 13.

3. JAPAN'S CHANGING AGRICULTURAL LANDSCAPE

1. Otsu Takamitsu, interview, Kumamoto City, June 4, 2014.

2. Shimada Toshio, interview, Mount Aso, June 17, 2017. Shimada's name has been changed to protect his privacy.

3. Shimada Toshio, interview, Kumamoto City, June 3, 2014.

4. Ministry of the Environment, "Wajimashi."

5. Ishizaki Hidezumi, interview, Kanakura, July 27, 2015.

6. Ishizaki, interview.

7. A controversial 2014 book by Masuda Hiroya, a former governor of Iwate Prefecture, predicted that nearly 900 cities, towns, and villages would be extinct by 2040. *Chihō shōmetsu*.

8. See also Hayami, *Japanese Agriculture under Siege*, 23–24; and Kelly, "Regional Japan," 214–18.

9. MAFF, "Nōgyō rōdōryoku ni kansuru tōkei."

10. US Department of Agriculture, "2017 Census of Agriculture Highlights: Producers."

11. Martha Henriques, "The Aging Crisis Threatening Farming," *BBC World News*, accessed July 2, 2020, http://www.bbc.com/future/bespoke/follow-the-food/the-ageing-crisis-threatening-farming/.

12. Honma, *Nōgyō mondai*, 30.

13. Noda Takeshi, LDP lower house member from Kumamoto Prefecture, interview, Tokyo, June 16, 2014.

14. This provision has helped fuel an increase over the years in the number of noncommercial farmers—that is, those who grow rice or other agricultural products solely for private use.

15. "JA Zenchū shihai hōkai zen'ya" [On the eve of the collapse of JA Zenchū dominance], *Daiyamondo*, November 29, 2014, 41–43. Due to lax enforcement of the tax code, farmers are eligible for reduced electricity and water rates for household—as well as farm-related—purposes simply by having their homes officially designated as an agricultural workplace (*nōsagyōsho*).

16. Otsu Takamitsu, interview, Kumamoto City, June 4, 2014.

17. "Japan's Food Self-Sufficiency Rate Hits Lowest Level in 25 Years Due to Drop in Wheat Production," *Japan Times*, August 6, 2019.

18. "Tanada iji, tanomi wa kankōkyaku, gen'eki jimoto nōka wa 1ken ni" [Number of active local farm households reduced to one, terraced rice paddy preservation now depends on tourists], *Asahi shimbun*, May 6, 2015.

19. For more on this point, see Mulgan, "Where Tradition Meets Change."

20. See Maclachlan, "Electoral Power." For comprehensive analyses of how the farm vote is changing, see Kawamura, "Seiken kōtai jidai no rieki dantai"; and especially Mulgan, "Where Tradition Meets Change."

21. Krauss and Pekkanen, *Rise and Fall*. See also Mulgan, "Where Tradition Meets Change," 271.

22. Mulgan, "Farm Lobby," 112–13, 117.

23. Honma Masayoshi, University of Tokyo, interview, May 29, 2014.

24. Maclachlan and Shimizu, "Kantei vs. the LDP."

25. Maclachlan and Shimizu, 179.

26. Takagi Yūki, "Fukudasōri himeta netsui" [Prime Minister Fukuda's hidden enthusiasm], *Yomiuri shimbun*, February 17, 2014; Yamashita Kazuhito, Canon Institute for Global Studies, interview, Berlin, May 18, 2015.

27. Seisankyoku and Keieikyoku officials (names withheld on request), interviews, Tokyo, July and August 2014.

28. See Takagi Yūki, "'Gurumi senkyo' ni shūshi" [Stopping "group-supported elections"], *Yomiuri shimbun*, March 15, 2014.

29. Mulgan, "Farm Lobby," 113; and Maclachlan and Shimizu, "Japanese Farmers in Flux," 455.

30. Yaguchi Hajime, former managing director of Zenchū, interview, Tokyo, September 7, 2015.

31. Nōgyō to keizai henshū iinkai, *Kīwādo de yomitoku*, 32.

32. Honma, *Nōgyō mondai*, 51–52. See also Davis, *Food Fights*; and Davis and Oh, "Repeal of the Rice Laws."

33. Honma, *Nōgyō mondai*, 15.

34. Honma, 53.

35. There has also been some effort over the years to price a portion of the country's rice supply at auction.

36. Mulgan, *Politics of Agriculture*, 625–26.

37. Mishima, "Revision of Japan's Basic Law," 259.

38. Indeed, and as Mulgan expertly explains, government intervention in the agricultural sphere was to remain a fixture in Japan for years to come. See Mulgan, *Japan's Interventionist State*; and Mulgan, *Japan's Agricultural Policy Regime*.

39. MAFF, "Basic Law on Food."

40. For an in-depth analysis of the New Basic Law, see Mulgan, "'Japan Inc.' in the Agricultural Sector."

41. Banno, "Japanese Agricultural Policy." As Banno writes, efficient and stable farm management "means farming on a level capable of bringing in a lifetime income comparable to that obtainable in other industries by working a similar number of hours."

42. See, for example, MAFF, "Ninaite akushon sapōto jigyō."

43. OECD, "Evaluation of Agricultural Policy Reforms," 61.

44. Figures calculated for various years from MAFF, "Nintei nōgyōshasū."

45. MAFF, "Kōhai nōchi no genjō to taisaku," 2.

46. MAFF, "FY2014 Annual Report," 5. Yamashita Kazuhito estimates that production costs for farms 15 ha or larger can be less than *half* that of Japan's smallest farms. Yamashita, *Nōkyō kaitai*, 151.

47. Yamashita, "Issues in the Farmland System."

48. See McDonald, "Agricultural Landholding in Japan."

49. McDonald, 64; and Honma, *Nōgyō mondai*, 57.

50. McDonald, "Agricultural Landholding in Japan"; and Hirasawa, "Frame and Emerging Reform of Agricultural Policy."

51. Yamashita, "Issues in the Farmland System."

52. MAFF, "FY2015 Annual Report," 20.

53. Honma, *Nōgyō mondai*, 81–82. See Jentzsch, "Tracing the Local Origins," for an analysis of the origins—both local and national—and content of this law.

54. Jones and Kimura, "Reforming Agriculture," 14.

55. A more literal translation of the term would be "Farmland Intermediary Management Organizations." For more on the FLCBs at the local level, see Jentzsch, "Abandoned Land."

56. MAFF, "FY2015 Annual Report," 20.

57. Conversion of arable land is also controlled by government regulation.

58. Honma Masayoshi, University of Tokyo, interview, Tokyo, January 15, 2015.

59. See Iiguni, "Kazoku keiei wo keizaigaku."

60. Sakai, "'Henyō' shitsutsu hattensuru kazoku nōgyō keiei," 3.

61. Takagi Yūki, "Nōgyō keieisha sodatsu kankyō ni" [Toward an environment for raising farm managers], *Yomiuri shimbun*, March 20, 2014.

62. Tashiro, "Hōjinka suisen seisaku," 16–17.

63. See Umemoto, "Nōgyō ni okeru hōjinka," 6.

64. The point here is that while family members—immediate or extended—may remain owners of the farm, its management can be left to "outsiders."

65. Shimada, interview, June 3, 2014.

66. Umemoto, *Nōgyō ni okeru*, 9–11.

67. MAFF, "2015 Census of Agriculture and Forestry."

68. Umemoto, *Nōgyō ni okeru*, 9.

69. Shimada, interview, June 3, 2014.

70. Tashiro, "Hōjinka suisen seisaku," 21.

71. Takagi, "Nōgyō keieisha sodatsu kankyō ni."

72. Tsutaya, *Kyōdo kumiai no jidai*, 149.

73. Shimizu Kazuaki, "Mizuinasaku chiiki," 303.

74. Nōgyō to keizai henshū iinkai, *Kīwādo*, 140.

75. For an analysis of the impact of HBFAs on the survival of rural communities, see Seki and Matsunaga, *Shūraku einō*.

76. Otsu, interview, June 4, 2014.

77. Otsu, interview.

78. Nōgyō to keizai henshū iinkai, *Kīwādo*, 141.

79. Hama Shimon, Japan Board of Audit, interview, Tokyo, June 11, 2015. For a rich analysis of related schemes for collectively managing farmland, see Jentzsch, "Tracing the Local Origins."

80. Otsu, interview, June 4, 2014.

81. Nōgyō to keizai henshū iinkai, *Kīwādo*, 194–95; OECD, "Evaluation of Agricultural Policy Reforms," 75.

82. OECD, "Evaluation of Agricultural Policy Reforms," 76.

83. OECD, 75; Nōgyō to keizai henshū iinkai, *Kīwādo*, 194.

84. MAFF, "Nōgyō seisan hōjin no nōgyō sannyū."

85. For a history of consumer preferences for safe food, see Maclachlan, *Consumer Politics*, chap. 7. Today, nationalist tendencies among Japanese consumers reflect a string of scandals during the late 1990s and 2000s involving tainted food imports, most notably from China.

86. Shimazaki, *Mōkaru nōgyō*, 67–68.

87. Shimizu Masao (director) and Terasaki Shinji, Agricultural Policy Division of the Agriculture, Forestry and Fisheries Department, Ishikawa Prefectural Government, interview, Kanazawa, July 28, 2015.

88. "Otehon nōka ga denjusuru mongaifushutsu no kasegu himitsu" [The jealously guarded earnings secrets passed down by model farmers]," *Daiyamondo*, February 6, 2016.

89. "Otehon nōka."

90. Daijōgo Yutaka and Kitamura Ayumu, Rokusei, interview, Kanazawa, July 29, 2015.

91. *Mokumoku*, or "billowing," evokes the smoke rising from the farm's smokehouses. *Tezukuri* means "handmade."

92. Kimura Osamu, Mokumoku Tezukuri Farm, interview, Mie Prefecture, July 22, 2015.

93. Yamashita, *Nōkyō kaitai*, 169.

94. For a history of these processing firms and their growing dependence on imports, see McDonald, "Food Firms and Food Flows."

95. Hamada Yasunari, Hamada Shoyū, interview, Kumamoto City, June 3, 2014.

96. Komoto, "Nō no 6 ji sangyōka e," 53.

97. "Shinkasuru shokuhin no chikara" [The power of evolving food products], *Asahi shimbun*, December 5, 2016.

98. "Agriculture Innovating to Secure Future," *Japan Times*, January 1, 2019.

99. For more on the relationship between large-scale retailers and the traditional distributional system, see Itoh, "Competition in the Japanese Distribution System."

100. Iwata Jun, transport company owner, interview, Kumamoto City, June 5, 2014.

101. See "Nōgyō saisei no shuyaku wa dare da" [Who's leading the revitalization of agriculture?], *Daiyamondo*, November 29, 2014, 44–57.

102. Saitoh, *Nōshōkō renkei*, 19–20.

103. Saitoh, 16.

104. Iwata Jun, interview, June 5, 2014.

105. Shimazaki, *Mōkaru nōgyō*, 108–9.

106. Yamashita Kazuhito, Canon Institute for Global Studies, interview, Tokyo, January 5, 2015.

107. See, for example, the MAFF's website on Food, Commerce and Industry Coordination, which was originally a METI program: http://www.maff.go.jp/j/shokusan/sanki/nosyoko, accessed June 27, 2020.

108. Kajiura, *Datsu nōkyō*, 44–45.

109. Yoshida Makoto, agricultural adviser to Mitsubishi Shōji, interview, Tokyo, June 18, 2016.

110. Kajiura, *Datsu nōkyō*, 45.

111. Shimazaki, *Mōkaru nōgyō*, esp. 106–11. See also Shimazaki, *Nōgyō Ishin*.

112. See, for example, "Kanenashi konenashi chishikinashi: nōka nyūmon kōza" [No money, no connections, no knowledge: an introductory course for farmers], *Daiyamondo*, November 29, 2014, 58–63.

113. Kimura, interview, July 22, 2015.

4. PUTTING FARMERS FIRST

1. Ostrom, *Governing the Commons*.

2. Agricultural cooperatives are not alone in their struggle to adapt to slow-moving structural changes; other nonprofit interest organizations, including labor unions, face similar challenges. Nor are the challenges confronting agricultural cooperatives confined to the West. The Republic of Korea, for instance, has been immersed in a debate following the conclusion of a comprehensive free trade agreement with the United States (KORUS) about how best to reorganize farm cooperatives. Similar debates are unfolding in the People's Republic of China.

3. USDA, "Agricultural Cooperatives," 7.

4. See, for example, Hogeland, "Managing Uncertainty."

5. Torgerson, "Critical Look," 15.

6. Nilsson, Svendsen, and Svendsen, "Are Large and Complex," 193.

7. OECD, "Agricultural Support."

8. Torgerson, "Critical Look," 15.

9. Hogeland, "Economic Culture."

10. Nilsson, Svendsen, and Svendsen, "Are Large and Complex," 191–92.

11. Hogeland, "Economic Culture," esp. 75.

12. Chaddad and Cook, "Understanding New Cooperative Models."

13. Coltrain, Barton, and Boland, "Differences"; and Kelley, "Introduction to New Generation Cooperatives."

14. Dunn, "Basic Cooperative Principles," 85.

15. Nilsson, "Co-operative Organizational Models," 453–54; and Bijman and Iliopoulos, "Farmers' Cooperatives in the EU," 505.

16. In the European Union, the number of transnational co-ops increased from just a handful during the 1990s to forty-six in 2012. Jos Bijman et al., "Support for Farmers' Cooperatives," 12.

17. Hogeland, "Economic Culture," 73.

18. Pempel, *Regime Shift*.

19. Ōtahara, *Nōkyō no taigi*, 9.

20. Kajiura, *Datsu nōkyō*, 44–45.

21. For a detailed account of this phenomenon, see Kajiura.

22. Kajiura, 70.

23. For accounts of these and related JA practices, see Kajiura and the writings of Yamashita Kazuhito, including *Nōkyō kaitai* and *Nihon nōgyō wa sekai ni kateru*.

24. Yurugi, "Zennō to keizairen," 142.

25. Fujita et al., "Kenrenshudōgata," 29.

26. JA Zenkyōren, "2018 Annual Report," 4.

27. Yurugi, "Zennō to keizairen," 139–40.

28. Yurugi, 142.

29. Fujita et al., "Kenrenshudōgata." For a definitive analysis of the relationship between co-ops and Hokuren, their regional economic federation, see Kajiura, *Datsu nōkyō*.

30. Yurugi, "Zennō to keizairen," 142.

31. Zennō, Kajiura wryly complained, was treating farmers like prey (*kuimono*). *Datsu nōkyō*, 52.

32. Ōtahara, *Nōkyō no taigi*, 14.

33. Yamashita Kazuhito, Canon Institute for Global Studies, interview, Tokyo, July 18, 2019.

34. Fujita et al., "Kenrenshudōgata," 33.

35. Hamada Yoshiyuki, former director general, Department of Agriculture, Forestry and Fisheries, Kumamoto Prefectural Government, interview, Kumamoto City, July 10, 2018.

36. Yamashita Kazuhito, Canon Institute for Global Studies, interview, Tokyo, October 7, 2017.

37. Nozawa Satoshi, *Nōgyō kyōdō kumiai shimbun*, interview, Tokyo, July 17, 2018.

38. Tanaka Yukio and Shimura Tomoya, JA Saku Asama employees, interviews, Saku City, Nagano Prefecture, July 23, 2018.

39. Ōtahara, *Nōkyō no taigi*, 15.

40. Unless otherwise indicated, the next two paragraphs are drawn from Tashiro, *Nōkyō kaikaku to heisei gappei*, 20, 36–60.

41. MAFF, "Nōgyō kyōdō kumiai sū."

42. MAFF, *Nōkyō ni tsuite*, April 2020, 2.

43. Yamaguchi and Morozumi, "Shokuin no ishiki kara mita," 69.

44. The total number of co-op branches in Japan decreased as a result of mergers from 16,623 in 1995 to 8,728 in 2010. In the past, the jurisdiction of each branch approximated that of an elementary school district. Today, branches roughly duplicate middle-school districts. Masuda Yoshiaki, "JA gabanansu no kōzō," 29.

45. MAFF, "Nōgyō kyōdō kumiai oyobi dō rengōkai."

46. Tashiro, *Nōkyō kaikaku to heisei gappei*, 59–60.

47. Yurugi, "Zennō to keizairen," 141.

48. Ōtahara, *Nōkyō no taigi*, 25.

49. Yamashita, *Nōkyō kaitai*, 104.

50. Ishida Masaaki, *Nōkyō wa chiiki ni*, 73–83.

51. Fukuda, "Nōkyō soshiki no gabanansu bunseki," 5.

52. Kitade, *Nōkyō wa kyōdō kumiai*, 105.

53. Masuda Yoshiaki, "JA gabanansu no kōzō," 34.

54. Masuda Yoshiaki, 35.

55. Ishida Masaaki, *Nōkyō wa chiiki ni*, 74.

56. Tsutaya, *Kyōdō kumiai no jidai*, 144.

57. In late 2018, JA Niigata resolved to reduce the total number of Niigata co-ops to five by 2023. "Kennai JA, 5kasho ni shūyaku, 5nengo medo, kentaikai kettei" [Prefectural convention decides to reduce prefectural co-ops to five in five years], *Asahi shimbun*, November 21, 2018.

58. MAFF, "Nōgyō kyōdō kumiai no keizai jigyō."

59. See, for example, JA Zenchū, *JA fakuto bukku*, 47; and JA Zennō Nagoya, "Tashikana ippo kara saki e" [From a solid first step toward the future], accessed July 10, 2020, https://www.nn.zennoh.or.jp/kaikaku/.

60. Hamada Yoshiyuki, director general, Department of Agriculture, Forestry and Fisheries, Kumamoto Prefectural Government, interview, Kumamoto City, June 17, 2017; Nozawa, interview, July 17, 2018; Kimura Osamu, Mokumoku Tezukuri Farm, interview, Mie Prefecture, July 22, 2015. From that amount, the farm household will have to pay taxes—which remain low for farmers—and cover the costs of agricultural production.

61. Of the co-ops that do publish past disclosure statements and other data sources online, some do not measure their data consistently over time.

62. Please contact the authors for access to the relevant data set.

63. We deliberately excluded major beef-, pork-, and dairy-producing prefectures—like Kagoshima, Miyazaki, and especially Hokkaido—from our data set, as these industries tend to be national outliers in terms of farm size (large), production costs (high), and the like. (It is for these reasons that MAFF often separates Hokkaido from its data on national agricultural trends.)

64. Co-op strategies for raising farmer incomes that we cannot explore include lowering input prices and commission rates. Unfortunately, there are no consistent, co-op-level data available in 2018 for either measure. However, we do know on the basis of co-op disclosure documents that the total volume of input sales was less than 50 percent of the total volume of sales of agricultural products for our 105 co-ops. Furthermore, since input costs tend to change far more slowly than the prices of agricultural output, we view the latter as a better indicator of individual co-op efforts to serve its farmer-members.

65. Ishida Masaaki, *Nōkyō wa chiiki ni*, 73.

66. Our definition of regular members focuses on individual farmer-members and excludes incorporated farm enterprises.

67. It would also be useful to calculate the amount of AMH per full-time co-op employee, but many co-ops do not disclose clear, consistent data on their employees.

68. There is an insurance system in place to protect farmers against excessive losses.

69. Odaka, "JA ni yoru nōsanbutsu," 6.

70. "Kome no kaitori hanbai: toriatsukai no 4 wari ni [Buy-up sales used for 40 percent of rice handled]," *Nōgyō kyōdō kumiai shimbun*, March 10, 2021, https://www.jacom.or.jp/noukyo/news/2021/03/210310-49945.php.

71. Odaka, "JA ni yoru nōsanbutsu."

72. Both commission rates and dividends are set by individual co-ops. Today, most co-ops have lowered their commission rates to approximately 3 percent of a product's final sales value. Since commission rates are product specific and fixed in relation to those final prices, it is in the co-op's (as well as the farmer's) interest to secure the highest possible wholesale prices. It should also be noted that raw product that travels up the keitō will be subject to *two* rounds of commission. Co-op dividends are calculated on the basis of the level of member patronage of co-op services.

73. A total of 676 of 679 co-ops surveyed in 2015 were profitable in insurance. MAFF, "Nōkyō ni tsuite," November 2017, 17.

74. See, for example, Tsutaya, "Nōkyō nōgyō kashidashi shinchō."

75. "JA Banku zentai de nōgyō kanren yūshi shea."

76. "JA Banku, nōgyō yūshi 3nen renzoku zō" [JA Bank increases its agricultural loans for the third year in a row], *Nihon nōgyō shimbun*, May 26, 2019.

77. Over 50 percent of regular members are over the age of seventy. MAFF, "Nōkyō ni tsuite," November 2017, 4.

78. The definitions of full-time and part-time farmers tend to vary across co-ops. There is, for example, no consistent measure—the number of days per year devoted to farm work or earnings from agriculture, and so on—for distinguishing between the two types of farmers.

79. Given our assumption that virtually all farmers are JA members regardless of the extent to which they use JA services, this measure of the general population should effectively mimic the ratio within our co-ops.

80. JA Zenchū, *JA fakuto bukku*, 47.

81. A 2008 Nōrinchūkin study found that profitable co-ops had AMH per member of 1.51 million yen, while co-ops in the red were at 650,000, or just 43 percent of their profitable counterparts (t-value of 5.236). In other words, profitable co-ops marketed and handled a lot more volume. Odaka, "Nōkyō ni okeru nōgyō," 56.

82. The co-ops can, of course, boost their AMH by reducing their payments to farmers. But we have yet to see concrete evidence of such practices.

83. See MAFF, "Nōkyō no genjō to kadai."

84. Inayoshi Masahiro, farmer, interview, Karuizawa, July 17, 2017.

85. The co-ops can also steer farmers into purchasing specific Zennō inputs through their agricultural consultation services (*einō shidō*).

86. Former top MAFF bureaucrat Okuhara Masaaki underscores this point in his book, *Nōsei kaikaku*, 117–18.

87. Masuda Yoshiaki, *Kinkyū tenken!*, 25–27.

88. Masuda Yoshiaki, 27.

89. Mahoney, "Path Dependence," 518.

90. Kobayashi, "JA no kiso soshiki."

91. Miyamoto Kenji, restaurant owner, interview, Kumamoto City, July 10, 2018.

92. Jentzsch, "Village Institutions."

93. Masuda Yoshiaki, "JA gabanansu no kōzō."

94. Kitade, *Nōkyō wa kyōdō kumiai*, 109.

5. A TALE OF TWO CO-OPS

1. Rankings are for total agricultural output for FY2017. Rankings for the six prefectures included in our data set (see chapter 4) are as follows: Chiba, fourth; Kumamoto, sixth; Niigata, twelfth; Nagano, thirteenth; Yamagata, fourteenth; and Shizuoka, fifteenth. MAFF, "Seisan nōgyō shotoku tōkei."

2. Figures drawn from 2018 disclosure statements of each co-op. Please contact authors for access to these data.

3. Iwata Jun, transport company owner, interview, Kumamoto City, June 5, 2014.

4. Hamada Yoshiyuki, director general, Department of Agriculture, Forestry and Fisheries, Kumamoto Prefectural Government, interview, June 5, 2014.

5. Hamada, interview; and Nozawa Satoshi, *Nōgyō kyōdō kumiai shimbun*, interview, Tokyo, July 17, 2018.

6. Unless otherwise specified, this section is based on two lengthy interviews with Kodama Kōyō, former JA Kamimashiki employee and head of the S. Mega-Farm, Kumamoto Prefecture, July 24, 2017, and July 9, 2018; unpublished megafarm documents provided by and discussed with Kodama; newspaper articles; two follow-up phone interviews with Kodama conducted on August 5, 2018, and July 24, 2019; and interviews with Hamada Yoshiyuki, Kumamoto City, June 4 and 5, 2014; June 17 and July 9, 2017; and July 10, 2018. Kodama's name and the name of his farm have been changed at his request, and newspaper references to him have been withheld.

7. A rate of arable land use of more than 100 percent means that local cultivators are producing more than one harvest per year.

8. Hamada Yoshiyuki, director general, Department of Agriculture, Forestry and Fisheries, Kumamoto Prefectural Government, interview, Kumamoto City, July 10, 2018.

9. Ishida Masaaki, *JA no rekishi*, 73.

10. Kodama, interview, July 9, 2018.

11. As discussed in chapters 4 and 6, this is known as the unconditional consignment sales (mujōken itaku hanbai) method.

12. Kodama, interview, July 9, 2018.

13. Kodama, interview.

14. Kodama, interview.

15. Hamada, interview, July 10, 2018.

16. Unless otherwise specified, this section is based on interviews with Tanaka Yukio and Shimura Tomoya, head of the vegetable section (*yasai ka*) of the agricultural consultation division (*einō shidō bu*) of JA Saku Asama, Saku City, July 23, 2018, and with Tanaka on August 8, 2018; unpublished co-op documents discussed with Shimura and Tanaka; and a follow-up phone interview conducted with Tanaka on July 24, 2019. Tanaka's and Shimura's names have been changed on request.

17. Tableland vegetables are grown in high elevation but relatively level areas.

18. Shimazaki, *Mōkaru nōgyō*, 126.

19. By "JA Nagano," we mean the prefecture's local multipurpose co-ops and various prefecturewide associations, including the chūōkai, the central organization affiliated with Zenchū that functions as the co-ops' main spokesperson.

20. JA Nagano has also introduced some noteworthy branding strategies for its top products. Due to space restrictions, we focus in this section on the prefecture's production and product collection strategies. We address branding and marketing (in Niigata Prefecture) in the next chapter.

21. Tanaka, interview, July 23, 2018.

22. Kaneshige Mikio, interview, Karuizawa, June 17, 2019.

23. Kaneshige, interview.

24. Tanaka, interview, July 23, 2018.

25. The rental service is designed to help small-scale farmers who cannot afford to purchase their own machinery. "Nōki rentaru shidō" [Agricultural machinery rentals activated], *Nihon nōgyō shimbun*, July 19, 2018.

26. Yanagisawa Toshihiko, interview, Karuizawa, July 23, 2018.

6. JA'S SANCTUARY

1. More specifically, as Mulgan writes, rice cultivation is "a way of profitably maintaining farmland as an asset inherited down through the generations." Mulgan, *Politics of Agriculture*, 24.

2. As of 2018, Japan's rate of national self-sufficiency in food production is 37 percent (in caloric terms). This is the lowest rate in the industrialized world. But with the exception of only a few years, Japan has enjoyed self-sufficiency—98 percent in 2018—in rice production for more than a half century. MAFF, "Kome wo meguru kankei shiryō," 4.

3. In the words of Emiko Ohnuki-Tierney, rice has been "a dominant metaphor of the Japanese." *Rice as Self*, 4–5.

4. Yamashita, *Nōkyō kaitai*, 177; and JA Zenchū, *JA fakuto bukku*, 48.

5. "Sanchi gisō giwaku ni nageuri mo JA gurūpu no fukai yami" [Suspicions that the JA Group's illicit practices include dumping camouflaged rice], *Daiyamondo*, February 18, 2017, 31–35.

6. Most "rice-centric co-ops" are located in eastern Japan.

7. Our argument reflects the sum of our interviews and analysis of numerous accounts of rice-centric co-ops.

8. Yamashita, *Nōkyō kaitai*, 180.

9. See Davis, *Food Fights*. For more on rice market changes before 1994, see Mulgan, *Politics of Agriculture*, 275–77.

10. Godo, "History of Japan's."

11. See MAFF, "Nōrin suisanbutsu," 1.

12. Yamashita, *Nōkyō kaitai*, 177; and JA Zenchū, *JA fakuto bukku*, 48.

13. JA Zenchū, *JA fakuto bukku*, 47.

14. MAFF, "Kokumin hitori."

15. Leo Lewis, "Japan: End of the Rice Age," *Financial Times*, September 21, 2015.

16. Ako Mari, "Naze tabenai! Kome no shōhi ga heritsuzukeru shin'in" [Why aren't they eating it! The causes of the continuing decline of rice consumption], *Tōyō keizai Online*, April 29, 2018, https://toyokeizai.net/articles/-/218173?page=2.

17. "Kome zōsan 1% domari, 18 nensan sakuzuke, gentan haishi de mo shinchō" [Rice production increases by only 1%; the 2018 planting remains cautious despite the end of gentan], *Nihon keizai shimbun*, October 3, 2018.

18. Donburi consists of vegetables, meat or chicken, and other ingredients that are simmered together and served over rice.

19. Yoshida Yūji, interview, Tokyo, May 31, 2019. Yoshida's name has been changed at his request.

20. Yamashita, "Rather than Being Abolished."

21. Doi Takero, "Kome no kakaku ga 3 nen de 3 wari mo jōshōshita konpon riyū" [The reason rice prices have risen 30 percent over the last 3 years], *Tōyō keizai Online*, April 30, 2018, https://toyokeizai.net/articles/-/218648.

22. "Konbini onigiri, gyūdon . . . kome busoku de aitsugu neage: hojokin nōsei ga maneita shissei no tsuke" [A succession of price increases for convenience store rice balls and beef bowls is caused by rice shortages; misgovernment caused by agricultural subsidy policies], *Business Insider*, January 30, 2018, https://www.businessinsider.jp/post-160976.

23. Yamashita, "Rather than Being Abolished."

24. Ohnuki-Tierney observed during the early 1990s that consumers were willing to pay top prices for good rice in part because they were eating less of it. *Rice as Self*, 40, 43. It is important to note, however, that households are more price sensitive now than they were a generation ago.

25. "Japan's Farmers Double Output of Premium Rice," *Nikkei Asian Review*, November 7, 2018, https://asia.nikkei.com/Business/Business-trends/Japan-s-farmers-double-output-of-premium-rice.

26. MAFF, "Heisei 30nensan kome." The data used are for rice harvested in the fall of 2017 and sold through October 2018.

27. MAFF, "Seisan nōgyō shotoku tōkei."

28. JA Echigo Jōetsu shares this distinction with many other co-ops—fifty-three others in February 2020. See "Reiwa gannen sanmai no shokumi rankingu" [Taste rankings of rice produced in 2019], *Shokuhin sangyō shimbunsha nyūsu Web*, February 27, 2020, https://www.ssnp.co.jp/news/rice/2020/02/2020-0227-1206-15.html.

29. MAFF, "Nōgyō kyōdō kumiai oyobi dō rengōkai," various years.

30. Unless otherwise specified, the following analysis of JA Uonuma Minami is based on interviews with Kaneko Kunio, head of the Special Rice Sales Section; Nishiyama Jun, head of the Farm Section (*einōbu*); and Tajima Seiji, head of the Organic Rice Section, Minami Jōetsu City, July 17, 2014. At their request, the names of these individuals have been changed.

31. MAFF, "Kome ni kansuru mansurī repōto," December 2018.

32. Beikoku antei kyōkyū kakuho shien kikō, "Heisei 30nensan suitō no hinshu betsu sakutsuke dōkō" [Planting trends of different rice varieties in 2018], Kome Net, April 11, 2019, http://www.komenet.jp/pdf/H30sakutuke.pdf.

33. Why so little attention to organic rice? The conventional argument that the JA Group discourages the elimination of agricultural chemicals because it lowers farmer demand for Zennō's inputs does not hold for JA Uonuma Minami, which directly imports most of its chemicals from abroad. The main reason is that organic production is hard work. For many farmers, the extra time needed to battle weeds and pests is simply not worth the modestly higher financial returns. Co-ops, for their part, must introduce a denser thicket of operational rules when producing organic rice, including stricter production monitoring, to ensure that their output meets the nation's high certification standards for organic foods. Since the March 2011 nuclear meltdown in Fukushima Prefecture, however, there has been an uptick in consumer demand for organic rice and other foods.

34. "JA Uonuma Minami: kome no seisan · hanbai to shizai kakaku teigen" [JA Uonuma Minami: the production and sale of rice and the reduction of input prices], *Nōgyō kyōdō kumiai shimbun*, July 24, 2018, https://www.jacom.or.jp/noukyo/rensai/2018/07/180724-35847.php.

35. Kaneko, interview, July 17, 2014.

36. MAFF, "Heisei 27nensan" and "Heisei 30nensan."

37. Since farmers would complain if the co-op made downward adjustments to its initial payments to farmers following a post-harvest drop in market prices, some co-ops would compensate by raising the costs of future rice collections and/or charging farmers higher commissions. Yamashita, *Nōkyō kaitai*, 138.

38. "JA Uonuma Minami: kome no seisan."

39. "Uonuma koshihikari, mamore burando, JAL kokusaibin no kinaishoku ni" [Uonuma koshihikari, a protected brand, to be served in in-flight meals on international flights], *Asahi shimbun*, May 12, 2012.

40. Kaneko, interview, July 17, 2014.

41. Kaneko, interview.

42. One indication of JA Uonuma Minami's status as a "good co-op" is its high rankings in periodic surveys conducted by the news magazine *Daiyamondo*. In the magazine's March 9, 2019, issue (see 60–61), the co-op received the highest overall farmer-member rankings among 116 co-ops on such measures as sales performance, input sales, perceptions of the co-op's willingness to engage in reform, and so on. Unfortunately, the response rates for these surveys tend to be very low; only eight farmer-members from JA Uonuma Minami responded to the 2019 survey.

43. "Tsubuzoroi no kome wo: shūkaku honban, Minami Uonuma de tōkyū kensa" [Toward rice of uniform excellence: the harvest and grade inspection at Minami Uonuma], *Asahi shimbun*, September 21, 2018.

44. "Uonuma koshihikari," *Asahi shimbun*, May 12, 2012.

45. "Kome banare, kuitometai: Minami Uonumashi · koshihikari jōrei 'motto chōshoku ni'" [We want to curb "the drift away from rice": Minami Uonuma City's koshihikari ordinance promotes more rice for breakfast], *Asahi shimbun*, October 22, 2013.

46. "Gyakufū no nōkyō: nōka no shotoku, zōdai sakusen" [Co-ops in the headwinds: farmer incomes and expansion strategies], *Asahi shimbun*, September 29, 2018.

47. Kaneko, interview, July 17, 2014.

48. "Yairo suika, ajiwatte, niigata de senden" [Yairo watermelon, something to be savored, according to Niigata advertising], *Asahi shimbun*, July 24, 2014.

49. "Yairo shiitake, nikuatsu shikoshiko no shokkan uri" [Yairo shiitake, selling a meaty, spongy texture], *Asahi shimbun*, September 12, 2012.

50. Uonuma Minami nōgyō kyōdō kumiai, "Disclosure 2018," 78.

51. "'JA Minami Uonuma' tanjō; tokuA fukkatsu koshi, senryaku kyōka" [The birth of "JA Minami Uonuma": a restored special-A rating for its koshihikari and strengthened strategies], *Asahi shimbun*, March 2, 2019.

52. "Jichitai no namae ga kawaru: Niigata" [The names of localities are changing: Niigata], *Asahi shimbun*, February 5, 2003.

53. "JA Niigata chūōkai, kennai 24 JA wo 5tsu ni saihen, 5nengo medo, saabisu no shitsu iji" [JA Niigata's Central Union of Agricultural Cooperatives to reorganize 24 local co-ops into 5 within next 5 years in order to maintain quality of service], *Nihon keizai shimbun*, November 21, 2018.

54. "'JA Minami Uonuma' tanjō."

55. Those regions are Jōetsu, Chūetsu, Uonuma, Kaetsu, and Sado.

56. "Sakerarenai: JA gappei" [It can't be avoided: JA mergers], *Tokyo yomiuri shimbun*, May 15, 2019.

57. "Uonumasan koshihikari, hajimete saikō hyōka nigasu, shokumi ranku" [For the first time, Uonumasan koshihikari misses the highest rating in taste ranks], *Nihon keizai shimbun*, February 28, 2018.

58. "Sanchi gisō giwaku," 31.

59. "Tsubuzoroi no kome wo."

60. Unless otherwise noted, the analysis in this section is based on interviews with Kikuchi Sado, farmer, and two employees of JA Eichgo Jōetsu's Sanwa branch, Inoue Yoshifumi (retired) and Kojima Daizō (head of agricultural consulting), Sanwa, November 21, 2018. At their request, the names of these individuals have been changed.

61. In Japan, some cities are divided into wards and others into towns. Towns are normally composed of villages, which are in turn divided into hamlets. But there are no uniform standards for the organization or naming of local communities and their component parts. Hence Jōetsu City's division into wards and hamlets.

62. "Matta nashi! Ninaitezukuri 'natsu no jin' ni zenryoku wo" [No time to wait! Let's go all out in nurturing the next generation of core farmers], *Nōgyō kyōdo kumiai shimbun*, July 5, 2006, https://www.jacom.or.jp/archive02/document/tokusyu/toku190/toko190k06070508.html.

63. Shimizu, "Mizuinasaku chiiki ni okeru," 309.

64. Twenty hectares is the magic number for Japanese rice farms. Economists argue that farms this size and larger are in a position to minimize the costs of rice cultivation and maximize profits.

65. Kikuchi, interview, November 21, 2018.

66. See also Shimizu, "Mizuinasaku chiiki ni okeru," 311.

67. Aoki Katsuaki, interview, Nagano City, August 3, 2019.

68. See also "JA Echigo Jōetsu x Jōetsushi: shūraku kan renkei de chiiki zukuri" [JA Echigo Jōetsu x Jōetsu City: building regions through inter-hamlet cooperation], *Nōgyō kyōdo kumiai shimbun*, October 17, 2016. http://www.jacom.or.jp/nousei/tokusyu/2016/10/161017-31115.php.

69. "JA Echigo Jōetsu."

70. Japan Grain Inspection Association, *Heiseigannen kara no tokuA*, 2.

71. Aoki, interview, August 3, 2019.

72. Inoue, interview, November 21, 2018.

73. "Suiden furu katsuyōshi hōfu na kome no shinazoroe" [Making full use of rice paddies and creating an abundant product lineup for rice], *Nōgyō kyōdo kumiai shimbun*, March 22, 2018, http://www.jacom.or.jp/kome/closeup/2018/180322-34885.php.

74. "Hanbaisaki to musubitsuki wo kyōka gyōmu・kakōyō ni mo taiō wo" [Working to strengthen ties with buyers, including processors], *Nōgyō kyōdō kumiai shimbun*, May 25, 2018, https://www.jacom.or.jp/nousei/tokusyu/2018/05/180525-35332.php.

75. "Gyōmuyō mo ichihayaku taiō: juyō ni ōji kome tsukuri" [Quickly dealing with the need for business rice: rice production that responds to demand], *Nihon nōgyō shimbun*, May 9, 2019.

76. "Hanbaisaki to musubitsuki wo."

77. Shimada Toshio, interview, Kumamoto City, June 3, 2014.

78. Lewis, "Japan." Tamaki Ichiro, a well-known rice farmer who now exports his rice to other countries, including the United States, argues that several brands of Japanese rice are now competitive abroad. Yamaguchi Ryōko, "Seisan kosuto hangen de kokusanmai wa sekai wo sekken suru!?" [At half the production costs, Japanese rice is conquering the world!?], *Wedge Report*, October 17, 2018, https://wedge.ismedia.jp/articles/-/14225.

79. MAFF, "Kome wo meguru kankei shiryō," 87.

80. The next four paragraphs are based on an interview with Kawai Naotada, former chairman of Ōtoya, Tokyo, July 9, 2014.

81. Some of the Southeast Asian farmers whom Ōtoya works with acquired their skills as short-term interns at farms in Japan.

82. Kawai, interview, July 9, 2014.

83. Yamashita Kazuhito, Canon Institute for Global Studies, interview, Tokyo, July 18, 2018.

84. Yamashita, "Can the Abe Administration Export Rice?"

85. Iida, *JA kaitai*, 24. Total rice exports, including those of exporters working outside of Zennō but excluding processed foods made from rice, were less than 10,000 tons in 2016—9,986 tons, to be exact. But that number has significantly increased since then. See MAFF, "Kome wo meguru kankei shiryō," esp. 87.

7. ABENOMICS, JA SELF-REFORM, AND THE FUTURE OF AGRICULTURAL COOPERATIVES IN JAPAN

1. Iida, *JA kaitai*, 81.

2. The farmland consolidation banks, which empower prefectural governments to serve as intermediaries in the supply and leasing of farmland, are viewed as a more effective variant of organizations introduced in 1970. By the end of 2014, all forty-seven prefectures had consolidation banks in place, and the level of farmland concentration was approximately 48 percent; by 2017, the concentration level had risen to 55.2 percent. See Yamashita, "Issues in the Farmland"; MAFF, "Nōchi chūkan kanri jigyō no 5nengo minaoshi ni tsuite," 3. See also Jentzsch, "Abandoned Land."

3. Mulgan, "Where Tradition Meets Change," 290.

4. See, for example, the various chapters in Taniguchi and Ishii, *Nihon nōgyō nenpō 61*.

5. On January 20, 2017, the day US president Donald Trump was sworn into office, the Japanese Diet ratified the TPP agreement. A few days later, President Trump eviscerated Abe's hard-won victory by officially withdrawing the United States from the pact. An eleven-nation version of the pact went into effect in late 2018 and is expected to boost not only Japanese farm exports but also some farm imports—most notably beef and pork. The increase in imports, however, is likely to be fairly modest.

6. Taniguchi, "Abenomikusu nōsei no zentaizō,"10–11.

7. See Mulgan, "Much Ado About Something?," 86.

8. See Honma, "Nōkyō wa doko e."

9. See Masuda Yoshiaki, "Nōkyo kaikaku," 13–15.

10. Masuda Yoshiaki, "Nōkyo kaikaku"; and Nishii, "Nōgyō kōzō no henka," 83–88.

11. Baba, "'JA gurūpu einō・keizai kakushin puran,'" 36–38.

12. See, for example, Okuhara, *Nōsei kaikaku*, esp. chap. 3.

13. Murata Yasuo, agricultural journalist, interview, Tokyo, May 20, 2016.

14. Okuhara experienced his formative moment as an agricultural reformer while serving in the Japanese embassy in West Germany following the 1989 collapse of the Berlin Wall. As he observed the gradual reintegration of the East and West German economies, he recognized in the moribund East German farm sector the perils of excessive

government intervention in agricultural markets. It was a cautionary tale, he concluded, for Japan. Okuhara, *Nōsei kaikaku*, 3, 16–18.

15. Okuhara, 107, 112.

16. Kanda, "Kurikaesareru 'nōkyō kaikaku ron.'"

17. Taniguchi, "Abenomikusu nōsei no zentaizō," 7; and Ishida Nobutaka, 'Nōkyō kaikaku,' 12–13.

18. Iida, *JA kaitai*, 100–101.

19. Iida, 99.

20. See, for example, Nōsangyoson bunka kyōkai, *Kisei kaikaku kaigi*.

21. For more on the content of reform and the myriad political trade-offs that preceded the passage of amendments to the Co-op Law, see Iida, *JA kaitai*; Maclachlan and Shimizu, "Japanese Agricultural Reform"; Mulgan, "Loosening the Ties"; and Mulgan, "Much Ado About Something?"

22. We concur with Mulgan's assessment that while limited, the Abe government's co-op reforms were unprecedented and hence "radical." Mulgan, "Much Ado About Something?"

23. The point here, of course, is that while co-ops are encouraged to pursue profits, those profits should be returned to farmers.

24. The Abe government did not limit its reform initiatives to JA in August 2015. It also introduced changes to local agricultural committees (nōgyō iinkai)—long a drag on the loosening of farmland regulations at the local level. Members will now be appointed by municipal mayors rather than elected by local farmers, and a majority of appointed members must be certified farmers, thus increasing the likelihood that the committees will support future government-led efforts to rationalize local farming. The Agricultural Land Act was also amended to raise the ceiling on nonfarm corporate ownership of farmland within the purview of agricultural production corporations from 25 percent to just under 50 percent. Maclachlan and Shimizu, "Japanese Farmers in Flux," 463–64.

25. See Mulgan, "Much Ado About Something?," for a comprehensive analysis of the details of these reforms.

26. Fujimoto Taku, assistant manager, Agricultural Policy Department, JA Zenchū, interview, Tokyo, July 23, 2015.

27. Shimizu Masao and Terasaki Shinji, officials with the Agricultural Policy Division of the Agriculture, Forestry and Fisheries Department, Ishikawa Prefecture, interview, Kanazawa, July 28, 2015.

28. This was not the first time farm zoku politicians bounced back after a spell in the political wilderness; as Mulgan observed in 2005, they have long demonstrated "impressive powers of political survival." Mulgan, "Where Tradition Meets Change," 284.

29. "Nihon no nōgyō kikan shisutemu mezasu: Aguri Hub Itō Shōichi CEO" [Toward a core system for Japanese agriculture: Aguri Hub's CEO, Itō Shōichi]," JAcom, August 21, 2020, https://www.jacom.or.jp/noukyo/rensai/2020/08/200821-45921.php.

30. Unless otherwise specified, the remainder of this section is based on an interview with Aoki Katsuaki, head of JA Echigo Jōetsu's management committee, Nagano City, August 3, 2019.

31. Aoki, interview.

32. The 2009 liberalization of farmland leasing rules to allow nonfarm corporations to lease farmland is viewed by many traditionalists as an unwelcome violation of this principle.

33. "Daikibo nōka ga kakaeru nayami wo sōgōteki ni kaiketsu" [Comprehensively solving the problems of large-scale farm households]," NikkeiBP, February 3, 2017, https://special.nikkeibp.co.jp/NBO/businessfarm/innovation/03.

34. Zennō official (name withheld on request), interviews, Tokyo, August 2, 2017, and July 4, 2018. TAC was introduced in part to help shore up Zennō's reputation, which was tarnished by media revelations of its misrepresentation of the prefectural origins of JA rice and illegal diversion of JA rice into more lucrative free-market channels. Ten years after the program was launched, only 264 local co-ops had TAC experts on board—fewer than half the total number (654) of co-ops at the time.

35. Aoki, interview, August 3, 2019.

36. Aoki, interview.

37. Hirose Sakae, mayor of Yabu City, interview, Tokyo, June 5, 2017; Daimon Rikio, Tani Yoshimi, Tsuruda Shinya, and Yoneda Kazuaki, Yabu City officials, interview, Yabu City, June 7, 2017.

EPILOGUE

1. Suge citizens and representatives, interview, Suge, June 2, 2014.

2. Unless otherwise specified, demographic data for Yamato in this and subsequent paragraphs taken from Yamato (website), accessed October 26, 2018, https://www.town.kumamoto-yamato.lg.jp/; and Yamato Town, "Yamato Database 2018."

3. Yamamoto Naoki, vice mayor of Yamato, interview, Yamato, June 2, 2014.

4. Yamamoto, interview.

5. In one such restaurant, located in a very old, renovated farmhouse in the nearby hills, we lunched on rice balls, soba, sweet tomatoes, and other local products. Sadly, we were the only diners in the restaurant.

6. Yamamoto, interview, June 2, 2014.

7. Umeda Yutaka, mayor of Yamato, interview, Yamato, June 16, 2017.

8. Umeda, interview.

9. Umeda, interview.

10. Yamato Town, "Yamato Database 2018."

11. Umeda, interview, June 16, 2017.

12. *Yamato deshika* literally means "Only in Yamato."

13. See Yamato Desica, accessed October 15, 2020, http://www.yamatodesica.com.

14. Yatsuda Shogo and Nakahata Yoshihirō, interview, Yamato, June 16, 2017.

Bibliography

Adler, Paul S., Paul du Gay, Glenn Morgan, and Mike Reed, eds. *The Oxford Handbook of Sociology, Social Theory, and Organizational Studies: Contemporary Currents.* Oxford: Oxford University Press, 2014.

Alho, Eeva. "Farmers' Self-Reported Value of Cooperative Membership: Evidence from Heterogeneous Business and Organization Structures." *Agricultural and Food Economics* 3, no. 23 (2015): 1–22. https://doi.org/10.1186/s40100-015-0041-6.

Ang, Yuen Yuen. *How China Escaped the Poverty Trap.* Ithaca, NY: Cornell University Press, 2016.

Arahata, Katsumi. *Gentan haishi—nōsei daitenkan no gokai to shinjitsu* [Abolishing gentan—the misunderstandings and truth of the great transformation of agricultural policy]. Tokyo: Nihon keizai shimbun shuppansha, 2015.

Baba, Toshihiko. "'JA gurūpu einō · keizai kakushin puran' no kihon mokuhyō to jūten senrakyu" [The basic goals and priority strategies of the JA Group's management and economic reform plan]. *Nōgyō to keizai* 80, no. 7 (2014): 34–43.

Babb, James. "Making Farmers Conservative: Japanese Farmers, Land Reform and Socialism." *Social Science Japan Journal* 8, no. 2 (2005): 175–95.

Banno, Yuko. "Japanese Agricultural Policy: Last Chance for Change." Tokyo Foundation, May 12, 2014, http://www.tokyofoundation.org/en/articles/2014/japanese-agricultural-policy.

Bates, Robert H. *Markets and States in Tropical Africa: The Political Basis of Agricultural Policies.* 2nd ed. Berkeley: University of California Press, 2005.

Benos, Theo, Nikos Kalogeras, Frans J. H. M. Verhees, Panagiota Sergaki, and Joost M. E. Pennings. "Cooperatives' Organizational Restructuring, Strategic Attributes, and Performance: The Case of Agribusiness Cooperatives in Greece." *Agribusiness* 32, no. 1 (2016): 127–50. https://doi.org/10.1002/agr.21429.

Bijman, Jos, and Constantine Iliopoulos. "Farmers' Cooperatives in the EU: Policies, Strategies, and Organization." *Annals of Public and Cooperative Economics* 85, no. 4 (2014): 497–508. https://doi.org/10.1111/apce.12048.

Bijman, Jos, Markus Hanisch and Ger van der Sangen. "Shifting Control? The Changes of Internal Governance in Agricultural Cooperatives in the EU." *Annals of Public and Cooperative Economics* 85, no. 4 (2014): 641–61. https://doi.org/10.1111/apce.12055.

Bijman, Jos, Constantine Iliopoulos, Krijn J. Poppe, Caroline Gijselinckx, Konrad Hagedorn, Markus Hanisch, George W. J. Hendrikse, Rainer Kühl, Petri Ollila, Perttu Pyykkönen, and Ger van der Sangen. "Support for Farmers' Cooperatives: Final Report." Brussels: European Commission, 2012.

Boas, Taylor C. "Conceptualizing Continuity and Change: The Composite-Standard Model of Path Dependence." *Journal of Theoretical Politics* 19, no. 1 (2007): 33–54.

Boettke, Peter J., and Christopher J. Coyne. "Context Matters: Institutions and Entrepreneurship." *Foundations and Trends in Entrepreneurship* 5, no. 3 (2009): 135–209. Reprinted as *Context Matters: Institutions and Entrepreneurship* (Hanover, MA: Now Publishers, 2009).

Boland, Michael, Julie A. Hogeland, and Greg McKee. "Current Issues in Strategy for Agricultural Cooperatives." *Choices* 26, no. 3 (2011). https://www.choicesmagazine

.org/choices-magazine/theme-articles/critical-issues-for-agricultural-coopera
tives/current-issues-in-strategy-for-agricultural-cooperatives.

Brinks, Daniel M. "Informal Institutions and the Rule of Law: The Judicial Response to State Killings in Buenos Aires and São Paulo in the 1990s." *Comparative Politics* 36, no. 1 (2003): 1–19.

Buccola, S. T. "Agricultural Cooperatives." In *Encyclopedia of Agriculture and Food Systems*, 2nd ed., edited by Neal K. Van Alfen, 71–80. Amsterdam: Elsevier, 2014. http://doi.org/10.1016/B978-0-444-52512-3.00125-X.

Bullock, Robert. "Nokyo: A Short Cultural History." Working Paper No. 41, Japan Policy Research Institute, Oakland, CA, December 1997.

Capoccia, Giovanni, and R. Daniel Keleman. "The Study of Critical Junctures: Theory, Narrative, and Counterfactuals in Historical Institutionalism." *World Politics* 59, no. 3 (2007): 341–69.

Chaddad, Fabio R., and Michael L. Cook. "Understanding New Cooperative Models: An Ownership-Control Rights Typology." *Review of Agricultural Economics* 26, no. 3 (2004): 348–60.

Collier, Ruth Berins, and David Collier. *Shaping the Political Arena: Critical Junctures, the Labor Movement, and Regime Dynamics in Latin America.* Princeton, NJ: Princeton University Press, 1991.

Coltrain, David, David Barton, and Michael Boland. "Differences between New Generation Cooperatives and Traditional Cooperatives." Manhattan, KS: Arthur Capper Cooperative Center, Kansas State University, May 2000. http://citeseerx.ist.psu .edu/viewdoc/download?doi=10.1.1.511.2195&rep=rep1&type=pdf#:~:text =New%20Generation%20Cooperatives%20differ%20from,market%2D%20 driven%20nature%20of%20NGCs.

Commons, John R. *Legal Foundations of Capitalism.* New York: Augustus M. Kelley, 1974.

Conkin, Paul K. *A Revolution down on the Farm: The Transformation of American Agriculture Since 1929.* Lexington: University Press of Kentucky, 2008.

Cook, Michael L. "The Future of U.S. Agricultural Cooperatives: A Neo-Institutional Approach." *American Journal of Agricultural Economics* 77, no. 5 (1995): 1153–59.

Cross, Robin, and Steven Buccola. "Adapting Cooperative Structure to the New Global Environment." *American Journal of Agricultural Economics* 86, no. 5 (2004): 1254–61.

Davis, Christina L. *Food Fights over Free Trade: How International Institutions Promote Agricultural Trade Liberalization.* Princeton, NJ: Princeton University Press, 2003.

Davis, Christina L., and Jennifer Oh. "Repeal of the Rice Laws in Japan: The Role of International Pressure to Overcome Vested Interests." *Comparative Politics* 40, no. 1 (2007): 21–40.

Dore, Ronald P. *Land Reform in Japan.* 2nd ed. London: Athlone, 1984.

Dunn, John R. "Basic Cooperative Principles and Their Relationship to Selected Practices." *Journal of Agricultural Cooperation* 3 (1988): 83–93.

Embree, John F. *Suye Mura: A Japanese Village.* Chicago: University of Chicago Press, 1939.

Filippi, Maryline. "Support for Farmers' Cooperatives: Country Report: France." Wageningen, Netherlands: Wageningen UR, 2012. https://edepot.wur.nl/244795.

——. "Using the Regional Advantage: French Agricultural Cooperatives' Economic and Governance Tool." *Annals of Public and Cooperative Economics* 85, no. 4 (2014): 597–615. https://onlinelibrary.wiley.com/doi/abs/10.1111/apce.12053.

Fioretos, Orfeo, Tulia G. Falleti, and Adam Sheingate, eds. *The Oxford Handbook of Historical Institutionalism.* Oxford: Oxford University Press, 2016.

Fuji, Shigeo. "JA Gurūpu no einō • keizai kakushin puran ni tsuite" [On the JA Group's management and economic reform plan]. *Nihon nōgyō no ugoki* 188 (2015): 66–97.

Fujita, Hisao, Kobayashi Kuniyuki, Tanahashi Tomoharu, Nakamura Masashi, and Sakashita Akihiko. "Kenrenshudōgata no nōkyō jigyō taisei to nōkyō gappei ni yoru ittaika" [Unification through prefectural federation-led cooperative business systems and co-op mergers]. *Hokkaido daigaku nōkei ronsō,* no. 69 (April 2014): 29–41.

Fujitani, Chikuji. "Nōkyō at a Crossroads." *Japan Quarterly* 39, no. 3 (1992): 369–80.

Fukuda, Jun. "Nōkyō soshiki no gabanansu bunseki" [Analysis of the governance of co-op organizations]. *Dai 20kai shinka keizaigakukai taikai,* March 26–27, 2016, 1–13.

Godo, Yoshihisa. "The Changing Political Dynamics of Japanese Agricultural Cooperatives." Paper presented to the conference of International Association of Agricultural Economists, Beijing, August 16–22, 2009.

——. "The History of Japan's Post-Pacific War Rice Policy." *FFTC Agricultural Policy Platform,* November 1, 2013. https://ap.fftc.org.tw/article/542.

——. "The Japanese Agricultural Cooperative System: An Outline." *FFTC Agricultural Policy Platform,* May 30, 2014. https://ap.fftc.org.tw/article/678.

——. *Sayonara nippon nōgyō* [Good-bye Japanese agriculture]. Tokyo: NHK shuppan, 2010.

Hall, Peter A. "Historical Institutionalism in Rationalist and Sociological Perspective." In *Explaining Institutional Change: Ambiguity, Agency, and Power,* edited by James Mahoney and Kathleen Thelen, 204–23. New York: Cambridge University Press, 2010.

——, ed. *The Political Power of Economic Ideas: Keynesianism Across Nations.* Princeton, NJ: Princeton University Press, 1989.

Hall, Peter A., and David Soskice. "An Introduction to Varieties of Capitalism." In *Varieties of Capitalism: The Institutional Foundations of Comparative Advantage,* edited by Peter A. Hall and David Soskice, 1–68. Oxford: Oxford University Press, 2001.

Havens, Thomas R. H. *Farm and Nation in Modern Japan: Agrarian Nationalism, 1879–1940.* Princeton, NJ: Princeton University Press, 1974.

Hayami, Yujiro. *Japanese Agriculture under Siege: The Political Economy of Agricultural Policies.* New York: St. Martin's, 1988.

Heclo, Hugh. *On Thinking Institutionally.* Oxford: Oxford University Press, 2008.

Helmke, Gretchen, and Steven Levitsky. "Informal Institutions and Comparative Politics: A Research Agenda." *Perspectives on Politics* 2, no. 4 (2004): 725–40.

Hirasawa, Akihiko. "Frame and Emerging Reform of Agricultural Policy in Japan." *FFTC Agricultural Policy Platform,* July 2, 2014. https://ap.fftc.org.tw/article/691.

Hogeland, Julie A. "The Economic Culture of U.S. Agricultural Cooperatives." *Culture and Agriculture* 28, no. 2 (2006): 67–79.

——. "Managing Uncertainty and Expectations: The Strategic Response of U.S. Agricultural Cooperatives to Agricultural Industrialization." *Journal of Co-operative Organization and Management* 3, no. 2 (2015): 60–71. https://doi.org/10.1016/j.jcom.2015.06.001.

Honma, Masayoshi. *Nōgyō mondai: TPP go, nōsei wa kō kawaru (Agricultural issues: how agricultural policies will change after TPP).* Tokyo: Chikuma shinsho, 2014.

——. "Nōkyō wa doko e mukau no ka: JA no kaikaku an wo megutte" [Where are agricultural cooperatives heading? Concerning the JA reform plan]. *Nōgyō to keizai* 80, no. 7 (2014): 25–33.

Honma, Masayoshi, and Yujiro Hayami. "Distortions to Agricultural Incentives in Japan, Korea and Taiwan." Agricultural Distortions Working Paper Series 48510, World Bank, 2008. http://doi.org/10.22004/ag.econ.48510.

Honma, Masayoshi, and Aurelia George Mulgan. "Political Economy of Agricultural Reform in Japan under Abe's Administration." Asian Economic Policy Review 13, no. 1 (2018): 128–44. https://doi.org/10.1111/aepr.12208.

Iida, Yasumichi. JA kaitai: 1,000 man kumiaiin no meiun [The dissolution of JA: the fate of ten million co-op members]. Tokyo: Tōyō keizai shinpōsha, 2015.

Iiguni, Yoshiaki. "Kazoku keiei wo keizaigaku de toraeru" [Grasping family management from the perspective of economics]. Nōgyō to keizai 80, no. 9 (2014): 33–43.

Ikeda, Tatsuo. "Nōkyō kaikaku no ugoki to ronten" [Shifts and issues in JA reform]. Nihon nōgyō no ugoki 188 (2015): 6–13.

Ishida, Masaaki. "Development of Agricultural Cooperatives in Japan (1): Agricultural Co-operatives of Today." Bulletin of the Faculty of Bioresources, Mie University 28 (2002): 19–34.

——. JA no rekishi to watashitachi no yakuwari: korekara no JA wo ninau shokuin no tame no [JA's history and our role: for officials who will be shouldering the future of JA]. Tokyo: Ie no hikari kyōkai, 2014.

——. Nōkyō wa chiiki ni nani ga dekiru ka: nō wo tsukuru · chiiki gurashi wo tsukuru · JA wo tsukuru [What can the co-ops do for rural areas? Constructing agriculture, local livelihoods, and JA]. Tokyo: Nōbunkyō, 2012.

Ishida, Nobutaka. "Nōkyō kaikaku" wo dō kangaeru ka: JA no sonzai ishiki to hatasubeki yakuwari [How should we think about "co-op reform"? JA's raison d'être and the roles it should play]. Tokyo: Ie no hikari kyōka, 2012.

Ishii, Hayato. "Nōsei undō no kakutai wa dono yō ni henkashitekita no ka" [How have the various organizations of the agricultural policy movement changed?]. Nihon nōgyō no ugoki 189 (2015): 6–13.

Itoh, Motoshige. "Competition in the Japanese Distribution System and Market Access from Abroad." In Deregulation and Interdependence in the Asia-Pacific Region, edited by Takatoshi Ito and Anne O. Krueger, 139–56. Chicago: University of Chicago Press, 2000.

"JA Banku zentai de nōgyō kanren yūshi shea wa 6wari teido" [JA Bank's agricultural loan share is about 60 percent]. Nōrinchūkin Bank Newsletter 1 (June 2018): 10. https://www.nochubank.or.jp/efforts/newsletter/pdf/newsletter2018_01_04.pdf.

JA Zenchū. JA fakuto bukku 2018 [JA fact book 2018]. Tokyo: JA Zenchū, February 2018.

JA Zenkyōren. "2018 Annual Report." Accessed July 10, 2020. https://www.ja-kyosai.or.jp/about/annual_report/pdf/2018annual.pdf.

Japan Grain Inspection Association. Heiseigannen kara no tokuA rankingu ranhyō [List of special A rankings since 1989]. https://www.kokken.or.jp/data/ranking_special A02.pdf.

Jentzsch, Hanno. "Abandoned Land, Corporate Farming, and Farmland Banks: A Local Perspective on the Process of Deregulating and Redistributing Farmland in Japan." Contemporary Japan 29, no. 1 (2017): 31–46.

——. Harvesting State Support: Institutional Change and Local Agency in Japanese Agriculture. Toronto: University of Toronto Press, 2021.

——. "Tracing the Local Origins of Farmland Policies in Japan—Local-National Policy Transfers and Endogenous Institutional Change." Social Science Japan Journal 20, no. 2 (2017): 243–60.

——. "Village Institutions and the Agricultural Reform Process in Japan." Paper presented to the annual meeting of the Association for Asian Studies, Chicago, March 26–29, 2015.

"Jigyō rieki no genshō tsuzuku: sōgōJA no kessan gaikyō" [Business profits continue to decline: outlook for the financial results of multipurpose cooperatives]. *Nōgyō kyōdō kumiai shimbun*, November 13, 2018. https://www.jacom.or.jp/noukyo/news /2018/11/181113-36642.php.

Jones, R. S., and S. Kimura. "Reforming Agriculture and Promoting Japan's Integration in the World Economy." OECD Economics Department Working Papers, no. 1053, OECD, Paris, 2013.

Kajiura, Yoshimasa. *Datsu nōkyō: Nihon nōgyō saisei e no michi* [Abandoning Nokyo: the road to Japanese agricultural regeneration]. Tokyo: Daiyamondosha, 1995.

Kanda, Kensaku. "Kurikaesareru 'nōkyō kaikaku ron' to kyōteki ichi" [The much repeated "cooperative reform theory" and its position today]. *Nōkyō to keizei* 80, no. 7–8 (2014): 5–14.

Kanda, Kensaku, ed. *Shinjiyūshugika no chiiki・nōgyō・nōkyō* [The regions, agriculture, and cooperatives under neoliberalism]. Tokyo: Tsukuba shobō, 2014.

Kanda, Kensaku, Ohashi Osamu, Wang Jing, Ozaki Toru, Katsuki Toshitaka, Zhou Xiaodong, Songe Xiaokai, Cao Bin, Hara Haruhisa, Fujishima Hiroji, Yamafuji Atsushi, Yang Yan, and Ishitsuka Satoshi. "Kyō no nōkyō kaikaku to nihongata sōgō nōkyō no igi: Aomoriken Somamura nōkyō no jirei" [The current restructuring of the agricultural cooperatives in Japan and the significance of Japanese-style multipurpose agricultural cooperatives: a case study of the Soma Agricultural Cooperative in Aomori Prefecture]. *Kiyō* 8 (2016): 73–82.

Kawamura, Kazunori. "Seiken kōtai jidai no rieki dantai to sono hen'yō: 2010nen san'insen de no nōgyōhyō no ikikata kara" [Interest groups and their transformation in the age of alternating political power: the farm vote and the 2010 upper house election]. *Kōmei* 75 (March 2012): 24–30.

Kelley, Kathy. "An Introduction to New Generation Cooperatives." Penn State Extension. Updated March 11, 2016. http://extension.psu.edu/an-introduction-to-new-gener ation-cooperatives.

Kelly, William W. "Japanese Farmers." *Wilson Quarterly* 14, no. 4 (Autumn 1990): 34–41.

——. "Regional Japan: The Price of Prosperity and the Benefits of Dependency." *Daedalus* 119, no. 3 (1990): 209–27.

Kishi, Yasuhiko. *Shoku to nō no sengōshi* [A postwar history of food and agriculture]. Tokyo: Nihon keizai shimbun shuppansha, 1996.

Kitade, Toshiaki. *Nōkyō wa kyōdō kumiai de aru: rekishi kara mita kadai to tenbō* [Nōkyō is a cooperative: problems and perspectives as seen from history]. Tokyo: Tsukuba shobō, 2014.

Knight, Jack. *Institutions and Social Conflict*. Cambridge: Cambridge University Press, 1992.

Kobayashi, Hajime. "JA no kiso soshiki to kadai" [JA's foundational organizations and issues]. In *JA wa dare no mono ka: tayōkasuru jidai no JA gabanansu* [Who does JA belong to? JA governance in the era of diversification], edited by Masuda Yoshiaki, 119–46. Tokyo: Ie no hikari kyōkai, 2013.

——. *Tsugi no sutēji ni mukau JA jiko kaikaku: tankiteki・chōkiteki senryaku de kiki wo norikoeru* [JA self-reform as it faces the next stage: overcoming crisis with short- and long-term strategies]. Tokyo: Ie no hikari kyōkai, 2013.

Komoto, Keishō. "Nō no 6 ji sangyōka e no ryūtsū senryaku [Distribution strategies for the sixth industrialization of agriculture]." In *Nō no 6 ji sangyōka to chiiki shinkō* [The sixth industrialization of agriculture and rural promotion], edited by Kumakura Isao and Yoneya Takefumi, 52–77. Tokyo: Shumpusha, 2015.

Krauss, Ellis S., and Robert J. Pekkanen. *The Rise and Fall of Japan's LDP: Political Party Organizations as Historical Institutions*. Ithaca, NY: Cornell University Press, 2011.

Kurimoto, Akira. "Agricultural Cooperatives in Japan: An Institutional Approach." *Journal of Rural Cooperation* 32, no. 2 (2004): 111–28.

Maclachlan, Patricia L. *Consumer Politics in Postwar Japan: The Institutional Boundaries of Consumer Advocacy*. New York: Columbia University Press, 2002.

——. "The Electoral Power of Japanese Interest Groups: An Organizational Perspective." *Journal of East Asian Studies* 14, no. 3 (2014): 429–58.

Maclachlan, Patricia L., and Kay Shimizu. "Japanese Agricultural Reform Under Abenomics." In *The Political Economy of the Abe Government and Abenomics Reforms*, edited by Takeo Hoshi and Phillip Y. Lipscy, 421–44. Cambridge: Cambridge University Press, 2021.

——. "Japanese Farmers in Flux: The Domestic Sources of Agricultural Reform." *Asian Survey* 56, no. 3 (2016): 442–65.

——. "The Kantei vs. the LDP: Agricultural Reform, the Organized Vote, and the 2014 Election." In *Japan Decides 2014: The Japanese General Election*, edited by Robert J. Pekkanen, Steven R. Reed, and Ethan Scheiner, 170–82. London: Palgrave, 2015.

MAFF—*see* Ministry of Agriculture, Forestry, and Fisheries

Mahoney, James. "Path Dependence in Historical Sociology." *Theory and Society* 29 (August 2000): 507–48.

Mahoney, James, and Kathleen Thelen, eds. *Explaining Institutional Change: Ambiguity, Agency, and Power*. Cambridge: Cambridge University Press, 2010.

——. "A Theory of Gradual Institutional Change." In *Explaining Institutional Change: Ambiguity, Agency, and Power*, edited by James Mahoney and Kathleen Thelen, 1–37. New York: Cambridge University Press, 2010.

March, James G., and Johan P. Olsen. "Elaborating the 'New Institutionalism.'" In *The Oxford Handbook of Political Institutions*, edited by R. A. W. Rhodes, Sarah A. Binder, and Bert A. Rockman, 3–20. Oxford: Oxford University Press, 2006.

Masuda, Hiroya. *Chihō shōmetsu: Tokyo ikkyoku shūchū ga maneku jinkō kyūgen* [Rural annihilation: population decline caused by overconcentration in Tokyo]. Tokyo: Chūō kōron shinsha, 2014.

Masuda, Yoshiaki. "JA gabanansu no kōzō to kadai" [JA governance structure and issues]. In *JA wa dare no mono ka: tayōkasuru jidai no JA gabanansu* [Who does JA belong to? JA governance in the era of diversification], edited by Masuda Yoshiaki, 11–38. Tokyo: Ie no hikari kyōkai, 2013.

——, ed. *JA wa dare no mono ka: tayōkasuru jidai no JA gabanansu* [Who does JA belong to? JA governance in the era of diversification]. Tokyo: Ie no hikari kyōkai, 2013.

——. *Kinkyū tenken! JA jiko kaikaku: kumiaiin mesen no soshiki • jigyō no saikōchiku* [Emergency inspection! JA self-reform: organizational and business reorganization from the perspective of coop members]. Tokyo: Ie no hikari kyōkai, 2017.

——. "Nōkyō kaikaku to jiko kaikaku: sono nerai to shinpo jōtai" [JA reform and self-reform; their aims and progress]. *Nōgyō to keizai* 84, no. 7 (2018): 6–16.

Matsuoka, Kōmei. "'Jidai e tsunagu kyōdō' wo kangaeru" [Thinking about "cooperation for connecting to the next generation"]. In *Shiten kyōdō katsudō de genki na JA zukuri: "jidai e tsunagu kyōdō" no susumekata* [Building healthy co-ops through the cooperative activities of branch offices: how to proceed with "cooperation for connecting to the next generation"], edited by Matsuoka Kōmei, Kobayashi Hajime, and Nishii Kengo, 9–38. Tokyo: Ie no hikari kyōkai, 2013.

Matsuoka, Kōmei, Kobayashi Hajime, and Nishii Kengo, eds. *Shiten kyōdō katsudō de genki na JA zukuri: "jidai e tsunagu kyōdō" no susumekata* [Building healthy co-ops through the cooperative activities of branch offices: how to proceed with "cooperation for connecting to the next generation"]. Tokyo: Ie no hikari kyōkai, 2013.

McDonald, Mary G. "Agricultural Landholding in Japan: Fifty Years after Land Reform." *Geoforum* 28, no. 1 (1997): 55–78.
——. "Food Firms and Food Flows in Japan, 1945–98." *World Development* 28, no. 3 (2000): 487–512.
Meyer, John W., and Brian Rowan. "Institutionalized Organizations: Formal Structure as Myth and Ceremony." In *The New Institutionalism in Organizational Analysis*, edited by Walter W. Powell and Paul J. DiMaggio, 41–62. Chicago: University of Chicago Press, 1991.
MIC—*see* Ministry of Internal Affairs and Communications
Milly, Deborah J. *New Policies for New Residents: Immigrants, Advocacy, and Governance in Japan and Beyond*. Ithaca, NY: Cornell University Press, 2014.
Ministry of Agriculture, Forestry, and Fisheries. "Annual Report on Food, Agricultural and Rural Areas in Japan." Accessed April 30, 2021. https://www.maff.go.jp/e/data/publish/#Annual.
——. "The Basic Law on Food, Agriculture and Rural Areas." Accessed May 15, 2021. https://www.maff.go.jp/j/kanbo/kihyo02/basic_law/pdf/basic_law_agri.pdf.
——. "Census of Agriculture and Forestry." Accessed June 29, 2020 https://www.maff.go.jp/j/tokei/census/afc/index.html.
——. "FY2014 Annual Report on Food, Agricultural and Rural Areas in Japan: Summary." 2015. https://www.maff.go.jp/e/data/publish/attach/pdf/index-5.pdf.
——. "FY2015 Annual Report on Food, Agricultural and Rural Areas in Japan: Summary." 2016. https://www.maff.go.jp/e/data/publish/attach/pdf/index-38.pdf.
——. "Heisei 27nensan kome no aitai torihiki kakaku・sūryō" [The prices and quantities of rice produced in 2018]. Accessed August 10, 2020. https://www.maff.go.jp/j/seisan/keikaku/soukatu/pdf/2710_27nensan_kakaku.pdf.
——. "Heisei 29nen todōfukenbetsu nōgyō sanshutsugaku oyobi seisan nōgyō shotoku" [2017 agricultural output and income by prefecture]. Accessed October 15, 2020. https://www.maff.go.jp/j/tokei/kouhyou/nougyou_sansyutu/.
——. "Heisei 30nensan kome no aitai torihiki kakaku・sūryō" [The prices and quantities of rice produced in 2018]. Accessed August 10, 2020. https://www.maff.go.jp/j/press/seisaku_tokatu/kikaku/attach/pdf/190517-1.pdf.
——. "Inasaku no genjō to sono kadai ni tsuite" [On the current state and problems of rice cultivation]. March 2017. https://jataff.or.jp/project/inasaku/koen/koen_h28_1.pdf.
——. "Kōhai nōchi no genjō to taisaku ni tsuite" [On the current state of and measures for wasted farmland]. April 2020. https://www.maff.go.jp/j/nousin/tikei/houkiti/Genzyo/PDF/Genzyo_0204.pdf.
——. "Kokumin hitori・ichinichi atari kyōkyū soshokuryō" [The people's daily food supply]. 2015. https://www.e-stat.go.jp/stat-search/files?page=1&layout=datalist&touk ei=00500300&tstat=000001017950&cycle=8&year=20151&month=0&tclass1 =000001032890&tclass2=000001098955&tclass3val=0.
——. "Kome, kome kakōhin no yushutsu wo meguru jōkyō" [The situation surrounding the export of rice and rice-based processed products]. Accessed May 26, 2021. https://www.maff.go.jp/j/syouan/keikaku/soukatu/kome_yusyutu/attach/pdf/kome_yusyutu-574.pdf.
——. "Kome ni kansuru mansurī repōto" [Monthly rice report]. Accessed October 20, 2020. https://www.maff.go.jp/j/seisan/keikaku/soukatu/mr.html.
——. "Kome wo meguru kankei shiryō" [Documents relating to rice]. March 2020. https://www.maff.go.jp/j/seisan/kikaku/attach/pdf/kome_siryou-480.pdf.
——. "Kome wo meguru sankō shiryō" [Reference materials for rice]. Accessed May 25, 2020. https://www.maff.go.jp/j/seisan/kikaku/attach/pdf/kome_siryou-480.pdf.

——. "Ninaite akushon sapōto jigyō" [Support services for core farmer action]. Accessed June 26, 2020. http://www.maff.go.jp/j/ninaite/n_zigyo/action_support/pdf/ac_suppo_21panph.pdf.

——. "Nintei nōgyōsha no nintei jōkyō" [Certification status of certified farm enterprises]. Accessed May 30, 2021. https://www.maff.go.jp/j/kobetu_ninaite/n_seido/attach/pdf/31b-1.pdf; and https://www.maff.go.jp/j/kobetu_ninaite/n_seido/nintei_zyokyo/31b.html.

——. "Nintei nōgyōshasū" [Number of certified farmers]. Accessed June 28, 2020. http://www.maff.go.jp/j/tokei/kouhyou/nintei/.

——. "Nōchi chūkan kanri jigyō no 5nengo minaoshi ni tsuite" [Post five-year review of farmland consolidation bank operations]. November 2018. https://www.maff.go.jp/j/keiei/koukai/kikou/attach/pdf/kikou_ichran-26.pdf.

——. "Nōgyō kyōdō kumiai no keizai jigyō ni kansuru ishiki・iko chōsa no kekka" [Results of a survey on awareness and intensions of JA's economic operations]. 2013. https://www.maff.go.jp/j/finding/mind/pdf/noukei.pdf.

——. "Nōgyō kyōdō kumiai oyobi dō rengōkai issei chōsa" [Simultaneous surveys of agricultural cooperatives and their federated organizations]. Accessed August 10, 2020. http://www.maff.go.jp/j/tokei/kouhyou/noukyo_rengokai/index.html.

——. "Nōgyō kyōdō kumiai sū nado no suii" [Number of JA co-ops over time]. September 2017. http://www.agri-mj.co.jp/toukei/17-9noukyou.pdf.

——. "Nōgyō rōdōryoku ni kansuru tōkei" [Agricultural workforce statistics]. Accessed May 31, 2021. http://www.maff.go.jp/j/tokei/sihyo/data/08.html.

——. "Nōgyō seisan hōjin no nōgyō san'nyū ni tsuite" [On the entry of agricultural production corporations into farming]. Accessed May 15, 2021. https://www.maff.go.jp/j/keiei/koukai/sannyu/pdf/seisan.pdf.

——. "Nōkyō ni tsuite" [About JA]. November 2017. Hard copy in possession of the authors.

——. "Nōkyō ni tsuite" [About JA]. April 2020. https://www.maff.go.jp/j/keiei/sosiki/kyosoka/k_kenkyu/attach/pdf/index-109.pdf.

——. "Nōkyō no genjō to kadai ni tsuite" [On the current conditions and issues of agricultural cooperatives]. May 2009. http://www.maff.go.jp/j/study/nokyo_kotiku/01/pdf/data2.pdf.

——. "Nōrin suisanbutsu hinmokubetsu sankō shiryō" [Reference materials for agricultural, forestry, and fisheries products]. November 2015. https://www.maff.go.jp/j/kanbo/tpp/pdf/151224_sankou.pdf.

——. "Report on the Results of the 2010 World Census of Agriculture, Forestry and Fisheries of Japan." Accessed May 30, 2021. https://www.e-stat.go.jp/en/stat-search/files?page=1&layout=datalist&toukei=00500209&tstat=000001032920&cycle=0&tclass1=000001038546&tclass2=000001049164&tclass3val=0.

——. "Seisan nōgyō shotoku tōkei" [Agricultural income statistics]. Accessed September 15, 2020. https://www.e-stat.go.jp/stat-search/files?page=1&layout=datalist&toukei=00500206&tstat=000001015617&cycle=7&year=20170&month=0&tclass1=000001019794&tclass2=000001127636.

——. "Shūraku einō jittai chōsa gaiyō" [Summary of the survey of hamlet-based farm associations]. 2020. https://www.e-stat.go.jp/stat-search/files?page=1&layout=datalist&toukei=00500238&tstat=000001015294&cycle=7&month=0&tclass1=000001032277&tclass2=000001145956&cycle_facet=tclass1%3Acycle&tclass3val=0.

——. "Statistical Yearbook of the Ministry of Agriculture, Forestry and Fisheries." Accessed May 30, 2021. https://www.maff.go.jp/e/data/stat/nenji_index.htm.

Ministry of Internal Affairs and Communications. *Dai69 Nihon tōkei nenkan: nōrinsui sangyō* [69th Japan statistical yearbook: agriculture, forestry and fisheries]. Accessed May 30, 2021. http://www.stat.go.jp/data/nenkan/69nenkan/08.html.

———. *Japan Statistical Yearbook.* Accessed June 15, 2021. https://www.stat.go.jp/english/data/nenkan/.

———. *Statistical Handbook of Japan.* Accessed May 30, 2021. http://www.stat.go.jp/english/data/handbook/index.html.

———. *Statistical Handbook of Japan: 2016.* Tokyo: Ministry of Internal Affairs and Communication, 2016. http://www.stat.go.jp/english/data/handbook/pdf/2016all.pdf.

———. "Tōkei kara mita waga kuni no kōreisha" [Our country's elderly as depicted by data]. 2020. https://www.stat.go.jp/data/topics/pdf/topics126.pdf.

Ministry of the Environment. "Wajimashi Machinomachi Kanakura" [Wajima City, Machino Town, Kanakura]. Accessed May 15, 2021. http://www.env.go.jp/nature/satoyama/satonavi/initiative/kokunai/pdf/103.pdf.

Mishima, Tokuzoh. "Revision of Japan's Basic Law on Agriculture and Its Features." *Review of Agricultural Economics* 60 (March 2004): 259–71.

Moe, Terry M. "Power and Political Institutions." In *Rethinking Political Institutions: The Art of the State*, edited by Ian Shapiro, Stephen Skowronek, and Daniel Galvin, 32–71. New York: New York University Press, 2006.

Moore, Barrington. *Social Origins of Dictatorship and Democracy.* Boston: Beacon, 1966.

Moriyama, Hiroshi. "Jimintō ga kangaeru nōkyō kaikaku" [The LDP's thinking on JA reform]. *Nihon nōgyō no ugoki* 188 (2015): 40–65.

Morris-Suzuki, Tessa. "Cooperatives and Grassroots Developments." In *Routledge Handbook of Modern Japanese History*, edited by Sven Saaler and Christopher W. A. Szpilman, 310–23. London: Routledge, 2018.

Mulgan, Aurelia George. *The Abe Administration and the Rise of the Prime Ministerial Executive.* London: Routledge, 2018.

———. "The Farm Lobby." In *Japanese Politics Today: From Karaoke to Kabuki Diplomacy*, edited by Takashi Inoguchi and Purnendra Jain, 109–26. New York: Palgrave Macmillan, 2011.

———. "'Japan, Inc.' in the Agricultural Sector: Reform or Regression?" *Asia Pacific Economic Papers*, no. 314 (April). Canberra: Australia-Japan Research Centre, 2001.

———. *Japan's Agricultural Policy Regime.* London: Routledge, 2006.

———. *Japan's Interventionist State: The Role of the MAFF.* London: RoutledgeCurzon, 2005.

———. "Loosening the Ties that Bind: Japan's Agricultural Policy Triangle and Reform of Cooperatives (JA)." *Journal of Japanese Studies* 42, no. 2 (2016): 221–46.

———. "Much Ado About Something? The Abe Government's Reform of Japan's Agricultural Cooperatives." *Japanese Studies* 36, no. 1 (2016): 83–103.

———. *The Politics of Agriculture in Japan.* London: Routledge, 2000.

———. "Where Tradition Meets Change: Japan's Agricultural Politics in Transition." *Journal of Japanese Studies* 31, no. 2 (2005): 261–98.

Murata, Yasuo. "'Kantei nōsei' de, shinjiyūshugi nōsei no tenkai" [The evolution of neoliberal agricultural policy via "the Kantei's agricultural policy"]. *Nihon nōgyō no ugoki* 191 (2016): 8–19.

Najita, Tetsuo. *Ordinary Economies in Japan: A Historical Perspective, 1750–1950.* Berkeley: University of California Press, 2009.

Naoi, Megumi. *Building Legislative Coalitions for Free Trade in Asia: Globalization as Legislation.* Cambridge: Cambridge University Press, 2015.

Nilsson, Jerker. "Co-operative Organizational Models as Reflections of the Business Environments." *Finnish Journal of Business Economics* 4 (1999): 449–70.

Nilsson, Jerker, Gunnar L. H. Svendsen, and Gert Tinggaard Svendsen. "Are Large and Complex Agricultural Cooperatives Losing Their Social Capital?" *Agribusiness* 28, no. 2 (2012): 187–204.

"Ninaite kōreika susumu" [The aging of core farmers continues]. *Nihon kyōdō kumiai shimbun*, May 12, 2020. https://www.jacom.or.jp/nousei/rensai/2020/05/200512 -44281.php.

Nishii, Kengo. "Nōgyō kōzō no henka to JA no jigyō・soshiki" [Structural change in agriculture and the business and organization of JA]. In *JA wa dare no mono ka: tayōkasuru jidai no JA gabanansu* [Who does JA belong to? JA governance in the era of diversification], edited by Masuda Yoshiaki, 71–96. Tokyo: Ie no hikari kyōkai, 2013.

Nōgyō to keizai henshū iinkai. *Kīwādo de yomitoku gendai nōgyō to shokuryō・kankyō* [Contemporary agriculture, food, and environment through a deciphering of keywords]. Tokyo: Shōwadō, 2011.

North, Douglass C. "Five Propositions about Institutional Change." In *Explaining Social Institutions*, edited by Jack Knight and Itai Sened, 15–26. Ann Arbor: University of Michigan Press, 1995.

——. *Institutions, Institutional Change and Economic Performance.* Cambridge, MA: Cambridge University Press, 1990.

——. *Structure and Change in Economic History.* New York: W. W. Norton, 1981.

——. *Understanding the Process of Economic Change.* Princeton, NJ: Princeton University Press, 2005.

Nōsangyoson bunka kyōkai, ed. *Kisei kaikaku kaigi no 'nōgyō kaikaku': 20shi no iken* [The Council on Regulatory Reform's "agricultural reform": twenty opinions]. Nōbunkyō pamphlet 11. Tokyo: Nōbunkyō, 2014.

Odaka, Megumi. "JA ni yoru nōsanbutsu kaitori hanbai no kadai" [Issues in the buy-up sales of agricultural products by JA]. *Chōsa to jōhō* 49 (July 2015): 6–7.

——. "Nōkyō ni okeru nōgyō kanren jigyō son'eki no genjo to kadai" [The current state and problems of agricultural business profits and losses in agricultural cooperatives]. *Nōrin kin'yū* 61, no. 4 (2008): 53–59.

OECD—*see* Organization for Economic Cooperation and Development

Ogura, Takekazu. *Agricultural Development in Modern Japan.* Tokyo: Japan FAO Association, 1963.

Ohnuki-Tierney, Emiko. *Rice as Self: Japanese Identities through Time.* Princeton, NJ: Princeton University Press, 1994.

Oizumi, Kazunuki. *Nōkyō no mirai: atarashii jidai no yakuwari to kanōsei* [The future of agricultural cooperatives: their roles and potential in a new era]. Tokyo: Keisō shobō, 2014.

Okuhara, Masaaki. *Nōsei kaikaku: gyōseikan no shigoto to sekinin* [Revolution in agricultural policy: the work and responsibilities of officials]. Tokyo: Nihon keizai shimbun shuppansha, 2019.

Organization for Economic Cooperation and Development. "Agricultural Support." Accessed July 28, 2021. https://data.oecd.org/agrpolicy/agricultural-support.htm.

——. *Evaluation of Agricultural Policy Reforms in Japan.* Paris: OECD, 2009. https://www .oecd.org/japan/42791674.pdf.

Ostrom, Elinor. *Governing the Commons: The Evolution of Institutions for Collective Action.* New York: Cambridge University Press, 1990.

Ōtahara, Takaaki. "JA no 'sōgōsei' to iu mondai" [The problem with JA's "comprehensiveness"]. *Nōgyō to keizai* 7 (2011): 5–13.

——. *Nōkyō no taigi* [The noble cause of agricultural cooperatives]. Nōbunkyō pamphlet 10. Tokyo: Nōbunkyō, 2014.

Pempel, T. J. *Regime Shift: Comparative Dynamics of the Japanese Political Economy*. Ithaca, NY: Cornell University Press, 1998.

Pierson, Paul. *Politics in Time: History, Institutions, and Social Analysis*. Princeton, NJ: Princeton University Press, 2004.

——. "Power in Historical Institutionalism." In *The Oxford Handbook of Historical Institutionalism*, edited by Orfeo Fioretos, Tulia G. Falleti, and Adam Sheingate, 124–41. Oxford: Oxford University Press, 2016.

Pierson, Paul, and Theda Skocpol. "Historical Institutionalism in Contemporary Political Science." In *Political Science: The State of the Discipline*, edited by Ira Katznelson and Helen V. Milner, 693–721. Washington, DC: W. W. Norton, 2002.

Powell, Walter W., and Paul J. DiMaggio. "Introduction." In *The New Institutionalism in Organizational Analysis*, edited by Walter W. Powell and Paul J. DiMaggio, 1–38. Chicago: University of Chicago Press, 1991.

——, eds. *The New Institutionalism in Organizational Analysis*. Chicago: University of Chicago Press, 1991.

Rhodes, R. A. W., Sarah A. Binder, and Bert A. Rockman, eds. *The Oxford Handbook of Political Institutions*. Oxford: Oxford University Press, 2006.

Rixen, Thomas, and Lora Anne Viola. "Putting Path Dependence in Its Place: Toward a Taxonomy of Institutional Change." *Journal of Theoretical Politics* 27, no. 2 (2015): 301–23.

Rothacher, Albrecht. *Japan's Agro-Food Sector: The Politics and Economics of Excess Protection*. New York: St. Martin's, 1989.

Ryū, Zesan. *Hieiri soshiki no keiei senryaku: JA keiei kaikaku no kēsu sutadi* [The management strategies of nonprofit organizations: a case study of JA management reform]. Tokyo: Chūō keizaisha, 2004.

Saitō, Ken. "Jimintō ga kangaeru abenomikusu nōsei no nerai" [The Abenomics agricultural policy aims as intended by the LDP]. *Nihon nōgyō no ugoki* 191 (2016): 20–44.

Saitō, Yuriko. "Shūraku soshiki no hen'yō to kaikaku hōkō: tayōsei to aratana kadai" [The transformation and direction of the reform of hamlet organizations: diversity and new challenges]. *Nōrin kin'yū* 58, no. 12 (2005): 18–34.

Saitoh, Osamu. *Nōshōkō renkei no senryaku: renkei no shinka ni yoru fūdo shisutemu no kakushin* [Strategies for coordination among agriculture, commerce, and industry: reforming the food system by deepening coordination]. Tokyo: Nōbunkyō, 2011.

Sakai, Tomio. "'Hen'yō' shitsutsu hattensuru kazoku nōgyō keiei" [Family agricultural management that develops through change]. *Nōgyō to keizai* 80, no. 9 (2014): 3.

Schaede, Ulrike. *Choose and Focus: Japanese Business Strategies for the 21st Century*. Ithaca, NY: Cornell University Press, 2008.

Schoppa, Leonard J. *Bargaining with Japan: What American Pressure Can and Cannot Do*. New York: Columbia University Press, 1997.

Scott, W. Richard. *Institutions and Organizations: Ideas, Interests, and Identities*. 4th ed. Los Angeles: SAGE, 2014.

Seipel, Michael F., and William D. Heffernan. "Cooperatives in a Changing Global Food System." USDA Rural Business-Cooperative Service, Research Report 157, 1997.

Seki, Mitsuhiro, and Matsunaga Keiko. *Shūraku einō: nōsanmura no mirai wo hiraku* [Hamlet-based farm associations: clearing the way for the future of farm villages]. Tokyo: Shinhyōron, 2012.

Shapiro, Ian, Stephen Skowronek, and Daniel Galvin, eds. *Rethinking Political Institutions: The Art of the State*. New York: New York University Press, 2006.

Shimazaki, Hideki. *Mōkaru nōgyō: 'doshirōto shūdan' no nōgyō kakumei* [Profitable agriculture: the agricultural revolution of a "group of amateurs"]. Tokyo: Takeshobō shinsho, 2009.

——. *Nōgyō ishin: 'apātogata nōjō' de kawaru kigyō no nōgyō san'nyū to chiiki kassei* [Agricultural restoration: how "apartment farms" are changing corporate participation in agriculture and rural revitalization]. Tokyo: Takeshobō shinsho, 2014.

Shimizu, Kazuaki. "Mizuinasaku chiiki ni okeru shūraku einō soshiki no tenkai to sono igi: Niigataken Jōetsushi Sanwaku wo jirei ni" [The development and significance of hamlet-based farm associations in paddy rice cultivation areas: the case of Sanwa Ward in Jōetsu City, Niigata Prefecture]. *Jinmon chiri* 65, no. 4 (2013): 302–21.

Shōgenji, Shin'ichi. *Nōgyō to nōsei no shiya: ronri no chikara to rekishi no omomi* [Perspectives on agriculture and agricultural policy: the power of logic and the weight of history]. Tokyo: Nōrin tōkei shuppan, 2017.

Steinmo, Sven. *The Evolution of Modern States: Sweden, Japan, and the United States.* Cambridge, MA: Cambridge University Press, 2010.

Suda, Yūji. "Nōkyō no nōsei undō to wa nani ka" [What is JA's agricultural policy movement?]. *Nihon nōgyō no ugoki* 189 (2015): 14–43.

Suzuki, Motoshi. *Globalization and the Politics of Institutional Reform in Japan.* Cheltenham: Edward Elgar, 2016.

Takamine, Hiromi. "Kumamotoken JA Ashikita no 6ji sangyōka" [The sixth industrialization of Kumamoto Prefecture's JA Ashikita]. *Keiei jitsumu*, March 2013, 18–23.

Taniguchi, Nobukazu. "Abenomikusu nōsei no 'zentaizō': zaikaishudōgata nōsei e no tenkan" [The "big picture" of agricultural policies under Abenomics: the switch to big business-led agricultural policy]. In *Nihon nōgyō nenpō 61: abenomikusu nōsei no ikikata: nōsei no kihon hōshin to minaoshi no ronten* [Yearbook of Japanese agriculture 61: the agricultural policy line of Abenomics; agricultural policy's basic aims and points for review], edited by Taniguchi Nobukazu and Ishii Kei'ichi, 1–22. Tokyo: Nōrin tōkei kyōkai, 2015.

Taniguchi, Nobukazu, and Ishii Keiichi, eds. *Nihon nōgyō nenpō 61: abenomikusu nōsei no ikikata: nōsei no kihon hōshin to minaoshi no ronten* [Yearbook of Japanese agriculture 61: the agricultural policy line of Abenomics; agricultural policy's basic aims and points for review]. Tokyo: Nōrin tōkei kyōkai, 2015.

Tashiro, Yōichi. "Hōjinka suisen seisaku no kōzai" [The strengths and weaknesses of policies to promote incorporation]. *Nōgyō to keizai* 80, no. 6 (2014): 14–24.

——. *Nōkyō kaikaku・post TPP・chiiki* [Agricultural cooperative reform: post-TPP; regions]. Tokyo: Tsukuba shobō, 2017.

——. *Nōkyō kaikaku to heisei gappei* [Agricultural cooperative reform and the Heisei mergers]. Tokyo: Tsukuba shobō, 2018.

Thelen, Kathleen. *How Institutions Evolve: The Political Economy of Skills in Germany, Britain, the United States, and Japan.* Cambridge, MA: Cambridge University Press, 2004.

Tokoyama, Hiromi, Egaitsu Fumio, and Nakashima Yasuhiro. *Fūdo shisutemu no keizaigaku* [The economics of food systems]. 5th ed. Tokyo: Ishayaku shuppan, 2013.

Torgerson, Randall E. "A Critical Look at New-Generation Cooperatives." *Rural Cooperatives* 68, no. 1 (2001): 15–19.

——. "Farmer Cooperatives." *Annals of the American Academy of Political and Social Science* 429 (January 1977): 91–102.

Tsai, Kellee S. "Adaptive Informal Institutions and Endogenous Institutional Change in China." *World Politics* 59, no. 1 (2006): 116–41.

Tsai, Lily M. "Solidarity Groups, Informal Accountability, and Local Public Goods Provision in Rural China." *American Political Science Review* 101, no. 2 (2007): 355–72.

Tsutaya, Eiichi. *Kyōdō kumiai no jidai to nōkyō no yakuwari* [The age of co-operation and the functions of agricultural cooperatives]. Tokyo: Ie no hikari kyōkai, 2010.

——. "Nōkyō nōgyō kashidashi shinchō no kyōteki igi to kadai" [Contemporary significance of and issues in the growth of agricultural lending by agricultural co-ops]. *Nōrin kin'yū* 5 (2010): 18–33.

Umemoto, Masaki. "Nōgyō ni okeru hōjinka no igi to kinō" [The significance and functions of incorporation in agriculture]. *Nōgyō to keizai* 80, no. 6 (2014): 5–13.

Uonuma Minami nōgyō kyōdō kumiai. "Disclosure 2018." February 2018. Hard copy in possession of the authors.

USDA—*see* US Department of Agriculture

US Department of Agriculture. "Agricultural Cooperatives in the 21st Century." Cooperative Information Report 60, Rural Business-Cooperative Service, 2002.

——. "Cooperative Statistics 2013." Service Report 75, Rural Business-Cooperative Service, 2014.

——. "Problems and Issues Facing Farmer Cooperatives." RBS Research Report 192, Rural Business-Cooperative Service, 2002.

——. "2017 Census of Agriculture Highlights: Producers." April 2019. https://www.nass.usda.gov/Publications/Highlights/2019/2017Census_Farm_Producers.pdf.

Valentinov, Vladislav, and Constantine Iliopoulos. "Economic Theories of Nonprofits and Agricultural Cooperatives Compared: New Perspectives for Nonprofit Scholars." *Nonprofit and Voluntary Sector Quarterly* 42, no. 1 (2013): 109–26.

Vogel, Steven K. *Freer Markets, More Rules: Regulatory Reform in Advanced Industrial Countries*. Ithaca, NY: Cornell University Press, 1996.

——. *Japan Remodeled: How Government and Industry Are Reforming Japanese Capitalism*. Ithaca, NY: Cornell University Press, 2006.

——. *Marketcraft: How Governments Make Markets Work*. Oxford: Oxford University Press, 2018.

Waswo, Ann, and Nishida Yoshiaki, eds. *Farmers and Village Life in Twentieth-Century Japan*. London: RoutledgeCurzon, 2003.

Watanabe, Hiroaki Richard. *Labor Market Deregulation in Japan and Italy: Worker Protection under Neoliberal Globalization*. London: Routledge, 2014.

Williamson, Oliver E. *The Economic Institutions of Capitalism: Firms, Markets, Relational Contracting*. New York: Free Press, 1985.

Yamaguchi, Yōhei, and Morozumi Kazuo. "Shokuin no ishiki kara mita nōkyō soshiki・jigyō taisei no mondai ten—Miyagiken nōkyō shokuin anketto chōsa no kekka kara" [Issues in co-op organization business structure from the standpoint of staff—from the results of a public opinion survey of Miyagi Prefecture co-op staff]. *Nōkyō keizai kenkyū hōkoku* 43 (February 2012): 69–81.

Yamashita, Kazuhito. "Can the Abe Administration Export Rice?" Canon Institute for Global Studies, October 24, 2017. https://cigs.canon/en/article/20171024_4551.html.

——. "Issues in the Farmland System." Tokyo Foundation, January 20, 2009. http://www.tokyofoundation.org/en/articles/2008/the-issues-in-the-farmland-system.

——. *Nihon nōgyō wa sekai ni kateru* [Japanese agriculture can win globally]. Tokyo: Nihon keizai shimbun shuppansha, 2015.

——. *Nōkyō kaitai* [The road to the dissolution of JA]. Tokyo: Takarajimasha, 2014.

——. "Rather than Being Abolished, the Gentan System Was Strengthened." Canon Institute for Global Studies, January 12, 2017. https://cigs.canon/en/article/20170112_4095.html.

——. *TPP ga nihon nōgyō wo tsuyokusuru* [TPP will strengthen Japanese agriculture]. Tokyo: Nihon keizai shimbun shuppansha, 2016.

Yamato Town. "Yamato Database 2018." Accessed October 26, 2018. https://www.town .kumamoto-yamato.lg.jp/kiji0036144/3_6144_3230_up_opkhow15.pdf.

Yayama, Tarō. *Kome jiyūka kakumei—korede ikikaeru nihon nōgyō* [Rice liberalization revolution—this is what will revive Japanese agriculture]. Tokyo: Shinchōsha, 1989.

Yomiuri shimbun keizaibu. *Nōgyō shin jidai* [A new era of agriculture]. Tokyo: Chūō kōron shinsha, 2017.

Yurugi, Takao. "Zennō to keizairen no tōgō zengo ni okeru jigyō shea to shūekisei no suii ni kansuru bunseki" [An analysis of changes in business shares and profitability after the unification of Zenno and the prefectural economic federations]. *Nihon nōgyō keizai kenkyū* 87, no. 2 (2015): 138–44.

Zeuli, Kimberly A., and Robert Cropp. "Cooperatives: Principles and Practices in the 21st Century." Cooperative Extension Publishing Report. Madison: University of Wisconsin, 2004.

Index

CPSIA information can be obtained
at www.ICGtesting.com
Printed in the USA
LVHW101243100722
723115LV00039B/40/J